ALSO BY ROBERT DALLEK

Democrat and Diplomat:
The Life of William E. Dodd

Franklin D. Roosevelt
and American Foreign Policy, 1932–1945

EDITED BY ROBERT DALLEK

1898: McKinley's Decision:
The United States Declares War on Spain

The Roosevelt Diplomacy and World War II

Western Europe, Volume I of
The Dynamics of World Power: A Documentary History
of United States Foreign Policy, 1945–73

The American Style
of Foreign Policy

THE AMERICAN STYLE OF FOREIGN POLICY

Cultural Politics and Foreign Affairs

By ROBERT DALLEK

Alfred A. Knopf   New York   1983

THIS IS A BORZOI BOOK
PUBLISHED BY ALFRED A. KNOPF, INC.

Library of Congress Cataloging in Publication Data

Dallek, Robert.   The American style of foreign policy: cultural politics and foreign affairs.

Includes bibliographical references and index.
1. United States—Foreign relations—20th century.
2. United States—Politics and government—20th century.
3. National characteristics, American.   I. Title.
E744.D22   1983   327.73   82-48877
ISBN 0-394-51360-6

Manufactured in the United States of America

FIRST EDITION

To the Memory of

RICHARD HOFSTADTER

Scholar, Teacher, Friend

Contents

Acknowledgments

This book has profited from the comments of colleagues and friends who have read all or parts of the manuscript. Robert Jervis, Lawrence W. Levine, Robert Schulzinger, Ronald Steel, Arthur Steiner, and Richard Weiss provided encouragement and criticism for which I am grateful. My wife, Geraldine R. Dallek, helped improve my prose and tighten my argument with a thoughtful critique of the whole work. I am indebted to Ashbel Green and the editorial staff of Alfred A. Knopf for holding me to a high standard. They made both substantive and stylistic improvements in the manuscript and saved me from a number of errors. I am grateful to the Rockefeller Foundation for a Humanities Fellowship which freed me from teaching for a year and hastened completion of the book. The UCLA Academic Senate provided grants which also facilitated my work. Finally, a word of thanks to the community of scholars whose writings make an interpretive study of this sort possible.

Los Angeles, California   R.D.
July 1982

Introduction

To treat them [political ideas] as the offspring of pure reason would be to assign to them a parentage about as mythological as that of Pallas Athene. What matters most is the underlying emotions, the music, to which ideas are a mere libretto....

L. B. Namier, "Human Nature and Politics" (1955)

Immediately after World War II, when the United States took unprecedented responsibility for international peace and security, curiosity about the American style of foreign policy was intense. Partly generated by a desire to avoid future blunders, interest understandably centered on past misdeeds—on why we had fought a seemingly pointless war with Spain, committed ourselves to unrealizable goals in World War I, retreated into political isolationism in the twenties, ignored transparent threats in the thirties, and emerged from World War II imperfectly prepared to act constructively in foreign affairs. The answers to these questions produced a rich and varied literature on American diplomatic history. Where some scholars saw selfish economic interest or an imperial drive to make the world safe for capitalism as the principal influence on national actions abroad, others stressed the importance of domestic politics, the use of external events to promote internal political control. Still others found the central ingredient of America's foreign misadventures in legalism or a reverence for the rule of law, evangelism or a Protestant sense of responsibility for the disadvantaged, moralism or a tradition of free security ignoring the importance of power.

By the 1970s, however, this cycle of interest had run its course. Historians continued to write about major episodes in American diplomatic history, but the search for broad influences or the impulse to write synthetic history describing underlying forces in foreign affairs had waned. Perhaps this was a consequence of Vietnam, of despair that after all the analysis of earlier shortcomings the country could still go so wrong in Southeast Asia. Whatever the cause, this retreat from understanding is not only intellectually impoverishing but also dangerous. In a nuclear age, when a wrong turning can lead to global destruction, we cannot afford the luxury of indifference to fundamental shortcomings in the American style of foreign policy.

This book aims to rekindle discussion about U.S. foreign affairs. More than that, it is an attempt to probe nonrational influences on foreign policy. After almost two decades of reading, thinking, and writing about American diplomatic history, I remain unsatisfied with existing explanations for past crusading fervor, visions of eternal peace, denials of basic realities, and overblown fears in response to events abroad. Were such distortions merely quaint relics of the past, one might see them as aberrations worthy of only casual attention. But their enduring hold on the American imagination in dealing with the outside world heightens my interest in explaining them. I share with the diplomat and historian George Kennan the belief that our current "preoccupation with nuclear war is a form of illness [which] can be understood only as some form of subconscious despair on the part of its devotees—some sort of death wish, a readiness to commit suicide for fear of death—a state of mind explicable only by some inability to face the normal hazards and vicissitudes of the human predicament—a lack of faith, or better a lack of strength that it takes to have faith, as countless of our generations have had it before us."[1]

This book, then, is an exploration of what I would describe as the hidden side of American foreign policy. I do not mean conspiratorial schemes consciously pursued by unscrupulous men. I mean those subjective influences that makers and backers of foreign policy barely glimpse themselves. It is a study of undercurrents, of mood, tone, or milieu, of a climate of feeling that almost imperceptibly insinuates itself into concrete ideas and actions. Like the atmosphere, these matters are not easily described. Yet they are there. More precisely, I am interested in the ways Americans have given foreign affairs symbolic meanings or made them into something other than what they actually were. I am concerned with foreign policy as a product of emotional displacement, of the impulse to make overseas affairs a vehicle for expressing unresolved internal tensions. For most Americans, the external world has been a remote, ill-defined sphere which can be molded into almost anything they wish. More often than we might care to think, this attitude has translated into foreign policies which have relieved and encouraged a nation struggling with tormenting domestic concerns.

These matters are not easily pinned down. They are not accessible through the conventional materials of historical study. To get at them, we need to draw on impressions and make connections which are not readily apparent. Stated another way, I have tried to come to grips with what the historian Bernard Bailyn has described as "latent" events. He writes:

> The problem of relating latent events . . . to events that register in the awareness of contemporaries . . . is becoming the central methodological problem of modern historiography. . . . For the essence and drama of history lie precisely in the relationship between latent conditions, which set boundaries of human existence, and the manifest problems with which people consciously struggle.

Though Bailyn is referring principally to "quantitative information . . . (shifts in birth rate, changes in family size and structure)," the proposition would seem to hold true for unconscious national impulses as well.[2] The objective underpinnings of human affairs, after all, are no more important than the subjective ones. As the historian Fritz Stern has stated the point, we "are trained to deal with ideas and events, not with a power of discontent as expressed in unreason and fantasy. But this kind of subterranean and neurotic force is intrinsically important, and sheds light on the more prominent and healthier elements of society as well."[3] These influences, of course, are more difficult to demonstrate than quantitative data, but this should not forestall us from trying. If we are going to carry the study of American foreign policy beyond the confines of where we have been, we will need to explore those unconscious feelings which create the perceptual framework for viewing our relations with the rest of the world.

None of this is to suggest that political, strategic, and economic interests played no part in what the United States did abroad. These substantive matters, especially after World War II, loomed large in the country's overseas actions. But material and psychological or symbolic aims are not mutually exclusive. In our approach to foreign affairs, style and substance have always gone hand in hand. The fact that I have so much less to say about traditional influences on foreign policy than about the psychological ones is not meant to suggest that I wish to replace one explanation with the other. My objective is to expand our understanding of American foreign affairs by looking at them in a somewhat different way. As the historian Richard Hofstadter concluded, "people not only seek their interests but also express and even in a measure define themselves in politics; that political life acts as a sounding board for identities, values, fears, and aspirations."[4]

What I have found particularly striking in pursuing this idea is how consistently domestic mood or climate of feeling registered in all its complexity on foreign policy. It is well known that before 1945 the country's shift from an agricultural, rural, largely homogeneous society to an industrial, urban one with a heterogeneous population spawned economic, political, and social unrest. It has been less clearly recognized that this development also found release in actions overseas. Indeed, I would go so far as to say that during these years foreign policy was less a reaction to events abroad than to conditions at home, where economic, political, and social change substantially blotted out overseas affairs and largely made them an irrational extension of internal hopes and fears.

The way America fought and ended the Spanish-American War, for instance, expressed yearnings across the whole society for a way out of the tensions between the modern industrialized world and the earlier rural culture. At one level the struggle with Spain became a celebration of old-style individualism and localism, while the peace arrangements reflected the contrary belief that new, worldwide responsibilities might compel the country to accommodate itself to modern trends. When it did not, the progressives used foreign policy in every part of the globe to encourage hopes for greater harmony, democracy, individual opportunity, and social justice in the United States. The Caribbean, with small island countries that barely registered on American thought, became a perfect focus for these domestic absorptions. Roosevelt's Corollary to Monroe's Doctrine and Wilson's Missionary Diplomacy said less about American intentions in the Caribbean than about the quest for progressive advance in the United States. To be sure, the Roosevelt and Wilson policies also served selfish national interests, but the emotional or symbolic satisfaction which their actions provided seems to have been foremost in American minds.

Remote areas like East Asia were particularly susceptible to this sort of symbolic politics: When Americans invested China with visions of self-determination or freedom from alien control, they were more intent on combatting corporate influences destroying autonomy at home than on assuring independence for the Chinese. Even Europe, the most familiar foreign area of the world for Americans, could not escape the national preoccupation with internal affairs. Although the Great European War of 1914-18 was the most compelling event of the progressive era, it also became enmeshed in domestic concerns: American participation in the war was as much a device for relieving frustrations at home as a means of advancing national interests abroad.

The triumph of political reaction in the twenties and the subsequent revival of liberalism in the thirties and forties did not alter this pattern. Tied to enduring tensions over national self-image, the impulse to attach domestic goals to foreign relations survived the shifts between progressive and conservative political control. After World War I, when social cleavages between city and town, foreign- and native-born, agitated the country and heightened longings for a homogeneous America, foreign affairs reflected both these trends: Economic nationalism and political isolationism expressed the reality of special interest struggles in the United States, while treaties limiting naval arms and outlawing war were more symbolic wishes for lost domestic unity than sensible advances toward world peace. Moreover, World War II, the most serious international crisis of the century, repeated the national habit of viewing foreign relations in domestic terms: Universalism in the forties was more a statement about felt American harmony than a realistic assessment of the possibilities for "one world."

This impulse to invest overseas affairs with domestic meanings made American foreign policy before 1945 highly erratic. False assumptions about the outside world abounded. But as long as national survival did not seem particularly threatened by external conditions, Americans were loath to give up this psychologically satisfying way of seeing foreign affairs. After World War II, however, when national security could no longer be taken for granted and democratic and anticommunist nations everywhere depended on American power for their safety, U.S. foreign policy became more realistic than it had been. Interest in the United States mounted not only in past failures overseas but also in understanding how other people thought and international relations worked. "Realism" became a kind of national obsession in everything to do with foreign affairs.

But this self-conscious effort to be rational and tough-minded about foreign relations could not entirely overturn traditional habits, especially because tensions over the character of American life continued to trouble the domestic scene. Though the New Deal persuaded Americans of the necessity of accommodating themselves to a more centralized society of large-scale organizations and less individual autonomy, nagging doubts remained. However considerable the success of the New Deal, however popular many of its ideas and its spirit of humane responsibility for the disadvantaged, it did not advance a new national self-image or fresh systematic conception of social relations to replace the old ideology of self-help and free enterprise. Consequently, the postwar period witnessed enduring tensions over national character and the proper role of federal authority in American life. Periodic bursts of organized demand for less government and greater freedom, culminating in the Reagan presidency, testify to continuing dreams of restoring an earlier, simpler style of life. Yet the country has been willing to follow this traditional ideology only up to a point, suggesting that it remains stuck somewhere between the new and the old, the modern technological world of huge bureaucracies and the nineteenth-century small-town culture of greater autonomy and personal control.

This ongoing conflict over national character partly explains the persistent irrationality in postwar foreign policy. A central element of the American response to the outside world in this period has been an unthinking anticommunism, an impulse to see a significant Communist threat to American security where it was either small or nonexistent. Policy toward Iran in the 1950s, Vietnam in the 1960s, and Chile in the 1970s reflected this distortion. The Eisenhower, Kennedy, Johnson, and Nixon administrations successively turned nationalistic movements in each of these countries into international Communist advances threatening dire harm to the United States. American ideas of what went on in these countries and what it meant to the United States were greatly at variance with the facts. As demonstrated by post-1975 events in Southeast Asia, for example, a Communist government in all Vietnam produced not Communist control throughout the area, but rather a clash of the two most powerful Communist countries in Asia—China and Vietnam. My point here is not to make a virtue out of the triumph of Communist arms in Vietnam but to consider why so many Americans reached false conclusions about the meaning of events in three widely separated countries over a long period of time.

As with the pre-1945 period, I see part of the answer in the response to changes in the United States. Shortly after World War II, the sociologist David Riesman suggested that Americans were uncomfortable with recent alterations in American life. ". . . Why is war so likely, when few people want it?" he asked. ". . . One reason—certainly not the only one!—is simply that great numbers of people do not in fact enjoy life enough. They are not passionately attached to their lives, but rather cling to them. . . . The person who is not autonomous," he explained, "loses much of the joy that comes through strength—through the effort to live one's life, not necessarily heroically, but come what may, in full commitment to it." Though feeling alienated and powerless, this "other-directed" person, as Riesman calls him, refuses to confront the sources of his distress. Instead, he lays the blame for his discontent on conditions beyond his reach: It is not the industrial culture of organized conformity which provides so much material comfort and against which he refuses to turn, but a distant external threat—Russian communism, for example—to which he ascribes his sense of dread. In short, the "Communist threat" has become a convenient excuse for not facing up to troubling domestic concerns.[5]

The Communist danger served yet another function. It justified the need for "togetherness," conformity, or organizational loyalty as a substitute for the traditional individualism to which so many Americans are still drawn. Tied to the material benefits provided by the impersonal machine culture, Americans rationalize its necessity by pointing to Communist threats. Though other influences contribute to this exaggerated fear, its usefulness as a device for encouraging "Americanism" or "belongingness" has been a consistent reason for its centrality in U.S. foreign policy since the Second World War.

The other side of the struggle over national character—the attraction to old-style individualism—has also made itself felt in the postwar debate on foreign affairs. Advocates of the idea that there is no substitute for victory in the contest with communism and that we may have to fight a nuclear war which we could survive see such policies as ultimately restoring a nineteenth-century world of greater personal freedom. The destruction of Communist power would end the Cold War, partly eliminate the need for a powerful centralized government, reduce the pressure for conformity, and allow the individual more leeway to follow his own star. Viewing the Cold War as a major contributor to conformity in American life, many proponents of traditional individualism favor all-out steps to bring it to an end. They have also expressed their commitment to individualism more benignly in repeated calls for national self-determination all over the globe. Vietnamization during Nixon's presidency, for example, had less to do with the unrealistic goal of turning a client state into an independent South Vietnam than with finding a way out of the war and symbolically reasserting personal liberty in the United States. Despite the considerable movement toward a more rational view of international relations in recent years, then, the country has continued to use foreign policy in nonrational ways to express current hopes and fears.

This destructive impulse in American relations with the

world has not received its due, and badly needs attention. And beyond this beckons the even larger field of comparative studies—the exploration of a similar phenomenon in other countries. While I am describing the *American* style of foreign policy, I do not mean to imply that the influence of nonrational domestic forces on foreign affairs is exclusive to the United States. Other nations have surely been subject to similar influences, which a study of the American experience can help illuminate.

The book that follows is a step in that direction. It is a first step, a venture onto largely uncharted ground. As such, it is meant to be suggestive and exploratory, the reflections of a scholar who has thought about these issues for some time. Its objective is to encourage discussion and to highlight the need for ongoing investigation into the unilluminated side of the American foreign policy tradition.

The American Style
of Foreign Policy

1

Imperialism: A Crisis in National Self-Confidence

... There seemed to be an epidemic of insanity in the country just at this time.

President Grover Cleveland, August 1896

America in the 1890s was a nation in turmoil. Industrialization, urbanization, depression, labor unrest, and mass migrations from Southern and Eastern Europe were undermining traditions of rural-agricultural life maintained by a largely homogeneous population of British Protestants. The rise of trusts and the apparent closing of the frontier, announced by the historian Frederick Jackson Turner in a famous paper of 1893, suggested an end to the tradition of competitive opportunities for the individual and left middle-class Americans with a sense of permanently diminished prospects. "We meet in the midst of a nation brought to the verge of moral, political, and material ruin," the Populist platform of 1892 declared.

> Corruption dominates the ballot-box, the legislatures, the Congress, and touches even the ermine of the bench. The people are demoralized; . . . the newspapers are largely subsidized or muzzled; public opinion silenced; business prostrated; our homes covered with mortgages;

labor impoverished; and the land concentrating in the hands of the capitalists. The urban workmen are denied the right of organization for self-protection. . . . The fruits of the toil of millions are boldly stolen to build up colossal fortunes for a few. . . . From the same prolific womb of governmental injustice we breed the two great classes—tramps and millionaires.

The discontent engendered by these developments found expression in protest, humanitarian, and utopian movements which threatened to revolutionize American life. ". . . The public mind seemed to be in an inflammable state, and a spark might kindle a conflagration," President Grover Cleveland confided to a friend in August 1896. The "conflagration" Cleveland feared took the form not of an internal upheaval but of a war with Spain over Cuba and the acquisition of an island empire after the fighting. Indeed, the war and its aftermath formed a three-part response to the domestic tensions of the nineties. The reasons for going to war, the way in which the country fought, and the decision to take colonies at the close of the fighting had more to do with relieving internal strains than with serving American interests abroad. ". . . War with monarchial, Catholic, Latin Spain," one historian has written, "had no purpose except to relieve emotion." By acting to rescue Cuba from Spain's destructive rule, Americans were also unconsciously rescuing themselves from oppressive conditions at home. Further, by fighting the war with local militia rather than with a well-integrated national army, Americans made the conflict into a celebration of individualism and small-town culture, prized virtues of their past. Lastly, by describing empire as a new path to national stability and advance, as many did, Americans turned the peacemaking into yet another means of dealing with domestic unrest. In short, the imperial outburst of 1898–99 was more the product of troubles at home than of opportunities abroad, and was the first in a succession of modern episodes in which foreign affairs had greater symbolic than substantive importance in the nation's life.[1]

The impulse toward overseas involvements did not simply appear at the close of the nineties; advocates of expansion had encouraged Americans to think about such things for some twenty-five years before the Spanish-American War. The driving force behind this development was a series of economic depressions that engulfed the country in the seventies, eighties, and nineties and sent American farmers and manufacturers in search of foreign markets. The results were spectacular. Between 1860 and 1897 American exports more than tripled, making the United States second only to Britain as a world trader.

Beginning in the 1870s, the need for overseas markets became a common theme of American business journals and some popular magazines. Foreign outlets for surplus production were essential to American well-being, these articles declared. "We must turn our eyes abroad, or they will soon look inward upon discontent." The popular protests and threatened social convulsions following the economic collapse of 1893 underscored this concern. It was up to the federal government, the journals asserted, to provide the foreign markets that could stabilize the economy and preserve the political system of the United States.

Political leaders were responsive to this appeal. The presidents and their secretaries of state in these years uniformly supported the idea of commercial expansion. "The question which now preemptorily challenges all thinking minds," Secretary of State William M. Evarts declared in 1877, "is how to create a foreign demand for those manufactures which are left after supplying our home demands. . . ." Secretary of State James G. Blaine announced in 1890: "I wish to declare the opinion that the United States has reached a point where one of its highest duties is to enlarge the area of its foreign trade." The nation's "prosperity ... depends largely upon [its] ability to sell surplus products in foreign markets at remunerative prices," Treasury Secretary John G. Carlisle said on behalf of the Cleveland administration in 1894.[2]

A growing conviction in the nineties that internal expansion had reached an end quickened the sense of urgency about finding overseas markets. In 1890–91, C. Wood Davis, a Kansas farmer and businessman, published a series of articles in which he described the exhaustion of the public lands and predicted that population in the United States during the next thirty years would expand more than three times faster than the available arable land. He argued that the disappearance of easily acquired fertile land, to which the unemployed could freely resort, foretold the end of American uniqueness and the emergence of a European caste system. As Turner stated the point in his memorable paper of 1893, "The Significance of the Frontier in American History": "And now, four centuries from the discovery of America, at the end of a hundred years of life under the Constitution, the frontier has gone, and with its going has closed the first period of American history." The solution Turner and others saw to this dilemma was the creation of a commercial frontier or the expansion of American trade to all corners of the globe.

By the 1890s the idea of American expansion was enjoying popular approval. Although many Americans described themselves as isolationists, a business journal noted in 1889, no one in the country opposed increased commercial ties abroad. In a book published in 1885, titled *Our Country,* the Reverend Josiah Strong preached the doctrine of "Anglo-Saxon Christian Imperialism," and over the following eight years the book sold some 160,000 copies. The Anglo-Saxon race, Strong declared, was destined to reshape the world in its own image.

There are no more new worlds. The unoccupied arable lands of the earth are limited, and will soon be taken.

6

The time is coming when the pressure of population on the means of subsistence will be felt here as it is now felt in Europe and Asia. Then the world will enter upon a new stage of its history—the final competition of races, for which the Anglo-Saxon is being schooled.

... Then this race of unequalled energy ... having developed peculiarly aggressive traits calculated to impress its institutions upon mankind, will spread itself over the earth.[3]

American schoolbooks—geographies, histories, and readers—of the late nineteenth century reflected this general acceptance of overseas expansion. Many of these texts urged the extension of U.S. political influence abroad and celebrated national power as a virtue worthy of a moral nation. Indeed, the enlargement of American political power around the globe was seen as a liberating force that would uplift "the indolent or barbarian nations of the passive races." This was particularly the case with Latin America, where there was "little hope for progress unless [it was] guided by the United States."[4]

Popular interest in furthering national influence abroad was a fact of late-nineteenth-century American life. Yet alongside domestic questions, it was a distinctly secondary concern. If Strong's book sold well, it did not approach the success of works describing internal solutions to American economic ills: Henry George's *Progress and Poverty* and Edward Bellamy's *Looking Backward* sold in the millions, while William Hope Harvey's *Coin's Financial School* reached a circulation of 300,000 copies in one year. Moreover, even Strong's book focused more on domestic issues than on solving American problems through expansion abroad. Also, while late-nineteenth-century schoolbooks spoke approvingly of U.S. influence overseas, they had nothing to say about acquiring foreign markets. Indeed, the picture of the American economy painted in these texts was of a robust machine following a line of inevitable progress toward greater material wealth and comfort. The periodic depressions were seen as aberrations produced by outbursts of unethical speculation. Poverty was the consequence of willful misbehavior or immoral idleness; the poor were victims of their own evil ways. Since traditional habits of honesty and industry were the only requirements for national economic health, the schoolbooks described no need for external markets.[5]

Even more telling is the fact that, despite impulses toward overseas involvements in the seventies, eighties, and early nineties, little actual expansion took place. Opportunities to gain Dominican, Hawaiian, and Haitian naval harbors were bypassed, while the Cuban insurrection of 1868–78 against Spain provoked no decisive action by the United States. Even if one grants that markets, not territories or overseas possessions, were the objective of the expansionists, it is difficult to explain why so few coaling stations that could promote foreign trade were obtained in these years. In the words of one historian: "Is not more to be learned about established national policy by asking not what proposals were made for acquisition of coaling stations in the Caribbean or elsewhere, but rather why so little came of them? Why were the possibilities dangled at various times by Portuguese, Danes, Liberians, Peruvians, and Koreans not accepted? Why was so little done before the War with Spain to turn such available sites as Pearl Harbor and Pago Pago to strategic advantage?" Although the United States joined Britain and Germany in establishing a protectorate over Samoa in 1889 and went to the brink of war with Chile over an insult to its honor in 1891, foreign affairs remained so inconsequential that in 1892 the New York *Herald* urged abolition of the State Department and the recall of "our farcical diplomats."[6]

Yet within three years foreign affairs gained center stage in the United States when Washington provoked a major crisis with Britain over the contested Venezuela–British Guiana boundary line. While the aim of preventing British seizure of Venezuelan territory, a wish to assure U.S. access to Latin

American markets, and a desire to improve the Cleveland administration's political standing by twisting the British lion's tail together go far to explain the crisis, its roots seem more fully lodged in the nation's emotional response to the depression of 1893–97. Characterized by bloody conflicts like the Pullman and Homestead strikes, marches of the unemployed on Washington, radical proposals from anarchists, free-silverites, populists, and socialists, the depression produced frustrations which also found release in national self-assertiveness or jingoism. As Richard Hofstadter pointed out, Americans responded to the depression with "two quite different moods": an intensification of protest and humanitarian reform, on the one hand, and national self-assertion, aggression, and expansion, on the other. "The motif of the first [mood] was social sympathy; of the second, national power." Yet, as one observer at the time obliquely noted, the two impulses were tied together, and one could be submerged in the other. "When you come to diagnose the country's internal ills," a Texas congressman wrote Secretary of State Richard Olney, "the possibilities of 'blood and iron' loom up immediately. Why, Mr. Secretary, just think of how angry the anarchistic, socialistic, and populistic boil appears on our political surface and who knows how deep its roots extend or ramify? One cannon shot across the bow of a British boat in defense of this [Venezuela] principle will knock more *pus* out of it than would suffice to inoculate and corrupt our people for the next two centuries."[7]

Both moods expressed themselves in the Venezuela boundary crisis. The justification most Americans gave for turning an apparently minor issue into a major controversy threatening war was the desire to prevent British exploitation of Venezuela and future violations of the Monroe Doctrine. "If Great Britain is to be permitted to . . . take the territory of Venezuela," Senator Henry Cabot Lodge asserted in 1895, "there is nothing to prevent her from taking the whole of Venezuela or any other South American State. . . . The supremacy of the Monroe Doctrine should be established and at once—peaceably if we can, forcibly if we must." In the Venezuela crisis, jingoism was to serve humanitarian ends; a weak Latin state was to be saved from imperial abuse.

But for all the bluster, Americans backed away from a war with Britain over Venezuela. Beset by difficulties with Russia in the Balkans and the Far East and with Germany over the Transvaal, London showed itself receptive to a negotiated settlement with the United States. Furthermore, a financial panic over a possible war turned much of the American business community against a conflict. But perhaps most important, Britain's alleged exploitation of Venezuela seemed an insufficient moral question over which to go to war. For suggesting it might be, Cleveland "received the most unanimous and crushing rebuke that the pulpit of this country ever addressed to a President." For Americans to go to war, they needed to believe that they were rescuing some helpless victim of undeserved exploitation. Victims of a terrible depression at home for which they had no cure, Americans identified with and found considerable appeal in rescuing other victims abroad. If Venezuela and Britain could not supply the right formula, Cuba and Spain did.[8]

In 1898, few government leaders wanted a conflict between Spain and the United States. Madrid saw little gain and much loss from an American war, while other European governments feared its impact on stability in Spain and their own homelands. In the United States as well, there was little enthusiasm among businessmen or in the McKinley administration for a potentially unsettling struggle, and the President and his State Department bent all their efforts toward avoiding a conflict. But they were inadequate to the task. McKinley himself was too much a reflector of the public mood to turn domestic currents away from war, while the department was little more than a passive instrument of the President's will. Staffed by a senile secretary (John Sherman), a diffident first secretary (William R. Day), and a nearly deaf second secretary (Alvey A. Adee), the department was described as having a head who "knows nothing," a first assistant who "says nothing," and a second assistant who "hears nothing."[9]

Yet even the strongest of leaders might have struggled in vain against the war passion gripping the United States in 1898. Indeed, what seems striking in the movement toward war with Spain is not that the McKinley administration failed to hold it back but that it took three years to gain its end. In 1895, shortly after a renewed outbreak of fighting against Spain in Cuba, "free Cuba" rallies occurred throughout the United States. Supported by Cuban-Americans, labor groups, patriotic societies, and anti-Catholic Protestant evangelists, the movement evoked widespread public enthusiasm and congressional resolutions favoring recognition of Cuban belligerency. "The issue let loose cascades of imperialistic and moralistic oratory," the historian Ernest May writes. If the United States failed to act in behalf of Cuba, one senator warned, "the time will come when there will be retribution upon us as a people, because we have not been true to the task assigned us by Providence."

Between the middle of 1895 and early 1898, pro-Cuban sentiment came in waves that rose and abated. The passion of 1895 petered out during the presidential campaign of 1896, but appeared again at the end of the year. Touched off by stories of Spanish treachery in the slaying of a rebel leader, pro-Cuban demonstrations spontaneously erupted across the country. Whereas the excitement of 1895 "had arisen among people disquieted over the political, moral, or religious health of the country," May explains, "that of 1896 occurred among people who were economically discontented." This excitement quieted somewhat when Cleveland made it clear that he would leave the solution of the Cuban problem to the incoming McKinley administration. After he assumed office in March 1897, McKinley kept jingoes in the country and the Congress at bay for almost a year by a series of diplomatic and political actions that gave the appearance of movement toward a resolution of the issue. In December 1897, for example, when Congress reconvened, McKinley held off legislative pressure by promising action in "the near future" if current Spanish efforts to arrange peace in Cuba came to naught.[10]

A series of incidents in early 1898, however, began pushing the Cuban problem beyond McKinley's control. Riots in Havana in January encouraged speculation in the United States of coming anarchy marked by wholesale massacres. Publication of a private letter by Spain's minister to Washington, Dupuy de Lôme, describing McKinley as "weak and a bidder for the admiration of the crowd," intensified antagonism to Spain. When the American battleship *Maine* blew up in Havana Harbor with the loss of 260 lives on February 15, "a sort of bellicose fury . . . seized the American nation." War talk was heard on street corners in widely scattered cities and towns; mobs burned effigies of Spanish statesmen; "theater audiences cheered, stamped, and wept at the playing of the Star Spangled Banner"; while one Missouri resident reported "patriotism . . . oozing out of every boy . . . old enough to pack feed to the pigs."[11]

The nation received a "final propulsion to war" in mid-March, when Senator Redfield Proctor of Vermont reported to the Senate on a recent visit to Cuba. A conservative who previously held no pronounced opinion on events in Cuba, Proctor provided a dispassionate account of conditions in the island. It confirmed the worst estimates of Spanish rule. "Desolation and distress, misery and starvation" were everywhere to be seen outside Havana. He witnessed "the spectacle of a million and a half of people, the entire native population of Cuba, struggling for freedom and deliverance from the worst misgovernment of which I ever had knowledge." Concluding that neither side could overcome the other in the struggle, Proctor recommended American intervention to end the conflict. Given wide attention because he was believed to be speaking for McKinley, his report had a dramatic impact. Businessmen, conservative newspapers, and numerous religious leaders announced themselves ready to fight Spain for humanitarian ends. Reluctant to appear unpatriotic and remain out of step with the national mood, conservative leaders fell into line with mass sentiment. No doubt some among them cynically recalled De Tocqueville's observation about the tyranny of the majority.[12]

The political pressure on McKinley to act now became irresistible. Senator Henry Cabot Lodge of Massachusetts warned in late March that a failure to confront the crisis in Cuba would send the Republican party "down in the greatest defeat ever known. . . . I know that . . . to threaten war for political reasons is a crime. . . . But to sacrifice a great party and bring free silver upon the country for a wrong policy is hardly less odious. On a great, broad question like this, when right & wrong are involved I believe profoundly in the popular instinct & what that instinct is no one who goes out among the people . . . can doubt for one moment."

By the beginning of April, it was clear to the administration that unless McKinley promised to put the issue before Congress should peace negotiations fail, the legislature would go ahead immediately on its own. If the administration did "not turn its face towards the front and lead instead of being pushed," Elihu Root wrote Theodore Roosevelt, ". . . it will be rolled over and crushed and the Republican party with it." The Democrats would ride to power in 1900, it was widely predicted, on a program of Free Cuba and Free Silver. Fearful that a Democratic success would open the way to revolutionary changes in American life and unable to persuade the Spanish to accept the possibility of Cuban independence as a condition of further negotiation, McKinley put a war message before the Congress on April 11, 1898. "Caught between the aggressive irrationality of his own people and the decadent irrationality of the ancient Latin power," Richard Hofstadter observed, McKinley reluctantly went to war.[13]

The driving force behind this decision to fight was spontaneous pressure from great numbers of Americans in every part of the country demanding Cuba's release from Spanish abuse. For three years stories had poured into the United States about Cuban suffering: men, women, and children hacked to death by machetes; starvation and disease everywhere; arbitrary expropriations of property. Daily newspaper headlines shrieked the atrocities: "Massacre!"; "Slaughter of Innocent Noncombatants Continues in Cuba"; "Untried Prisoners Shot in Squads"; "Bodies Thrown into Trenches and Left Unburied." For most Americans war seemed justified on strict humanitarian grounds.[14]

But behind this sincerely enunciated desire to act selflessly in behalf of Cuba's suffering masses were inarticulated feelings or unspoken tensions which were finding release in a war with Spain. For farmers and laborers, who had lost their land and jobs and were the principal victims of the economic distress of the nineties, a war served two functions: On the one hand, it gave them the sense of supporting victims of ruthless exploitation—Cubans writhing under Spanish rule with whom Americans injured by economic forces beyond their control could readily identify; on the other, it gave them the sense of striking out against the perpetrators of these ills—decadent Spain in Cuba and conservative business interests in America, which had opposed government aid to farmers and unionization for workers, had backed McKinley against Bryan in 1896, and now resisted a war. The verdict of 1896, one historian notes, "was thus appealed and, in its probusiness aspect, symbolically overturned in the preliminaries to the Spanish American War." Advocates of intervention in Cuba denounced "the eminently respectable porcine citizens who ... consider the starvation of ... inoffensive men, women and children, and the murder of

250 American sailors . . . of less importance than a fall of two points in a price of stocks."[15]

Yet it was not just economically distressed Americans who plumped for war; middle-class citizens as well demanded action. Like their less fortunate fellow Americans, middle-class men and women used a humanitarian crusade against Spain as a release for unfocused feelings about their lives. For them, the Spanish-American War was largely a release from an oppressive life-style fastened on them by what the historian John Higham has called "the gathering restrictions of a highly industrialized society." They lived in cities, sat in rooms "cluttered with bric-a-brac," limited the size of their families, accepted the authority of professional elites, masked "their aggressions behind a thickening facade of gentility," and comforted "themselves with a faith in automatic material progress." Above all, they "learned to conform to the discipline of machinery."

Struggling with the frustrations of an urban-industrial culture, middle-class Americans gave vent to their feelings through a rising interest in sports and recreation and a fascination with untamed nature. The craze in the 1890s for football, basketball, boxing, bicycling, hiking, camping, and bird-watching was symptomatic of these trends. This athleticism was coupled with a new jingoism which Theodore Roosevelt perfectly expressed in a famous speech of 1899, "The Strenuous Life." Rejecting "the soft spirit of the cloistered life" and "the base spirit of gain," Roosevelt urged a "life of Strife," of "hard and dangerous endeavor" which could "win the goal of true national greatness." The tie between this athleticism and jingoism, John Higham explains, "was especially evident in the yellow press: William Randolph Hearst's *New York Journal* created the modern sports page in 1896, just when its front page filled with atrocity stories of the bloody treachery of Spanish brutes in Cuba." The Splendid Little War, the crusade against a decadent Spain, was a logical culmination to a decade in which an absorption with action and heroics had expressed the middle-class quest for a release from the staid conditions of industrial life.[16]

A war with Spain offered similar attractions to intellectuals, politicians, and publicists from "good families," Americans of Anglo-Saxon stock with a patrician outlook. For Brooks Adams, Albert Beveridge, Henry Cabot Lodge, Robert La Follette, Alfred T. Mahan, Theodore Roosevelt, and others like them in Union League clubs and patriotic societies, a war promised to blunt economic and social antagonisms, counter a spiritually debilitating materialism, and make possible the fulfillment of the promise of American life. The vitality released by war might "hammer us into decency," William James asserted. The Spanish-American War, Brooks Adams said, refuted his belief that the whole of Western civilization was heading toward decay; the war was promoting a revival of national energy and demonstrating that Americans were "the people of destiny." Albert Beveridge was more rhapsodic: "No sections any more but a Nation. . . . No, not *a* Nation, but the Nation, The Nation, God's chosen people." Theodore Roosevelt declared: "We will have this war for the freedom of Cuba in spite of the timidity of the commercial interests." And there was also his characteristic pronouncement that "The people that have lost the fighting edge, that have lost the virile virtues, occupy a position as dangerous as it is ignoble." Americans needed a war to rejuvenate their society.

What most of these men did not remark was that a war, which put them in conflict with much of the new business elite, allowed them a sense of resurgent influence in the society. Suffering an erosion of their status, feeling displaced by a new class of business wealth, they saw their and America's resurgence in a fight against Spain as one and the same. "In the case of some of the war enthusiasts," Richard Hofstadter observes, "it is not clear whether they favored action more because they bled for the sufferings of the Cubans or because they hated the materialism and the flaccid pacifism of the *haute bourgeoisie.*"[17]

If all segments of American society found psychic satisfaction in saving Cuba, they also agreed that Spain was an appropriate enemy. Judging from nineteenth-century schoolbooks and contemporary comments, most Americans saw Spain as a greedy, indolent, degenerate, and particularly cruel nation. Indeed, no people fared worse in the American mind than the Spanish. Their history was "a syllabus of barbarism," and "no single good thing in law, or science, or art, or literature" had come from Spain's presence in America. Its flag was the symbol of "rapine and pillage." One correspondent advised McKinley that "A Spaniard cannot buy a basket of eggs without intrigue." Spain was "three hundred years behind all the rest of the world," Henry Cabot Lodge declared. "What seems to us brutal treachery seems to them all right." Spain's General Valeriano Weyler in Cuba was "the voice of the Middle Ages." His "smileless cruel face" wore an expression of "brutal determination." Current Spanish actions in Cuba were simply extensions of what Americans remembered from schoolbooks: The Spanish stretched Mexicans on beds of hot coals, cut off the hands of prisoners, burned them at the stake, worked them to death, or tore them to bits with bloodhounds. Americans were almost unanimous in their belief that Spain had no redeeming features. "I would like to see Spain . . . swept from the face of the earth," said suffragist leader Elizabeth Cady Stanton. Spain was America's ideal enemy in a war.[18]

If the Spanish-American War was largely the product of mass emotions which had more to do with domestic tensions than with external concerns, we need to ask what happened to these anxieties after the conflict began. Although the war provided a release for pent-up feelings, and returning prosperity relieved the suffering of farmers and laborers, the psychic tensions over a society moving in new directions toward concentrated wealth and power in corporations and urban political machines continued to make themselves felt in foreign affairs.

The American response to the Spanish conflict is illustrative. Americans saw the fighting as less a victory of the United States over a feeble Spain than as a triumph of traditional individualism over modern centralizing trends. Indeed, in their imagination, the war with Spain became less a celebration of U.S. power than a vindication of individual initiative and small-town America over impersonal corporate forces dominating late-nineteenth-century national life. By viewing the war this way, Americans vented the tensions which had driven them into it in the first place. A celebration of traditional virtues, the conflict expressed American wishes to meet current economic and social problems by returning to an older, simpler style of life. In short, the war revealed less about what Americans hoped to achieve abroad than what they wished to see at home.

Resistance to submerging the National Guard in the Regular Army illustrates the point. To many Americans, it was essential that the career Army take a secondary role in the war to volunteers organized in National Guard units representing the states and localities. "There was in fact nothing national about the National Guards," Walter Millis has observed. "They were 'forty-five little state armies,' with no unity of organization, equipment or expertise." Efforts to bring them under the full control of the federal government met effective resistance. Under pressure from the states, Congress agreed to leave Guard units intact, with all their officers appointed upon the recommendation of the governors. The war was to be fought by hometown military units acting as extensions of their communities.

The principal virtue Americans saw in a volunteer or National Guard army was the chance to exercise personal initiative and avoid subjection to military "martinets." It was feared that service in the Regular Army under professional West

Pointers would convert hometown boys into interchangeable parts, cogs in a machine deprived of the chance to make a personal mark. Pressures for discipline and regimentation in National Guard units were vigorously resisted. Volunteers, for example, hated the salute and castigated officers who insisted on it. "Didn't yo' hear me shout ATTENTION?" an officer rebuked a volunteer. "Sure I did," he replied. "I thought yo' jest wanted me to look alive to somethin' interestin'." The 7th New York, one of the best National Guard regiments in the country, refused induction into federal service for fear it would have to serve under West Point graduates.

The war, historian Gerald Linderman points out, had to be one of personal encounter, of hating the enemy and grappling directly with him. The charge up San Juan Hill was the fulfillment of what many Americans hoped their share in a war would be. The assault began with so few men that "it seemed as if someone had made an awful and terrible mistake." Soldiers advanced without any command and began firing of their own accord. "Men were crazy," one trooper said of the battle. "Someone said, 'Let us charge' and someone sounded 'Let us charge' on a bugle . . . [and] that pack of demons swept forward. . . ." Stephen Crane described it as a soldiers' battle fought by those without orders and those who disobeyed whatever orders they had. "I got mine," one trooper told another after killing a Spaniard. "Now you go an' git yours." Spanish prisoners objected to the American style of fighting. "They tried to catch us with their hands," one of them complained.[19]

No individual and no military unit embodied American attitudes toward the war more clearly than Theodore Roosevelt and his Rough Riders. One of three federal volunteer cavalry regiments, the Rough Riders, as TR portrayed them in a popular account, were "natural fighters, men of great intelligence, . . . courage, . . . hardihood, and physical prowess. . . . Already good individual fighters, skilled in the use of the horse and rifle," they had no need of the training given to raw recruits. To have treated these men "from the standpoint of the martinet and military pedant would have been almost . . . fatal." There was to be no "militarism" among the Rough Riders, no attempt to deaden "the power of individual initiative" or suppress the "individual will." Only the "essentials of discipline" were needed to turn them into a magnificent fighting unit.

In TR's widely read postwar account, character and will repeatedly triumphed over adverse circumstances and technology. Mix-ups on the railway line into Port Tampa compelled the Rough Riders to seize coal cars which were backed down the nine miles of track into the port. A "shade" readier in "individual initiative" than were two other regiments, the Rough Riders boarded one of the limited number of transports ahead of them. Taking advantage of the chance to be among the first to land in Cuba and pushing ahead of other regiments by a quick march, the Rough Riders fought in the first battle of the campaign. Feelings of helplessness at confronting a hidden enemy using rifles with smokeless powder were overcome by "a mad drive" to the front. The charge up San Juan and Kettle hills was "the best moment of anybody's life." In it TR realized the American preconception of a Spanish-American War: personal combat in which he killed a Spaniard with his own hand. " 'T' was revelling in victory," his sister later wrote. "He had just 'doubled up' a Spanish officer like a jack-rabbit," as the Spaniard retreated from a blockhouse. In his description of the Cuban fighting, Linderman concludes, Roosevelt "fused the highest personal and social values in a single experience and had merged himself, temporarily at least, with his society."[20]

The consequences of this resistance to greater centralization and tighter organization were a poorly prepared Army and Navy. At the outbreak of the fighting a United States Army of 28,000 regulars confronted the task of dislodging 80,000 Spanish troops from Cuba. A call for volunteers quickly swelled the U.S. force to 200,000 men. But it had little resemblance to an effective army. The regular forces lacked high organization, training in combined operations, "provision for the assembling or transportation of an overseas expedition, or for the handling of any large body of troops whatever." Volunteers were even worse off; lacking modern rifles and tropical uniforms, they had to use almost worthless Springfield carbines and heavy clothing suitable for duty in Alaska. "A desperately overworked and understaffed War Department" could barely find the time to deal with these problems; regular working hours in the department were largely given over to answering the requests of high officials pressing for special privileges.

Plans to send a 25,000-man invasion force from Tampa Bay to Santiago highlighted these deficiencies. Regiments arrived at the port without uniforms, arms, blankets, tents, or medical supplies. Trains loaded with war matériel reached Tampa without bills of lading that would indicate their contents. Officers had to hunt through railroad cars to find the guns, ammunition, clothing, and commissary stores needed for the troops. "No word can paint the confusion," Theodore Roosevelt wrote of what he saw. "No head; a breakdown of both the railroad and military system of the country." Loading troops on the transports proved as confusing. With room on the ships for only 16,000 of the 25,000 men assembled for the invasion, a mad scramble occurred for the limited places. Regiments commandeered trains to travel from their camps to the port and then seized the first ship they could reach, holding it at gunpoint against other contending regiments. Once aboard, the troops sweltered in Tampa Bay for six days when false reports of Spanish vessels lying in wait to attack the convoy delayed its departure. Under way at last, the disorganized expedition of thirty-two transports, which could not keep in line and repeatedly lost sight of one another, took five and a half days to reach Santiago.[21]

Confusion and inadequate preparations continued to dog the American Army in Cuba. The journalist Richard Harding Davis considered the Cuban campaign a severe test of the axiom that "God takes care of drunken men, sailors, and the United States." In the first major engagement at Las Guásimas on the road to Santiago, "Fighting Joe" Wheeler, an ex-Confederate general, initiated the battle against the orders of General William R. Shafter, his commanding officer, and avoided the need for a humiliating rescue only when the Spanish broke and ran. "We've got the Yankees on the run," Wheeler shouted as the Spanish retreated. A week later, American victories at El Caney and San Juan and Kettle hills could not mask the Army's distressing failings. Outdated field guns and Springfields using black powder revealed U.S. positions at every shot and cost numerous casualties. The Navy was not much better off. Though relying on slow, thinly armored vessels manned by poorly trained gunners, it won surprisingly lopsided victories against Spain's inept Navy, losing but one man and no ships against 700 Spanish dead and the destruction of Spain's two main fleets.[22]

To some contemporaries, the conquest of a hopelessly outmatched Spain by a blundering United States in a series of relatively bloodless battles discredited the whole enterprise. "If the'se wan thing I'm prouder iv thin another in me past life," proclaimed Mr. Dooley, Finley Peter Dunne's comic character, " 'tis that whin me counthry called me to go to th' Spanish war, I was out. . . . Be hivins, Hinnissy, if a man's brought befure a judge on a charge iv larceny, th' coort says: 'Any prevyous convictions?' 'No,' says th' polisman. 'Five years,' says th' judge. 'But he was a hayro iv th' Cubian war.' 'Make it life,' says th' judge."[23] In retrospect, the conflict was less a war than a quasi-comic opera or farce in which an enfeebled Spain outdid the United States in military ineptitude.

Yet most Americans did not see the war that way. Instead, they shared John Hay's perception that it was "a splendid little war; begun with the highest motives, carried on with magnificent intelligence and spirit, favored by that fortune which loves the brave."[24] Most Americans saw it not as a demonstration of the country's military shortcomings or need for a modern army and navy, but as a testimony to the superiority of traditional individualism over modern technology and organization. Why, for example, did the widely known failings of the military not produce a significant outcry for change? Because what the country wanted was not a well-oiled military machine but the kind of individual heroics TR celebrated in his book. Indeed, Americans took the victory of inadequately prepared and equipped forces not as a prod to military reform but as a further inducement to resist current movements toward large-scale organization in domestic life.

The vast majority of Americans entered the war against Spain with no intention beyond freeing Cuba. Colonies or an imperial domain for the United States were on almost no one's agenda. Self-determination, antimilitarism, and opposition to absorbing "inferior peoples" into the Union stood as traditional bars to American colonialism. The congressional resolution for intervention in Cuba had included a self-denying proposition against U.S. "sovereignty, jurisdiction or control" over the island. The Philippines and other Spanish possessions in the Pacific were even more remote from American minds. There was nothing resembling a popular interest in the retention of these islands before the war. And even if McKinley was stretching the truth when he later said that Admiral Dewey's victory had surprised him completely and that he "could not have told where those darned islands were within 2,000 miles," it was symptomatic of how little forethought had been given to the Philippines.

Yet within days after Dewey had destroyed the Spanish fleet in Manila Bay, voices began to be heard in the United States for annexations. The most immediate impact was on Hawaii. In the spring of 1898, annexationists had been unable to push a joint resolution through the Congress. By the summer, however, after the war and Dewey's victory had convinced popular opinion that Honolulu had become a way station on the route to Manila and that Hawaii was essential to the defense of the Pacific coast, the House and the Senate approved annexation by two-to-one votes.

The swing on the Philippines was even more pronounced. In the six months after Dewey's victory at the beginning of May opinion in the United States moved from ignorance and indifference to widespread demand that the archipelago be brought under American control. In the middle of May one prominent businessman told the Republican Club of New York that clippings coming to him from newspapers all over the country indicated "a strong feeling . . . spreading over the whole land in favor of colonial expansion. The people are infatuated with the idea. . . . This feeling is getting so strong that it will mean the political death of any man to oppose it pretty soon." A survey of leading Republican newspapers in July showed them all favorable to annexation. By September many of the best known and most widely circulated papers supported retention of the Philippines. By then, one of McKinley's biographers writes, "all media available to the President indicated that the people favored retaining the islands." To test public sentiment, McKinley made a speaking tour of five midwestern states in October. Relying on stenographers and his own ears to record the intensity and duration of response to his comments on the Philippines, the President concluded that "there was no alternative" to taking the islands. "You and I don't want the Philippines," a Cabinet member wrote a friend, "but it's no use disguising the fact that an overwhelming majority of the people do. . . ."[25]

Historians have offered different explanations for the causes of this transformation. Some have said that imperialists and navalists—Theodore Roosevelt, Henry Cabot Lodge, Albert Beveridge, John Hay, Albert Shaw, Walter Hines Page, Henry and Brooks Adams, Admiral Mahan—presented the country with a *fait accompli*. By sending Dewey's fleet into Manila Bay and troops to invade the islands, by capturing Manila and occupying the city, bay, and harbor, and by extending U.S. military rule to the entire archipelago before the Senate could debate the wisdom of taking the islands, the expansionists made it difficult for the country to resist annexation. Some historians have emphasized in this the role of economic forces and businessmen. Although conservative business leaders had initially opposed a war with Spain as disruptive to national economic stability, they shifted ground after the prospect of seizing the Philippines arose. Believing that America's economic and political stability ultimately depended on finding overseas markets for surplus goods, businessmen now saw the Philippines as essential to the nation's Asian trade. Since mass opinion in the country accepted the need for foreign markets, it was now ready to break with the anticolonial tradition and favor the acquisition of a limited empire.[26]

Other historians have cited Manifest Destiny and Social Darwinism as reasons for American actions. An argument for preordained American acquisition of additional territories in the first half of the nineteenth century, the Manifest Destiny tradition made more sense to Americans in the circumstances of 1898–99 than customary anti-imperialism. In somewhat different form, Manifest Destiny became the rationale for the imperial outburst of the late nineties. Yet another historian sees Social Darwinism playing this role. Persuaded that international affairs were a struggle for survival among nations and that a country must expand or die, Americans accepted a war with Spain and colonial acquisitions as their "duty" and "destiny." When confronted with the opportunity to take the Philippines, they concluded that their own national survival required them to bring the islands under their control.[27]

Two other schools of thought have stressed "psychic" and foreign influences in accounting for American expansion following the war. According to the first interpretation, the taking of colonies represented a working off of domestic tensions or an outlet for pent-up emotions generated by internal upheavals. It argues the idea that "the widespread anxieties and discontents of the era, clearly had important bearings on questions of war and empire, and must be seen as major instrumentalities of history." According to the second explanation, the impact of British and European examples on Americans, or an awareness of foreign fashions in the United States, combined with Manifest Destiny, Social Darwinism, economic pressures, and psychological turmoil to make a policy of imperial expansion temporarily more appealing than the country's anticolonial tradition.[28]

Certainly each of these influences, in varying degrees, did play a part in launching the United States on its imperial course. Traditional Manifest Destiny and foreign thought and actions influenced America's imperial elite, economic considerations were uppermost with business leaders and some politicians, and Social Darwinism loomed large in the minds of American religious leaders, while a prospective release of personal frustrations appealed strongly to the mass public. These influences did not work exclusively on a single group; economic considerations and "psychic" tensions, for example, also had some impact on America's imperial elite. In short, these ideas and pressures cut across all groups in the society, creating a consensus for imperial domain.

Another, possibly more fundamental influence contributed to this general agreement—namely, a conviction reaching into all segments of the society that a turn toward colonial empire might end the economic and social tensions of the last twenty-five years by setting the nation on a new, more purposeful and settling course. As William James shrewdly foresaw, the war gave Americans a renewed "sense of mastery" that readily translated into a demand for colonies and a larger role in world affairs. To Henry Watterson, the editor of the Louisville *Courier-Journal*, the new empire abroad promised a degree of social cohesion at home the nation had not experienced in years:

> From a nation of shopkeepers we become a nation of warriors. We escape the menace and peril of socialism and agrarianism, as England has escaped them, by a policy of colonization and conquest. From a provincial huddle of petty sovereignties held together by a rope of sand we rise to the dignity and prowess of an imperial republic incomparably greater than Rome. It is true that we exchange domestic dangers for foreign dangers; but in every direction we multiply the opportunities of the people. We risk Caesarism, certainly; but even Caesarism is preferable to anarchism. . . . In short, anything is better than the pace we were going before these present forces were started into life.[29]

Other voices carried the same message. "Our country at the close of this war," the Daughters of the American Revolution announced, "will enter upon a new career, grander and more imposing than anything that has distinguished her in the past." And a prominent midwestern business leader declared: ". . . A nation cannot safely absorb itself in its own affairs. . . . It breeds strange and dangerous disorders. The most wholesome influence upon our home politics will be exerted by getting interested in questions that concern the whole world." Referring to the growth of domestic strife in the United States during the debate over colonial annexations, Senator E. O. Wolcott of Colorado said: "It may well be that this people have found, through the outlet which the results of war with Spain compelled us to take, the one course which shall lead to the perpetuity of our institutions and the safety and stability of the Republic." American clergymen preached the idea that the United States needed to expand in order to purify itself internally. ". . . We are to have a better America through cherishing larger responsibilities," one of them said. "Many who spoke for annexation of Hawaii, the Philippines, or other territories," Ernest May has pointed out, "claimed to be arguing for the nation's self-fulfillment as a propagator of liberty, democracy, and progress." The widely enunciated theme of expand or decline may have reflected the Social Darwinian mood of the time, but it also spoke to the American hope that a new career as a colonial power would permanently set aside the nation's domestic unrest.[30]

The expectation was short-lived. For about a year after the Senate approved annexation of the Philippines in February 1899 the surge toward expansion continued. In the summer of 1899 the *Literary Digest* found "a strong undercurrent of opinion in favor" of annexing Cuba. At the start of 1900, rumors circulated of secret negotiations to buy the Danish West Indies, and Americans responded to news of antiforeign violence in China with declarations of intent to join the Europeans in determining that country's political and economic future. Popular writings now also appeared forecasting ultimate American control over most of the Pacific and East Asia. The reasons remained the same as before: not a desire for territory as such, but "the extension of civilization" and the preservation of a vital America. "I believe in the expansion of great nations," Theodore Roosevelt wrote in December 1899. "India has done an incalculable amount for the English character. If we do our work well in the Philippines and the West Indies, it will do a great deal for our character."

Between 1900 and 1903, however, traditional anticolonialism regained its dominant position in the United States. Instead of joining in a partition of China, the McKinley administration called for an open door trade policy and the preservation of China's territorial and administrative integrity. The government also announced its intention to honor the Platt Amendment's commitment to Cuban independence, and prominent Americans began to predict eventual freedom for the Philippines. By 1903, Senator Henry Cabot Lodge believed that Americans had "lost all interest" in further colonial expansion.

This change in mood chiefly resulted from the conviction that imperialism brought not a new stability and optimism to America but the additional tensions and dangers foretold by opponents of empire. The most important influence in changing opinion was the Filipino rebellion against American rule. Lasting from the beginning of 1899 to the summer of 1901, Emilio Aguinaldo's rebels compelled an increase in American troops from 30,000 to 60,000 and burdened Washington with additional costs for pacifying the islands. Worse yet, U.S. forces now imitated their Spanish predecessors by torturing captured rebels, setting up concentration camps, and aiming "to kill and burn and make a howling wilderness" of a rebel stronghold. If the Philippine experience were not enough to disabuse Americans of their romantic hopes about colonialism, the British conflict with the Boers in South Africa clinched the point; extending from late 1899 to early 1902, the war cost Britain a heavy price in blood, treasure, and morale. Echoing the warnings of anti-imperialists that colonialism would violate America's tradition of self-determination, burden the country with heavy costs, spawn militarism, and ultimately destroy U.S. democratic institutions, the Filipino uprising shattered American hopes for a new cohesion and stability at home through expansion abroad.[31]

Contemporaries rationalized the Spanish-American War and its aftermath, the taking of a colonial empire, in a number of ways—economic and strategic needs, duty, Manifest Destiny, and the imperative to imitate and outdo other nations or die. The fact that people described these as their motives makes them central to any explanation of American imperialism at the turn of the century. But the crucial or deciding force in these events seems to have registered less clearly on Americans or been part of an unconscious process the nation was less ready to confront. The impulse toward war provided an outlet for feelings of frustration caused by the economic and social dislocations sweeping the United States in the late nineteenth century. The war itself became the occasion for a celebration of traditional virtues—of individualism and localism and small-town America. The war became a vehicle for expressing American desires for a return to an older, more familiar, less threatening way of life.

By contrast, the taking of colonies reflected an attempt to forge a new synthesis, a fresh means by which cohesion and hope would replace the divisiveness and pessimism troubling American society. The wounds opened up by industrialization, urbanization, immigration, and economic depression were now to be healed by meeting challenges abroad—the management of a far-flung empire and competition with other nations for world power. When the failings of this solution to the country's domestic ills quickly became apparent, Americans once more turned inward, seeking to meet their difficulties at home through a broad program of progressive reform. It is true that, though war and colonial acquisitions now fell out of favor, progressivism also had its imperialistic side. As the prominent progressive intellectual Herbert Croly saw it, the Spanish-American War ushered in the progressive era by arousing "national aspirations" and giving "a tremendous impulse to the work of national reform." Still, the imperialism of the progressive period never captured American enthusiasm or dominated American thinking as fully as during the Spanish fighting, nor did it spawn a drive for colonies as at the close of the Spanish war.[32]

The impulse to fight, the war itself, and colonial expansion represented three parts of a short-lived answer to domestic difficulties. The first served as a catharsis for pent-up feelings; the second embodied unrealizable hopes of returning to the past;

and the third reflected an imperfect vision of how to secure America's future. Taken together, they demonstrated a wish not simply to return to the past or to embrace the desirable features of the present, but to invest the modern world with as many symbols and practices of earlier times as possible. The inadequacy of this as an answer to the crisis in self-confidence gave it but a temporary hold on the American imagination. And although imperialism would continue to play a part in life during the progressive era, it would not again appeal to the country as a cure-all for its domestic woes.

2

The Progressive Style of Foreign Policy: Theodore Roosevelt

And never did a President before so reflect the quality of his time.

H. G. Wells[1]

The progressive era, extending roughly from 1901 to 1918, was a time of new hopes and great effort to fulfill the traditional promise of American life. Unburdened by the economic depressions of the late nineteenth century, reformers directly confronted the nation's various ills: a moral code more appropriate to an agricultural, village culture than an industrial, urban society; undemocratic concentrations of wealth and power in corporations and political machines; exploitation of women and children; neglect of the aged and the incompetent; and a growing population of impoverished rural and foreign migrants to burgeoning cities. As general solutions to these problems, progressives urged greater government control over industry, finance, transportation, natural resources, agriculture, and labor; wider social justice and democracy; larger opportunities for the individual; and greater morality or a return to the rule of law. They hoped that specific reforms would promote a new sense of control and order which would translate into a fresh sense of mastery over national affairs.

Though the progressives had their share of gains, antitrust actions, banking reforms, conservation measures, humane labor laws, more power to the electorate and less for the bosses, their victories were often more symbolic than real, more an amelioration than a fundamental change in social conditions. When particular problems proved beyond their ability to resolve or an innate conservatism restrained them from seeking meaningful reform, they settled for the appearance of advance, illusory gains providing psychic encouragement to keep up the good fight. This was the principal function of foreign affairs for the majority of progressives during the first ten years of the century. Little interested in international questions, most progressives responded to them in domestic terms or as extensions of the battles engaging them at home. Effective assertions of American power and influence abroad impressed them as triumphs not of the country's self-interest but of progressive ideals over reactionary opponents of change. Success in meeting a challenge overseas echoed in progressive minds as an advance against stubborn problems in the United States. In all this Theodore Roosevelt played a central and compelling role.

Few Americans in the country's history have captured the national limelight as completely as Theodore Roosevelt in the first decade of this century. An aristocrat, an author, a cowboy in the western badlands, a state assemblyman, a civil service commissioner, president of the New York City Board of Police Commissioners, assistant secretary of the navy, hero of the Spanish fighting, governor of New York, Vice President and President, Roosevelt, an English visitor said, was second only to Niagara Falls among the country's natural wonders. More important, in the words of Wisconsin Senator Robert La Follette, TR was "the ablest living interpreter of . . . the superficial public sentiment of a given time. . . ." One historian describes

Roosevelt as having "anticipated unerringly, often subconsciously, the wishes of the bulk of Americans."

This was especially true of foreign affairs, where popular opinion warmly supported all his major initiatives. In his aggressive nationalism, moralism, promotion of peace and progress, Roosevelt embodied the contradictory impulses that dominated American thinking about foreign policy in the progressive era. By policing the hemisphere, building the Panama Canal, restoring peace in Asia, and assisting it in Europe, he helped renew the sense of mastery and self-confidence that the social and economic upheavals of the late nineteenth century had largely dissolved in the United States. His actions also spoke to the progressive preoccupation with restoring the nation's moral health, which was being undermined by ruthless corporations and political machines. By making disorderly nations pay their debts, building a canal beneficial to world commerce, and promoting peace and international justice, TR imposed the kind of morality abroad that progressives were struggling to revive at home. His foreign actions provided symbolic victories over intractable domestic forces progressives could only partly change. Roosevelt's psychological function, Richard Hofstadter observes, was to relieve the widespread anxieties caused by the "frantic growth and rapid industrial expansion that filled America in his lifetime. . . . Hardened and trained by a long fight with his own insecurity, he was the master therapist of the middle classes."[2]

In his direction of foreign affairs Theodore Roosevelt was always more realistic than the bulk of his countrymen. Forty years before the Japanese attack on Pearl Harbor shattered American attachments to isolationism, TR preached national involvement in world affairs. "The increasing interdependence and complexity of international political and economic relations," he told Congress in 1902, "render it incumbent on all civilized and orderly powers to insist on the proper policing of the world." The principal component of this involvement, he emphasized throughout his public life, was power and the willingness to use it. "It is contemptible, for a nation, as for an individual, to . . . proclaim its purposes, or to take positions which are ridiculous if unsupported by potential force, and then to refuse to provide this force," he said. "I never take a step in foreign policy," he declared on another occasion, "unless I am assured that I shall be able eventually to carry out my will by force." He saw nations acting not for universal good but for selfish motives. National self-interest governed what happened in international affairs, and world peace came not from human kindness or moral restraint but from balanced power, equilibriums of force restraining the selfish aims of nation-states.[3]

Yet at the same time that Roosevelt celebrated the virtues of realism, he was also the consummate jingoist—nationalistic, moralistic, and ever ready for war. Just as in domestic affairs, where he aggressively struck out against businessmen, labor unions, and political machines putting special interest above national interest, so in foreign relations he led the charge against nations and peoples holding back civilized advance.

If most Americans in Roosevelt's day were unprepared to accept his realism as a guideline for current and future actions abroad, they found his national assertiveness in behalf of moral good exhilarating. His Big Stick diplomacy in the Caribbean appealed to the nationalist, anti-European, anti-British bias of rural populists while also exciting the patriotic fervor of middle-class progressives in all parts of the country. The source of this enthusiasm, one suspects, was the sense of mastery it gave to so many Americans aching for a new sense of control and order in domestic life. Dominance in the Caribbean was a vicarious means of relieving frustrations over an unruly society at home.[4] At the same time it satisfied the progressive impulse to do good, to take personal responsibility for encouraging public morality.

In progressive eyes, building a Panama Canal would serve not only national advantage but also international well-being. Taking over the finances of profligate nations and generally policing their behavior were seen chiefly as preserving them from self-destructive actions and averting European interventions that could end in war. In short, saving Caribbean peoples from evil was another version of the progressive crusade to overcome moral degeneration in the United States.[5]

Roosevelt's actions in acquiring the Canal Zone touched all these progressive concerns. First and foremost, they satisfied the yearnings of progressives for a renewed sense of control over their lives. In 1900, when Secretary of State John Hay reached a formal agreement with Britain that the United States would single-handedly construct and operate a canal which, like Suez, would be unfortified and open to all vessels in time of war as well as peace, TR struck a responsive chord with the public by objecting to the inhibition on American power. An unfortified canal would be a menace to the United States in time of war; fortified, it would become a potent source of sea strength. "The American people mean to have the canal, and they mean to control it," Henry Cabot Lodge wrote at the time. The revision of the treaty in 1901 to allow the United States to do whatever was necessary to guard the canal "against lawlessness and disorder" was one of the first acts of the Roosevelt administration to win broad popular acclaim.[6]

Roosevelt's high-handed dealings with Colombia over the canal in 1903 were no less popular. In January, John Hay and Colombia's minister, Tomás Herrán, signed a treaty authorizing the United States to acquire the rights given a French company to build a canal across the Isthmus of Panama and granting U.S. control over a six-mile-wide canal zone for $10,000,000 and an annual rent of $250,000. Convinced, however, that it was entitled to more money, especially a share of the $40,000,-000 the United States intended to pay the French company, and that the agreement would compromise Colombia's sovereignty in the canal zone, Bogotá showed little interest in ratifying the treaty.

Though Colombia's leaders were "politically high-minded men of character," acting out of a genuine desire to ensure their national interest and honor, Americans, led by Roosevelt and Hay, saw them as "blackmailers," "bandits," and "homicidal corruptionists." The general perception in the United States was not of a weak country trying to defend its interests against a great power but of immoral Latin leaders, comparable to Robber Barons, motivated by greed and indifferent to what was fair to the United States and advantageous to all civilization. The Colombian government would defeat the treaty, the New York *World* reported in June, because of its greed for a largely increased payment. Since the United States had spent millions of dollars determining that Panama was the best route and since two treaties had been signed granting rights-of-way across the Isthmus, "it would be unfair to the United States," the *World* concluded, "if the best route be not obtained." TR wrote Hay: "I do not think that the Bogotá lot of jack rabbits should be allowed permanently to bar one of the future highways of civilization. . . . What we do now will be of consequence, not merely decades, but centuries hence. . . ."

In taking Colombia to task for failing to ratify the Hay-Herrán Treaty and advance the building of the canal, Roosevelt was seen as challenging unscrupulous men who, with small regard for the larger issue of human progress, were trying to extort money from or "hold up" the United States. Framed in these terms, his assault was little different from the general progressive attack on the great corporations or trusts that seemed ruthlessly to enrich themselves and deny millions of Americans a chance for a better life. With little knowledge of or interest in Colombia, the administration in Washington and American progressives in general viewed that remote nation only in terms of stereotypes—its leaders seemed to combine the worst features of Latin American politicians and self-serving corporate chiefs.

Indeed, the attitude toward Colombia closely resembled TR's popular attack upon the Northern Securities Company in 1902 and 1903. A giant holding company organized by the Morgan and Rockefeller interests to monopolize the railroads of the Northwest, Northern Securities symbolized the Wall Street financial and industrial oligarchy in progressive minds. Its dissolution as a result of Roosevelt's actions produced the conviction that the people now controlled the corporations rather than the other way around. "Even Morgan no longer rules the earth," one journalist declared. When TR denounced Colombia's leaders as "bandits" and "corruptionists," it was no doubt seen as an extension of his opposition to the "dull, purblind folly of the very rich men; their greed and arrogance . . . and the corruption in business. . . ."[7]

This sort of thinking provided an easy rationalization for American support of a Panamanian revolution. In September and October 1903, first Hay and then Roosevelt indicated to revolutionary leaders that they could expect the United States to stop Colombia from landing troops to quell an uprising. Though TR refused to make any explicit commitments, he told one architect of the independence movement that Colombia had forfeited all claims on the United States and that he had no use for Colombia's government. If this individual had failed to grasp what his administration intended to do, TR later remarked, "he would have been a very dull man." Consequently, on November 4, 1903, the day after an insurrection had begun in Panama, an American warship prevented Colombian troops from reinforcing a weak force on the Isthmus. Sending nine more gunboats to the area in the next few days, the United States ensured the success of Panama's revolution. During the following week the administration guaranteed the survival of the new nation by granting formal recognition and signing a treaty which allowed the United States to build a canal and take full control of a ten-mile-wide canal zone "in perpetuity."[8]

Roosevelt's actions provoked legal and moral recriminations in the United States and Latin America. His signals to the Panama conspirators that he would immediately aid their cause were seen as a direct incitement to revolution. His use of force to inhibit the movement of Colombian troops was denounced as an "indefensible interpretation" of a U.S.-Colombian treaty guaranteeing transit across the Isthmus. His recognition of the new republic before it demonstrated its stability was described as a contravention of normal diplomatic practice and a further demonstration of unseemly American backing for the revolution. Critics at home and abroad condemned Roosevelt's involvement as "piracy," a "scandal," a "crime," a "disgrace," one of the "most discreditable" episodes in American history, and an "act of sordid conquest." Explaining and defending his actions during a Cabinet meeting, TR asked Secretary of War Elihu Root: "Have I answered the charges? Have I defended myself?" "You certainly have, Mr. President," Root replied. "You have shown that you were accused of seduction and you have conclusively proved that you were guilty of rape."

The bulk of progressive opinion did not fix on the legal and moral weaknesses in Roosevelt's case but focused, instead, on the justifications for his actions—justifications that had an especially compelling appeal for progressive citizens concerned to bring order out of chaos, assure democracy, and promote morality. The experience of more than half a century showed "Colombia to be utterly incapable of keeping order on the Isthmus," TR told Congress.

> . . . Had it not been for the exercise by the United States of the police power in her interest, her connection with the Isthmus would have been sundered long ago. . . . In other words, the government of Colombia, though wholly unable to maintain order on the Isthmus, has nevertheless declined to ratify a treaty the conclusion of which opened the only chance to secure its own stability

and to guarantee permanent peace on, and the construction of a canal across, the Isthmus.

Roosevelt also emphasized that Panama's independence was serving democracy.

The people of Panama had long been discontented with the Republic of Colombia, and they had been kept quiet only by the prospect of the conclusion of the treaty.... When it became evident that the treaty was hopelessly lost, the people of Panama rose literally as one man.... The Colombian troops stationed on the Isthmus ... made common cause with the people of Panama, and with astonishing unanimity the new republic was started.

Here was a triumph of democratic rule, a case of power to a people oppressed by a remote, indifferent force. As described by TR, it was a variation of the progressive struggle against antidemocratic forces in the United States.

Equally important, Roosevelt's justification of the "Panama business" repeatedly invoked the idea of moral advance, of setting civilization on a higher plane. "For 400 years, ever since shortly after the discovery of this hemisphere, the canal across the Isthmus has been planned," he declared. "For two-score years it has been worked at. When made it is to last for the ages. It is to alter the geography of a continent and the trade routes of the world." He was "bound not merely by treaty obligations, but by the interests of civilization," Roosevelt told the Congress, "to see that the peaceful traffic of the world across the Isthmus of Panama shall no longer be disturbed by a constant succession of unnecessary and wasteful civil wars." He would not hold up the great enterprise of building the inter-oceanic canal "to gratify the whims, or ... the even more sinister and evil peculiarities, of people who ... assert an unreal supremacy over the territory. The possession of a territory fraught with such peculiar capacities as the Isthmus in question carries with it obligations to mankind. The course of events has shown that this canal cannot be built by private enterprise, or by any other nation than our own; therefore it must be built by the United States."[9]

Roosevelt's appeal to moral considerations for what some saw as immoral actions was but one of several ironies in the progressive mood and world view. Not only had the United States casually overridden Colombia's legitimate self-interest and ignored customary international legal and moral constraints for the sake of a higher good, but it had also favored revolutionary disorder in the name of order and described its imperial control of a canal zone as Panamanian self-rule.

These were not so much expressions of blatant hypocrisy on the part of Roosevelt and his fellow progressives as reflections of basic contradictions in the whole progressive outlook. While the progressives, for example, made much of the need for institutional reform, they were too conservative to support basic changes in a society in which they were typically prosperous and respectable figures. In place of far-reaching legislative change, they happily settled for symbolic advance, for "a feeling that action was taking place" and that the country was experiencing moral uplift. Likewise, the progressives were of two minds about the trusts and great corporations they brought under attack. On the one hand, they perceived big business as undermining the traditions of economic opportunity and political democracy, and on the other, they valued the modern technology and material benefits the giant corporations did so much to advance. Thus, though Roosevelt broke up the Northern Securities Company, his administration did little to dissolve other corporate monopolies. The progressives were both repelled and seduced by the consequences of the industrial discipline: The destruction of individualistic values deeply troubled them, while the organization of industrial life provided comforts they refused to forsake. In short, the progressives were drawn in two directions at once—toward the old and the new. In foreign affairs, the contradictions, illustrated by Panama, were as pronounced as in domestic concerns: For the sake of civilization, the country acted in uncivilized ways; in the name of freedom and self-determination, the United States exercised imperial control. These were the deeds not of conscienceless men and women but of a genuinely divided people struggling with conflicting impulses in their daily lives.[10]

To leaders of the Roosevelt administration, the acquisition of the Canal Zone was a logical culmination of America's growing power in the Caribbean. We "must certainly bring the West Indies, from the point of Florida to the gateway of the Isthmian Canal, under the political and naval control of the United States," Elihu Root wrote early in 1902, "and must with equal certainty create special economic relations between them and the United States quite different from those which they or we bear to the rest of the world. Speaking in a broad way the first is in our interest; the second is theirs." In a speech in July, TR announced:

> The course of the last few years has made more evident than ever before that this nation must in time to come have pecuniary interests on the Isthmus connecting the two Americas and in the waters and among the islands adjacent thereto. Nationally we cannot occupy the position toward these regions that we did toward others where our interests are far less, and this is doubly true now that Congress . . . has provided for the building of an inter-oceanic canal.

For Roosevelt, Root, Hay, Beveridge, Lodge, Mahan, and other "realists," American strategic interests or the nation's position as a world power dictated that it make the Western Hemisphere into an area under its control.

U.S. progressives shared this goal, but less out of national strategic considerations than out of emotional ones tied to domestic aims: Their intense preoccupation with gaining a greater sense of control over their lives, creating a new social order, and promoting moral advance found symbolic and substantive expression through American power in the Caribbean. The U.S. response to events in the area between 1902 and 1905 illustrates the point. At the start of his presidency, TR publicly identified himself with Monroe's prohibition on territorial aggrandizement in Latin America. But he did not interpret this as a bar to European action against a Latin state that had failed to meet its financial obligations. "If any South American state misbehaves toward any European country," he wrote a German friend in July 1901, "let the European country spank it." And in his first State of the Union message, he announced that "We do not guarantee any State against punishment if it misconducts itself." European intervention in Latin America to compel proper behavior did not initially impress Roosevelt as a threat to America's national interest.[11]

The public response to Anglo-German action against Venezuela in the winter of 1902–03 changed his mind. In December and January, in an attempt to force payments on debts owed their nationals, Britain and Germany seized Venezuelan gunboats, bombarded some of its forts, and blockaded five ports. Americans reacted angrily, with organized opinion expressing fears that "England and Germany will overstep the limits prescribed by the Monroe Doctrine." Animated less by considerations of rational self-interest than by emotional demands for exclusive U.S. control in the Caribbean, concerned Americans pushed Roosevelt into seeking an end to European intervention of any kind in the southern republics. ". . . The chances of complications from a long and irritating little war between the European powers and Venezuela," TR said in December, "were sufficiently great to make me feel most earnestly that the situation should be brought to a peaceful end if possible." Undoubtedly recalling the emotional outburst in the United States that had led to the War of '98, Roosevelt was eager in this instance to keep the American consensus under control.

To this end, he helped arrange arbitration of the dispute between Venezuela and its European creditors, and he began formulating plans to prevent future European interventions in hemisphere affairs. In March 1903, when the German ambassador suggested international control of Venezuela's finances, Roosevelt rejected the idea as likely to agitate domestic opinion, which would interpret it as placing an American republic under European control. The United States, he told the ambassador, might have to solve the problem by establishing a protectorate over all of South and Central America.[12]

Conditions in Santo Domingo moved Roosevelt partly to implement this idea. In January 1904, under threat of intervention from France, Germany, and Italy, the Dominican government asked Roosevelt to assume a protectorate over the island. He had "about the same desire to annex it as a gorged boa constrictor might have to swallow a porcupine wrong-end-to," TR privately remarked. But he recognized that if he were to prevent foreign interventions that would arouse public feeling, the United States would have to take responsibility for ordering Latin American finances. "Sooner or later," he wrote his son in February 1904, "it seems to me inevitable that the United States should assume an attitude of protection and regulation in regard to all these little states in the neighborhood of the Caribbean."

He gave public voice to these sentiments in May. In a letter to Elihu Root read at a Cuban independence-day celebration, TR declared that he hailed "what had been done in Cuba not merely for its own sake, but as showing the purpose and desire of this nation toward all the nations south of us. . . . All that we desire is to see all neighboring countries stable, orderly and prosperous. . . . If a nation shows that it knows how to act with decency in industrial and political matters, if it keeps order and pays its obligations, then it need fear no interference from the United States. Brutal wrongdoing, or an impotence which results in a general loosening of the ties of civilized society, may finally require intervention by some civilized nation, and in the Western Hemisphere the United States cannot ignore this duty. . . ."[13]

Roosevelt's letter reflected the concerns of progressives with stability, order, decency, and moral restraint. Having won popular support at home for his efforts as an arbiter and upholder of civic virtue in a coal miners' strike of 1902, when he defended the public interest by forcing arbitration of the dispute, TR had little reason to think that Americans would object to a similar role abroad, especially since they had refused to have any other nation be the policeman for the Western Hemisphere. But 1904 was an election year, and his proposal to police the Caribbean raised a partisan outcry which angered him. ". . . What I wrote," he told Root, "is the simplest common sense, and only the fool or the coward can treat it as aught else. If we are willing to let Germany or England act as the policeman of the Caribbean, then we can afford not to interfere when gross wrongdoing occurs. But if we intend to say 'Hands off' to the powers of Europe, then sooner or later we must keep order ourselves." Although convinced that his proposal would ultimately win majority support, he refused to do anything which might give the Democrats ammunition against him in the campaign.

In December, however, after a Republican "sweep," Roosevelt formally announced his Corollary to Monroe's Doctrine. Using much the same language as he had in May, he declared his intention to "exercise . . . an international police power." He believed it "very much wiser . . . to concern ourselves here at home than with trying to better the condition of things in other nations. We have plenty of sins of our own to war against, and under ordinary circumstances we can do more for the general uplifting of humanity by striving with heart and soul to put a stop to civic corruption, to brutal lawlessness and violent race prejudices here at home than by passing resolutions about wrong-doing elsewhere." But as a "last resort," when it became evident that an injustice "had violated the rights of the United States or had invited foreign aggression," he would intervene in the affairs of our southern neighbors.[14]

Implementing his Corollary in Santo Domingo in 1905, Roosevelt again emphasized that he was acting in behalf of progressive principles. Conditions in Santo Domingo, he announced in explanation of American intervention, had reached a point at which "all society was on the verge of dissolution" and foreign intervention was "imminent." To prevent these developments, the United States had answered a Dominican request for help. The consequences of this intervention, he predicted, would be a greater measure of "stability and order" than Santo Domingo had enjoyed in a long time, a diminution of the danger of foreign intervention, and greater likelihood of true independence or eventual self-government than ever before. Order out of chaos, self-rule, and justice to legitimate creditors—all were virtues no American progressive could fault. And, indeed, most progressives had no objection to, or were even enthusiastic about, TR's assertion of the national will. The U.S. Senate took exception to Roosevelt's action by refusing to act on a treaty formalizing American intervention in the Dominican Republic; but this had more to do with partisan politics and his insensitivity to its institutional independence than with meaningful objections to what he did. By and large, progressive America was content with its President, who impressed it as being not an exploitative imperialist but a principled leader intent on exporting the same order and virtue, the same Square Deal, he was promoting at home.[15]

. . .

For most Americans in the first decade of the twentieth century, the Far East—China, Japan, and Korea—was as remote as the moon. For Roosevelt, Hay, Mahan, and other internationalists, East Asia was a strategic hot spot which the United States could not afford to ignore. Not only did the area hold out the promise of substantial trade, but it was also a potential battleground for the great powers, a locale where the principal competitors for world influence might come to blows and touch off a larger struggle involving the United States. China particularly concerned these internationalists. The economic supremacy of the next century, Brooks Adams predicted, rested on the fate of China. Admiral Mahan expected the great imperial battle of the twentieth century to be fought out in China between an aggressive Russia in the north and a combination of sea powers—Britain, Germany, Japan, and the United States—in the south. Roosevelt shared their views. "Owing to the rapid growth of our power and our interests on the Pacific," he said in his State of the Union message of 1901, "whatever happens in China must be of the keenest national concern to us." And in 1905 he declared: "Our future history will be more determined by our position on the Pacific facing China than by our position on the Atlantic facing Europe." To Roosevelt and a handful of like-minded Americans, then, there were, as in the Caribbean, compelling economic and strategic reasons for America to involve itself in East Asia's power politics.

But to the bulk of progressive America, this was unpersuasive doctrine. Beset by domestic worries absorbing most of their energies, progressives found little appeal in a distant power struggle that could distract them from compelling problems at home. "Public opinion is dull on the question of China," TR complained in 1901. Though by 1903 it was "understanding the situation more and more," it was still "not so far awake" that he could "go to the extent" he wished in China. Indeed, it was transparent to him in the summer of 1903 that "we cannot fight to keep Manchuria open." Public opinion, John Hay also concluded, would not support "any scheme of concerted action. . . ."[16]

In the face of popular reluctance to use force in East Asia, America's imperialists, led first by Hay and then by TR, resorted to the idea of the Open Door. In September 1899, hoping to preserve commercial opportunity in China, Hay asked the powers not to discriminate in favor of their nationals in foreign leaseholds. Further, in July 1900, when foreign suppression of the Boxer rebellion raised the possibility of China's further dismemberment and a repudiation of the Open Door, Hay extended the principle to include the preservation of China's territorial and administrative integrity, and commercial equality in "all parts" of China. In both forms, the Open Door idea was good progressive doctrine grounded in the anti-monopoly and prodemocratic attitudes of the time. As such, it won support in the United States for a limited involvement which more realistic assertions of power and interest could not command. Appealing to progressive concerns with self-rule, justice, and the triumph of equal opportunity over concentrations of economic and political power, the Open Door in China captured the imagination of progressive America by echoing the reform agenda in the United States.

In Roosevelt's hands, the program became the assertion of balance-of-power diplomacy in the name of progressive principles. Where he saw himself defending the national interest and international morality through an open door in East Asia, progressive America viewed his policy as chiefly an instrument for moral good. From the start of his presidential tenure, TR worried about trade monopolies and concentrations of power which would limit America's share of the China market and provoke a military conflict destructive to the "civilized" nations. Down to the outbreak of the Russo-Japanese War in 1904, he regarded Russian expansion in Manchuria as evidence of these developments, and he warmly sympathized with

Japanese efforts to check this aggression. "I have a strong liking and respect [for the Russians]," TR wrote early in 1904, "but unless they change in some marked way they contain the chance of menace to the higher life of the world. Our people have become suspicious of Russia and I personally share this view." By contrast, he perceived of Japan's becoming "the leading industrial nation of the Pacific," and he described it as "a great civilized nation" capable of teaching us "some things."

When Japan staged an effective surprise attack on the Russian fleet at Port Arthur in February 1904, TR believed that "Japan is playing our game" by restoring the East Asian balance of power. If the balance were to endure, however, Japan must not be fully victorious. "If the Japanese win out," he wrote shortly after the start of the war, "not only the Slav, but all of us will have to reckon with a great new force in eastern Asia." A Japanese victory, he speculated a few months later, "may possibly mean a struggle between them and us in the future. . . ." It was his chief hope that "the two powers will fight until both are fairly well exhausted, and that then peace will come on terms which will not mean the creation of either a yellow peril or a Slav peril."[17]

To this end, Roosevelt tried to assume the role of mediator early in the conflict. By putting himself between the belligerents, he aimed to check the dominance of either power in China, assure the survival of the Open Door, and encourage the growth of an international moral order. Having given the nation a Square Deal at home, he now wished to ensure evenhandedness abroad. It was a fiercely difficult task, especially dealing with Russia. Humiliated by a series of defeats on land and at sea, the Russians were loath to enter peace negotiations from a position of little strength. "Neither the Czar nor the Russian Government nor the Russian people are willing to face the facts as they are," TR complained in June 1905. "They are hopeless creatures with whom to deal. They are utterly insincere and treacherous; they have no conception of the truth, . . .

no knowledge of their own strength or weakness." To Hay he lamented: "The Czar is a preposterous little creature. . . . He has been unable to make war, and he is now unable to make peace." And he confided to an intimate: "Oh Lord! I have been growing nearly mad in the effort to get Russia and Japan together. The more I see of the Czar, the Kaiser, and the Mikado the better I am content with democracy, even if we have to include the American newspaper as one of the assets." These foreign leaders again resembled U.S. businessmen who drove Roosevelt to his "wits end" by their "arrogant stupidity." But, as with J. P. Morgan and the coal mine operators, TR intended to apply "sound chastisement" to these foreign versions of American corporate heads.

After eighteen months of fighting, Russian military defeats combined with Japanese financial exhaustion to bring both sides to the peace table. Presiding over the talks in Portsmouth, New Hampshire, Roosevelt struggled for three weeks in August 1905 to reach a settlement. "Dealing with these peace envoys has been an even tougher job" than dealing with U.S. senators, he told the French ambassador. "To be polite and sympathetic and patient in explaining for the hundredth time something perfectly obvious, when what I really want to do is to give utterance to whoops of rage and jump up and knock their heads together—well, all I can hope is that self-repression will be ultimately helpful to my character." His patience paid off handsomely when the belligerents agreed to terms that promised to preserve the Open Door. For its victories, Japan received Port Arthur, Russian-controlled railroads in Manchuria, the southern half of Sakhalin Island, and recognition of its "predominant" interests in Korea. At the same time Manchuria was to remain part of China, where all the nations were to be free to trade and invest, and Russia was not fully driven from East Asia. Instead, as Roosevelt saw it, it was "left face to face with Japan so that each may have a moderative action on the other."[18]

Roosevelt's successful efforts won him worldwide acclaim. Approval at home, where Americans found deep satisfaction in the influence their President and nation exerted on world affairs, was particularly strong. "Wasn't that a grand move . . . in getting Japan and Russia together in a Peace Conference, and especially getting them to meet and hold it in this country," one isolationist senator crowed. "The very thought that a great power of the Orient and one of the great powers of Europe have come here to America to settle their disputes is enough to make an old fellow like me swell up with more pride in our country than ever." "We are," Henry Cabot Lodge wrote TR, "the strongest moral force—also physical—now extant, and the peace of the world rests largely with us." And a prominent businessman wrote the President that "Nothing you have done in your whole official career has appealed more strongly to human sympathies and understanding."

American satisfaction with the Peace of Portsmouth had little to do with any clear sense of national advantage derived from the settlement. In celebrating the President's achievement, progressives did not fix on the material or strategic gains that might come to the United States from an international balance of power in East Asia. Instead, TR's supporters focused on his ability to master seemingly uncontrollable forces and, in so doing, advance the cause of moral order. For most progressives, including TR, his handling of the Russians and the Japanese was an extension of what he described as his "fundamental fight for *morality*" in American public life. In American minds, Russia and Japan were little different from the powerful self-seeking organizations in the United States operating with small concern for individual or social good. To most Americans, then, the Peace of Portsmouth was less an episode in international affairs and East Asian history than another means of persuading themselves that they were overcoming selfish undemocratic forces at home. The negotiations and their outcome provided a discharge for frustrations over the fight against intractable domestic conditions. Carrying on a reform campaign in which there were few clear substantive triumphs over corporations or political bosses, the progressives needed all the symbolic victories they could find.[19]

The Treaty of Portsmouth also produced a number of ironic twists. Roosevelt, the staunch imperialist who chafed under popular opposition to protecting American interests in China with force, won the Nobel Peace Prize for negotiating an end to the Russo-Japanese War. The combatants themselves, who had been saved from additional fighting that would have been costly to both in blood, treasure, and domestic stability, erupted in antagonism against Roosevelt and the United States—the Russians complained of having paid too high a price for peace, and the Japanese objected to having gained so little. The principle of the Open Door, which was supposedly endorsed in the treaty, now received short shrift in Korea, where the Japanese had considerable investments and 100,000 troops. Lacking the means or desire to contest Japan on the peninsula and more interested in an accommodation that included a Japanese promise against interference in the Philippines, TR recognized Tokyo's exclusive control by withdrawing the American legation from Seoul in November 1905. Though a clear violation of the Open Door, Roosevelt's action evoked little response in the United States. It was further evidence that the principle was more a projection of progressive concerns abroad than a national commitment to a particular policy for East Asia.[20]

Public absorption with domestic affairs at the expense of East Asian realities plagued Roosevelt during the remainder of his presidential term. In 1906 Californians, preoccupied with local economic and social issues, provoked a war scare with Japan. Agitated by the competition from Japanese laborers willing to work for lower wages, and fearing racial complications damaging to the homogeneity of their society, Californians demanded an end to Oriental migration, and the San

Francisco School Board restricted Oriental children to a segregated school. The Roosevelt administration and the eastern press were incensed at these displays of insensitivity to Japan. TR privately denounced "the idiots of the California legislature" and the "infernal fools in California" who threaten to lead the nation "into a war in which it was wrong." In public, he warned that arbitrary treatment of Japanese residents "may be fraught with the gravest consequences to the Nation" and described such behavior as a "confession of inferiority in our civilization."[21]

At the same time, however, the President shared the stock prejudices of progressive Americans, who thought in terms of "inferior" and "superior" races and could speak of "big-boned, blond, long-haired" Anglo-Saxons with "clean Aryan blood." Though he did not regard "backward peoples" as permanently or inherently inferior, distinguished between the Chinese and the Japanese, and genuinely regretted abuse of resident Orientals on the West Coast, Roosevelt shared the progressive impulse to maintain Northern European white control by restricting mass migration to the United States of Asians and Eastern and Southern Europeans. Indeed, his solution to the crisis over California race prejudice was not to challenge that discrimination head-on, despite public suggestions that he would, but to negotiate a gentlemen's agreement that halted all unwanted traffic between the two countries and specifically slowed the migration of Japanese laborers to America to a trickle.

The essential difference between Roosevelt and the mass of Americans was less in his attitude toward Japanese "coolie" laborers than in his recognition of the consequences that blatant expressions of contempt for Japanese migrants would have for America's international position. Whereas most progressives thought only about building a harmonious society at home by barring migrants from abroad, Roosevelt also focused on the impact of such a policy on international affairs. He worried that it might provoke a war with Japan which would be destructive to American interests in East Asia and the Pacific. Consequently, when jingoistic declarations of readiness for a conflict with Japan suggested a repeat of the mass hysteria that had provoked war in 1898, Roosevelt attempted to eliminate the condition agitating Californians and undermining friendship with Tokyo.[22]

The jingoism that flared in the crisis with Japan may be seen as another expression of mass agitation about foreign problems dating from the 1890s. To be sure, differences of degree and extent marked public responses to the various foreign crises involving the United States in the years 1890 to 1910, but they all seem to have been more a way for mass sentiment to work off frustrations over domestic tensions than expressions of· realistic concern about American needs abroad. As a shrewd interpreter of public sentiment, Roosevelt was able not only to dampen this public excitement before it got out of hand but also to encourage it when it served his advantage. His dispatch of the battle fleet on a global cruise is a good case in point.

In the summer of 1907, Roosevelt decided to send all of the country's sixteen battleships on a well-publicized trip around the world. Though many at the time, and he himself later, stressed the impact such a cruise would and did have on Japanese jingoes, the President's decision to send the fleet was not principally a response to a Japanese war threat. Instead, his motives had largely to do with domestic politics. Eager to enhance Republican party strength on the West Coast, which had been damaged by his opposition to California's treatment of the Japanese and by his conservation program for public lands, Roosevelt hoped to repair political fences by a show of determination to defend the Pacific coast from a possible Japanese attack. In addition, he desired to revive public and congressional support for naval expansion by focusing national attention on American naval power. He accurately foresaw that the cruise of the battle fleet would be "the most effective instrument of navalist propaganda since the Spanish-American War." It also caused the country's jingo press "to whip up a first class war scare," which undoubtedly had more to do with releasing tensions over intractable domestic problems than with the realities of Japanese-American relations. Thus, by tying mass desire for a sense of mastery and mass need to ventilate anger to a worldwide show of American power, Roosevelt cleverly strengthened the Republican party and won support for a larger navy.[23]

At the same time Roosevelt did not wish to make the cruise the occasion for another round of tension with Japan. Quite the contrary, he took great pleasure in the fact that fleet visits to Yokohama and Tokyo received wildly enthusiastic receptions and helped clear the air of war talk. More substantively, he responded warmly to a Japanese proposal in October 1908 that the United States and Japan reaffirm their friendship in a formal agreement. Preferring an informal statement of friendship, which would not have to come under congressional scrutiny, Roosevelt fostered the Root-Takahira Agreement of November 30, 1908, an exchange of diplomatic notes between the secretary of state and the Japanese ambassador. The two countries agreed to maintain the status quo in the Pacific and respect each other's territorial possessions in the region. They also reaffirmed their commitment to the Open Door in China, endorsing that country's "independence and integrity."

Roosevelt chiefly aimed the agreement at progressive opinion in the United States. Though he had little fear of Japanese aggression against America's Pacific possessions and little reason to think that an informal agreement would deter them from an attack in their interest, he endorsed the pronouncements on the status quo and territorial possessions because they quieted American suspicions of Japanese intentions toward the Philippines. In addition, he joined Tokyo in publicly reaffirming the Open Door not because he thought that the agreement would end Japanese violations occurring in Manchuria against the doctrine since 1905 but because it would please the progressive public and weaken its suspicions of Japan. Again, as with all of Roosevelt's actions toward East Asia during his term, moralistic pronouncements were enough to satisfy progressive Americans whose domestic preoccupations made them largely indifferent to the realities of East Asian affairs.[24]

International arbitration was a hallmark of Roosevelt's presidency. Yet this was more in spite than because of TR. Privately he had little use for the idea. "I have no sympathy with . . . [the] arbitration treaty business," he wrote after leaving office. ". . . As a model for world treaties, . . . I think it is absurd. . . . The whole business is tainted by that noxious form of silliness which always accompanies the sentimental refusal to look facts in the face." But as with so much else during his White House years, Roosevelt took his cue from the dominant progressive mood. And for the progressive middle classes, arbitration was highly appealing, especially in disputes between the more advanced Western nations. Indeed, whereas progressives could view aggressive action against "backward peoples" as necessary and desirable, they found it less appealing among "civilized" states, whose greater regard for law, moral restraint, and order made them more likely to accept mediation over war. To progressive thinking, conflicts among Western nations were like clashes between selfish interests in the United States; they injured society as a whole unless checked by an arbiter serving all the "people." The salvation of America, progressives believed, required justice to all classes. The preservation of "civilized" peoples depended on justice to all advanced nations. Just as Roosevelt had prevented open strife between the "criminal rich" and the "lunatic" left at home, so his progressive backers wished him to support mediation between selfish nations threatening war abroad.[25]

Roosevelt reluctantly followed the progressive lead. In 1903, he grudgingly accepted arbitration of a disputed boundary line between Alaska and Canada. The dispute dated from 1896, when gold was discovered in Canada's northwest Klondike region. Eager for an outlet to the sea for these gold fields, the Canadians asserted that their territory extended to the inlets on the southernmost coast of Alaska rather than to the headlands of the coastal peninsulas. Theodore Roosevelt and most other Americans who knew anything about the case regarded the Canadian claim as "outrageous and indefensible." But TR agreed to accept arbitration of the dispute when the Canadians requested it as a face-saving device that would largely favor the United States. To ensure that the decision would satisfy American claims, he appointed not three "impartial jurists," as called for in the agreement, but three men who were certain to reject the Canadian claim. In addition, he sent private warnings to London, where the tribunal met, that a failure to side with the United States would lead him to send armed forces to decide the boundary line. The subsequent decision favoring the United States suggested that the procedure was essentially a sham arbitration. But from the President's perspective, it had two salutary effects: It removed a potentially dangerous irritant from Anglo-American relations, and it raised his standing with progressive Americans, who believed that governance by legal rules, whether in domestic or in international affairs, was bound to improve the lot of humankind.[26]

Between 1904 and 1907, Roosevelt repeatedly catered to this progressive attraction to arbitration or the settlement of international disputes between "civilized" states by judicial means. In 1904, in the midst of the Russo-Japanese War, with American peace advocates urging a reconvening of the Hague Peace Conference of 1899, Roosevelt publicly called for a new meeting. The domestic consequences of such a step during the presidential campaign of 1904 were not lost on Finley Peter Dunne's Mr. Dooley: "Sicrity Cortilyou authorizes me to deny th' infamous rayport that th' Prizidint was iver at San Joon

Hill. At th' time iv this gloryous an' lamintable performance, th' good man was down with measles conthracted at th' Internaytional Peace Convintion." The following year, after the Portsmouth Treaty, Roosevelt was relieved when the czar took the lead in sponsoring the conference. ". . . I particularly do *not* want to appear as a professional peace advocate . . . ," TR wrote Elihu Root. "For the last six months most of what I have done in connection with foreign affairs . . . has been on an exclusively altruistic basis; and I do not want people to get the idea that I never consider American interests at all, or still worse, that I am posing as never considering them."[27]

Under pressure from progressives, Roosevelt made an arbitration agreement his principal goal for the Hague meeting. In 1905, in "the belief" that he "had the sentiment of my party and of the country behind me," he had put twelve arbitration treaties before the Senate for confirmation. But when considerations of senatorial prerogative produced amendments which made the treaties "an expression of barren intention," in the words of sympathetic newspapers, or "shams," as TR called them, he abandoned the effort. Public pressure, however, for a permanent international court of justice that would be "dominated solely by jurisprudence" and "unaffected by national and diplomatic considerations" moved the President to press the case for a general arbitration agreement at the Hague Conference of 1907. "Personally I think that the strengthening of the Hague Court is of more consequence than disarmament," he wrote Britain's foreign secretary, Sir Edward Grey. "Every effort should be made to extend the number of possible international disputes which are to be subjected to arbitration." But he had no desire to go too far; a nation's "vital interests" were not to be arbitrated, and he wished "not to raise such high anticipations as will insure disappointment with the actual outcome." He urged the public to understand: ". . . There is only a partial and imperfect analogy between international law and internal or municipal law, because there is no sanction of force for executing the former, while there is in the case of the latter."[28]

Roosevelt's caution was well advised, for the Hague Conference accomplished next to nothing, giving far more attention to the regulation than to the prevention of war. The deliberations, Mr. Dooley observed, fixed on "th' larger question iv how future wars shud be conducted in the best inthrests iv peace." But progressive America would not let go of the arbitration issue. Unyielding in the conviction that human advance depended on the rule of law, progressives were eager for even the smallest international gain in that direction. Consequently, in 1908 Secretary of State Root negotiated twenty-four symbolic agreements which excluded arbitration of "the honor, independence, and vital interests" of the contracting nations and included requirements for future Senate agreement to arbitration of any specific dispute.[29]

More significantly, Roosevelt helped arbitrate the 1905–06 Franco-German dispute over Morocco. A classic exercise in European power politics, the crisis aroused traditional isolationist sentiments in the United States. American interests in Morocco, newspapers and congressional leaders pointed out, were negligible, and involvement in the conflict in any form might draw the United States into a European war. Yet only the year before, in 1904, public sentiment about military action over events in Morocco had been all the other way. When TR had responded to the kidnapping of Ion Perdicaris, a naturalized American, by Raisuli, a native chieftain, with gunboats in Moroccan waters and a ringing declaration, "Perdicaris alive or Raisuli dead," Americans had thrilled to the challenge. For most Americans this had been a case of warfare against a "backward people" who did not operate under "civilized" rules. By contrast, involvement in a European war over Morocco meant a breakdown of the social order and of the legal restraints progressives were so eager to advance. Moreover, the fact that "civilized" nations were involved in this latest Moroccan crisis made arbitration an appealing idea.

Asked by the Germans to help negotiate an end to the crisis, Roosevelt was initially reluctant. Not only did he anticipate "the bitterest attacks" in Congress were he to involve himself in Morocco, but he would be distracted from the Caribbean and Far Eastern crises he was then trying to manage. Still, believing that a European war would be "a real calamity to civilization" and undoubtedly convinced that a successful mediation would silence isolationist complaints, he took up the challenge. His instincts were right. His part in arranging and agreeing to participate in a conference at Algeciras, Spain, provoked a storm of criticism, but the successful resolution of the conflict at the conference brought American opinion to Roosevelt's side. The picture of the President standing the Kaiser "on his head with great decision," as Roosevelt privately described his role in the conference, appealed again to the American sense of mastery and national pride. Further, the portrait of Roosevelt and America as a deciding force for moral order in a tumultuous world spoke to the progressives' innermost concern with overcoming organized power ready to ride roughshod over majority interests. The settlement at Algeciras was another symbolic victory in the progressive struggle against the evils of modern life.[30]

"Theodore Roosevelt," the political scientist Robert E. Osgood has written,

> was not plagued . . . by a refractory public opinion. He experienced remarkably little difficulty in leading the nation to its most active participation in international affairs since the days of the French alliance. But his success can scarcely be attributed to any sudden burst of realism in the popular attitude toward world politics.

Rather it was due to Roosevelt's political genius, his consummate skill in tapping the resources of aroused nationalism and directing them into new channels. By bold deeds . . . he was able to capture the public imagination and dramatize the emergence of the United States as a great power, capable of inspiring awe and respect in all parts of the world.[31]

But there was something more than this. Roosevelt's success in winning public support for his foreign initiatives, whether in Latin America, East Asia, or Europe, rested in large measure on an instinctive ability to relate overseas actions to progressive concerns. Taking the Canal Zone, policing the Caribbean, supporting the Open Door, mediating the Russo-Japanese War, settling differences with Japan, sailing the battleship fleet around the globe, and promoting the Algeciras settlement became extensions of the progressive struggle to advance morality, democracy, law, and social order. They also gave progressives an exhilarating feeling of power, of a newfound ability to control seemingly unmanageable forces like the ones besetting them at home. Frustrated by their inability to find effective solutions to the country's deeply troubling problems, progressive crusaders took comfort from Roosevelt's seeming mastery of world affairs.

3

The Progressive Style
of Foreign Policy:
Woodrow Wilson

The ear of the leader must ring with the voices of the people. He
cannot be of the school of the prophets; he must be of the number of those who studiously serve the slow-paced daily demand.

Woodrow Wilson, 1890

It is possible to observe in certain lives, where conspicuously superior abilities are united with serious deficiencies, . . . a curve
plotted over and over again and always dropping from some
flight of achievement to a steep descent into failure.

Edmund Wilson, "Woodrow Wilson at Princeton,"
Shores of Light (1952)

It is customary to distinguish between the Roosevelt and Wilson foreign policies as, respectively, "Big Stick" and "Missionary" diplomacy. According to these formulations, the former
took its impulse from strategic and military or power considerations, while the latter rested on an overriding concern with morality and a determination to extend the benefits of American
democracy to other parts of the globe. As with all labels, the
terms "Big Stick" and "Missionary" hide as much as they tell.
The Roosevelt and Wilson foreign policies had more in common than these descriptions suggest. Like Wilson, TR was intensely moralistic about foreign relations, talking often about

America's civilizing role in the world. Similarly, Wilson resembled Roosevelt in his use of force. For all his pacifistic talk against interference in other people's affairs and "being too proud to fight," Wilson relied heavily on military power to gain his ends in world politics.

Yet the Roosevelt and Wilson foreign policies *were* different. No one scrutinizing the events of the two administrations can ignore the distinction in style between Wilson's measured, reflective rhetoric and TR's constant invocation of "hairy-chested Darwinian virtues." The contrast between Roosevelt's attacks on the "timidity" and "soft living" of those without "the high gallantry of entire indifference to life" in war and Wilson's legalistic pronouncements on how individuals and nations need behave is too striking to miss. But the difference was more than stylistic; it was also substantive. Roosevelt, a cosmopolitan internationalist with a lifelong interest in world affairs, fashioned his foreign policy out of a mixture of progressive concerns and traditional power politics. Progressive visions of a more civilized or just world operating by rules of law went hand in hand with the national self-interest. Wilson, a more parochial American with limited interest in and knowledge of foreign affairs, made foreign policy largely an expression of progressive hopes and aims. Whether in the Caribbean, China, Mexico, or Europe, where the great powers descended into the "barbarism" of all-out war, the Wilson policy sought the same ends: more democracy and law; greater justice; less power to the interests and more to the people. If these were central features of TR's foreign policy, they thoroughly dominated what Wilson did, reaching extraordinary proportions after 1917, when the country was supposed to turn the entire world from its wicked ways and convert it into a kind of global United States.[1]

This preoccupation with progressive principles in foreign affairs was not simply the product of differences in outlook between Roosevelt and Wilson. It also reflected an intensification of the progressive mood. After four frustrating years under Taft, a progressive tide swamped the country. From 1913 to 1918 no public action or policy could succeed unless it was couched in progressive terms. The need to save democracy through programs of progressive reform became a widespread article of faith. This determination to assure greater economic and political democracy also extended to foreign affairs. Indeed, it is striking that down to the progressive era Americans had been largely content to deal with autocratic governments abroad and had taken comfort in the thought that the United States was different from these corrupt, decadent regimes. A democratic, moral America was to keep these old-world countries and habits at arm's length while going its own way. Then, in the progressive period, Americans became intensely concerned to rescue these foreign peoples from themselves or to lead them along democratic paths earlier Americans assumed they could never travel.[2]

What explains this reversal? Anxiety in the nation about rescuing itself may tell much. In the midst of an age when Americans worried about the weakening of democratic institutions, when they saw economic and political power being concentrated in fewer and fewer hands, they sought reassurance in a drive to promote democracy abroad. Agitated by the thought that democracy might no longer work in the United States, Americans bolstered their confidence with brave words about restoring it at home and extending it overseas. Like a troubled man angered by his own uncertainty, the country aggressively demanded international conformity to democratic goals it now believed might be slipping out of domestic reach.

Wilson was the ideal leader to preside over this mood. As Arthur Link, his biographer, has written, "the United States, Wilson believed, had been born that men might be free." As Wilson himself put it, "I believe that God planted in us the vision of liberty; ... and, therefore, I cannot be deprived of the hope that we are chosen, and prominently chosen, to show the way to the nations of the world how they shall walk in the paths of liberty." The moral fervor, the evangelism behind these words strongly appealed to a generation of Americans plagued by threats to traditional habits. The comforting thought that Providence had chosen their nation to lead the world toward the divine goal of freedom relieved doubts that it was in jeopardy in the United States.[3]

The Wilson policy toward Latin America offers a case in point. Wilson's election to the presidency and the appointment of William Jennings Bryan as secretary of state prompted forecasts of a radical change in Latin American policy. A respect for the independence and equality of all nations now seemed certain to replace the "imperialism" and Dollar Diplomacy of the preceding Republican administrations. Wilson's rhetoric during his first year in the White House encouraged this expectation. "We can have no sympathy with those who seek to seize the power of government to advance their own personal interests or ambition," he said in his first formal declaration of a Latin American policy. He would not support any "special group or interest" to exploit the southern republics, he simultaneously told the press. He shortly predicted the freeing of the Latin states from foreign economic exploitation and declared the United States the champion of constitutional government in the Americas.

In a surprisingly short time, however, the Wilson administration "violated all its generous professions in its relations with Mexico, Central America, and the island countries" of the Caribbean. Political and military interventions in Nicaragua, Haiti, the Dominican Republic, and Mexico quickly went beyond anything TR and Taft had done in the area. Whatever their intentions, Wilson and Bryan could not escape the consequences of earlier Republican actions. "The possession of the Panama Canal and its defense have . . . given to the territories in and about the Caribbean Sea a new importance from the standpoint of our national safety," Robert Lansing, Wilson's second secretary of state, told the President. "It is vital to the interests of this country that European political domination should in no way be extended over these regions. . . . Our national safety . . . requires that the United States should intervene and aid in the establishment and maintenance of a stable and honest government, if no other way seems possible to attain that end."[4]

National security was a central consideration in determining policy in the Americas. But a missionary zeal to promote democracy and constitutional government was an even larger concern. In Nicaragua, for example, where the Taft administration had sent marines and negotiated a treaty encouraging dependence on the United States, the Wilson administration maintained the forces and added treaty provisions making Nicaragua a U.S. protectorate. The government gave three reasons for its actions: It could not abandon the Taft policy without throwing Nicaragua into revolutionary chaos; it could not repudiate Taft's actions without jeopardizing the security of the Panama Canal and ultimately of the United States; and most important, Christian conscience obliged the United States to act as a good neighbor. "Those Latin republics are our political children. . . ," Bryan said in a public address. ". . . They not only look to us but pattern after us. It is written that much is required of them to whom much is given. . . . The commandment is to 'Love thy neighbor as thyself.' It is the only precept on which we can safely build, so we want to be friends with those countries and help them." If Bryan's appeal to Missionary Diplomacy struck some as a cynical rationalization for a new round of imperialism, it made sense to a public little interested in or excited by sophisticated arguments about national security. More to the point, it made sense to an America preoccupied with the triumph of virtue and democracy in all public questions.

In dealings with Haiti and the Dominican Republic as well, the emphasis was on democracy and stability. In the summer of 1915, when revolutionary upheaval and bloodshed swept Haiti, Wilson saw nothing to do "but to take the bull by the horns and restore order." He wished the Haitian leaders to understand "that we consider it our duty to insist on constitutional government there and will, if necessary . . . take charge of elections and see that a real government is erected which we can support." Likewise, in November 1916, when the collapse of civil authority in the Dominican Republic brought an American military occupation, it was regarded in Washington as the fulfillment of an obligation to help eliminate revolutionary movements and establish "a regular and constitutional government."

Wilson felt no compulsion to justify these actions to the nation, probably because his general comments on the Americas made any explanation seem redundant. In an address to a Pan-American scientific congress in January 1916, for example, he said:

> . . . revolution tears up the very roots of everything that makes life go steadily forward and the light grow from generation to generation. . . . It is just as much to our interest to assist each other to the orderly processes within our own borders as it is to orderly processes in our controversies with one another. These are very practical suggestions which . . . are based . . . upon the solid eternal foundations of justice and humanity. No man can turn away from these things without turning away from the hope of the world. . . . God grant that it may be granted to America to lift this light on high for the illumination of the world.

It was the nation's self-evident duty to export stability and democracy to its southern neighbors. For most Americans, Wilson's appeal made irresistible good sense and needed no repetition in relation to small Caribbean countries with which they had little concern.[5]

Besides, the issue was being directly confronted over Mexico. From the start of his term, Wilson had insisted on a constitutional, popular government in Mexico as a prerequisite for formal relations. When he came into office in March 1913, a counterrevolutionary government under Victoriano Huerta was asking for recognition. But having gained control in the previous month by deposing and murdering Francisco Madero, an idealistic reformer, the Huerta regime failed Wilson's tests of constitutionality and popularity. "I will not recognize a government of butchers," Wilson said privately. Instead, he put his hopes in a new revolutionary group, the Constitutionalists, led by Venustiano Carranza.

In the name of constitutionality and a higher morality, Wilson now tried to impose a solution on Mexico's internal problem. In a note of June 14 he proposed an armistice between the warring factions and early and free elections in which Huerta would not be a presidential candidate. When the latter rejected this interference in Mexico's affairs as a breach of sovereignty, Wilson put his case before the American people. "The peace, prosperity, and contentment of Mexico mean more, much more, to us than merely an enlarged field for our commerce and enterprise," he announced. "They mean an enlargement of the field of self-government and the realization of the hopes and rights of a nation with whose best aspirations, so long suppressed and disappointed, we deeply sympathize." The United States, the President also emphasized, was acting not out of any selfish motive but in behalf of Mexico's best interests and the principle of self-government. This, he added, expressed the spirit and will of the American people for whom his administration spoke. In a word, Wilson had enunciated the proposition that for all practical purposes, Mexico's internal affairs were subject to the same standards applied in the

United States and that most of his countrymen shared this view. There is good reason to believe that he was accurately assessing the national mood. By insisting on democratic rule under law, he was extending abroad what he had been elected to achieve at home.[6]

Mexican resistance to Wilson's pressure increased his determination to bend Mexico to his will. When, with the apparent approval of British oil interests and the British government, Huerta imprisoned the members of the Chamber of Deputies and established a military dictatorship, Wilson again spoke out. In a nationally publicized speech he identified Mexico more clearly than ever with America's domestic concerns. "What is at the heart of all our national problems?" he asked. "It is that we have seen . . . material interests threaten constitutional freedom in the United States. Therefore," he observed with reference to British influence in Mexico, "we will now know how to sympathize with those in the rest of America who have to contend with such powers, not only within their borders but from outside their borders also. . . . In emphasizing the points which must unite us in sympathy . . . with the Latin American peoples we are only emphasizing the points of *our own life,* and we should prove ourselves *untrue to our own traditions* if we proved ourselves untrue friends to them."* Once more Wilson urged Americans to believe that the struggle for constitutional liberties and individual freedom against powerful interests in Mexico was simply an extension of their own battle. He made it clear that he would now try to drive Huerta from power, and by so doing, he expected to draw Latin America in general and Mexico in particular "closer and closer" to the United States.[7]

His campaign led him and the country along paths they did not care to take. In November 1913, Wilson began working to topple Huerta and, as he put it to an English envoy, "teach the

---

* Author's italics.

South American republics to elect good men." Five months later Huerta was still in power, and Wilson's frustration boiled over into military action. Seizing upon a minor incident at Tampico, in which a handful of American sailors had been briefly detained by Huertista forces, Wilson asked Congress for permission to retaliate. But even before both houses could act, the President ordered the Navy to prevent large supplies of ammunition from reaching the Huertistas by occupying Veracruz. The ensuing action on April 21–22 cost 126 Mexican and 19 American lives. In taking this action, Wilson quickly realized that he had overreached himself. Whereas American opinion had sympathized with his policy of overturning Huerta, it objected to the use of force and the prospect of full-scale war with Mexico. Newspapers, mass meetings, petitions, White House and congressional mail registered strong objections to military action and threw Wilson on the defensive. "I never went into battle," he shortly said in a speech, ". . . but I fancy . . . that it is just as hard to do your duty when men are sneering at you as when they are shooting at you. . . . The cheers of the moment are not what a man ought to think about, but the verdict of his conscience and of the consciences of mankind."

Wilson, however, had no intention of going beyond this limited action in Veracruz. When Argentina, Brazil, and Chile proposed mediation, he quickly accepted. But, confident that American opinion still supported his fundamental aim, he publicly reiterated his determination to oust "those in de facto control of the [Mexican] government." His "sole object" in Mexico, he said, was "to help the people secure the liberty which . . . is fully theirs by right. . . . What we desire to do . . . is to show our neighbors to the south of us that their interests are identical with our interests; that we have no plans or any thoughts of our own exaltation, but have in view only the peace and prosperity of the people in our hemisphere." Again, despite Wilson's unquestionable faith in his own and the nation's altruism, the drive to assure constitutional freedom in Mexico rested on a compelling belief in an identity of interests between the two nations. In some not quite conscious way, Wilson and progressive America had incorporated the struggle in Mexico into their own national fight for democracy and social justice under law.[8]

And nothing less would suffice. In the summer of 1914, when Carranza finally overturned Huerta, Wilson could not bring himself to recognize the new regime. For months before he came to power, Carranza had made it abundantly clear that he would not accept guidance from the United States. Moreover, Francisco (Pancho) Villa seemed to offer an alternative. Having helped Carranza to power, he promptly went into revolt against his rule. Championing the downtrodden masses, Villa publicly called for immediate land reform and privately indicated his willingness to follow Wilson's lead.

The administration now took up Villa's cause—but to no avail. Between the fall of 1914 and the spring of 1915, Carranza skillfully mobilized public support for his regime and effectively used his armies to defeat Villa's forces. In response to mounting pressure in the United States to halt what seemed like an endless, devastating struggle, Wilson announced his intention on June 2 to intervene "to help Mexico save herself" unless its leaders stopped fighting and restored order in a very short time. Events during the next four months, however, persuaded the President to back away from this plan. A mounting crisis with Germany over submarine warfare made intervention to the south an unwanted distraction from the country's central foreign policy concern. Further, the consolidation of Carranza's hold on his country left no alternative to the Constitutionalists. Consequently, in October Wilson finally gave de facto recognition to Carranza's regime. Though armed provocations by Villa during the next seventeen months repeatedly brought the administration to the edge of full-scale war and kept his country very much in American minds, the idealistic vision of an altruistic America leading Mexico toward democratic reform now faded from Wilson's discussion of Mexican affairs. The administration did demonstrate a liberal regard for Mexico's right to work out its own destiny by not succumbing to interventionist pressures from conservative opponents of Carranza's revolutionary regime, but the missionary impulse to assure democracy's triumph outside the United States now shifted to other corners of the globe.[9]

No area of the world served as a better surrogate for progressive assumptions and hopes than East Asia, where a weak China struggling to create a republican government suffered exploitation at the hands of the great powers. China was an ideal place for progressive Americans to do psychic battle with their domestic foes. Whereas the progressives struggled for liberation from ruthless corporations and political bosses indifferent to equal opportunity and individual rights, China battled to free itself from self-serving alien powers hostile to its self-determination. A democratic China, of course, would also serve American national interests by placing a large country with a huge population on the side of the United States. A progressive China would, in other words, satisfy practical as well as symbolic American concerns.

From the start of his term, Wilson faithfully enunciated the progressive view. During his first month in office he repudiated American participation in an international bankers' consortium in China and gave formal recognition to a new republican government at Nanking. Denouncing the consortium as a threat to China's independence and refusing to follow the other powers in withholding recognition until the Nanking government confirmed the continuity of foreign concessions in China, Wilson won wide acclaim in the United States. His pronouncement that the United States wished to aid "the great Chinese people" in every way "consistent with their untrammeled development and its own immemorial principles" evoked the comment that now "Humanity is to be placed higher than Property in our international affairs."[10]

Although Wilson and his fellow progressives vocally lined up behind the idea of a new democratic state in China, it is difficult to take their pronouncements at face value. They were far more ambivalent about Asians and their ability to emulate American democracy than their expressions of support suggest. A controversy over Japanese landownership in California during Wilson's first months in office is more revealing of what progressive Americans thought of Asian capacity to conform to American ways: With the tacit approval of the national administration, California lawmakers excluded Japanese aliens from owning land in their state. The objective, Californians freely admitted, was to prevent "mongrelization." The Japanese were "a non-assimilable people," and unless checked, they would flood into California, where they would turn the state into "a Japanese plantation and republican institutions [would] perish." Their presence, a Californian declared, would lead to "race antipathy" and "prevent democratic development, just as it has done in the South." Wilson and a majority of Americans, Arthur Link believes, shared these anti-Japanese prejudices.

There is little evidence that Americans had more regard for the Chinese, who, after 1882, were barred, along with "imbeciles, paupers, and prostitutes," from migrating to the United States or becoming citizens. Theodore Roosevelt expressed a significant element of popular feeling when he described the Chinese as an "immoral, degraded and worthless race." While Americans warmly supported democracy and independence for China, they doubted its ability to achieve these goals. In backing them, they impulsively urged for China what they hoped to see in the United States. For Americans, then, there were two Chinas: the real China, in which there would continue to be great-power influence, and the China of the American imagination, which shared progressive concerns and dreams.[11]

The U.S. response to Japan's entrance into World War I and to its twenty-one demands on China in 1915 further illustrates the point. Despite initial pronouncements from the Wilson administration in behalf of China's independence, Japan's decision to join the fighting by seizing the Shantung Peninsula from Germany evoked no call in the United States for a restoration of China's territorial or administrative integrity. Of course, Tokyo did help forestall such an outcry by promising to consider the eventual return of the area to China, but this assured nothing. Nevertheless, the American government would go no further than a private expression of "satisfaction" at Japan's intention to forgo any territorial aggrandizement in China.

Likewise, the twenty-one demands produced an ambivalent response in Washington. Hoping to take advantage of European weakness in Asia caused by the war, Japan set a body of demands and "requests" before China which would have transformed it from "a ward of all the powers" into a protectorate of Tokyo. The initial reaction from the Wilson administration was not an expression of indignation at Japan's blatant "imperialism" but a recognition of the fact that "territorial contiguity creates special relations between Japan" and Shantung, South Manchuria, and Inner Mongolia, where Tokyo had asked for favored treatment. Then and later, the U.S. government made a point of emphasizing its concern for the "sovereign rights of China" and refused to recognize any agreement impairing American treaty rights in China or the political or territorial integrity of that country. Moreover, as Japanese intentions became known in America, they caused an uproar in the press. Nevertheless, what remains striking about the "crisis" over the twenty-one demands is how restrained Americans were in taking up China's cause. For all the talk of "independence" and "integrity," China's freedom from intervention and exploitation had greater symbolic than substantive importance to Americans; the impulse to make China democratic and free told more about American hopes for themselves than for the Chinese.[12]

Events during and immediately after World War I show the same pattern. Forceful professions of concern for China's independent development were coupled with diplomatic concessions to Japan for greater control in China. In the fall of 1917, five months after the United States had entered the war, Wilson and Lansing answered renewed demands for recognition of Tokyo's "paramount" political and economic interests in China by publicly acknowledging its "special interests" in Chinese areas "contiguous" with Japanese possessions. The administration also reaffirmed the Open Door and China's territorial integrity and rejected the assertion that "special interests" had any political implications, but the Lansing-Ishii Agreement, as it was known, was widely interpreted as a surrender of principle. Similarly, although strenuously defending China's right of self-determination at the Paris Peace Conference, Wilson agreed to continued Japanese control of Shantung Province. As with other compromises of China's integrity, the agreement included a fresh affirmation of Chinese independence: a verbal promise from Tokyo to restore China's political sovereignty in Shantung in the near future.

A number of considerations beyond U.S. control help explain these agreements with Japan. Reluctance to alienate a powerful ally in the struggle against Germany was of major importance in persuading the Wilson administration to accept Japan's claim to "special interests" in China in 1917. Prior European commitments and Japanese threats to reject the peace agreement and participation in the League of Nations in 1918 and 1919 moved Wilson to concede the Japanese demand on Shantung. While these constraints go far to explain American compromises on China, they do not tell the whole story. There was also U.S. ambivalence about China. However warmly they might support Chinese independence in principle, Americans doubted China's ability to maintain its independence in practice. Consequently, they showed little inclination to abandon the unequal treaties imposed on the Asian nation by the great powers.

To most Americans, including Wilson and Bryan, China was an abstraction, a prism through which they filtered their highest public hopes. It was a remote nation in which they found it more satisfying to invest idealized dreams than to confront unwelcome realities. Though recognizing that great power encroachments and internal disarray were the actualities in China, Americans spoke of the country as if it were an extension of theirs: a "great people" ready to free themselves from selfish powers indifferent to humane rules of law. The glaring contradictions in China policy between rhetoric and fact, then, suggest not the hypocrisy of cynical men but the inability of progressive America to look outward and free itself from strictly internal concerns.[13]

No event abroad during Wilson's eight years in office better demonstrates the progressive style of foreign policy than the First World War. A cataclysm which increasingly forced itself on American attention, the conflict evoked a series of responses which strikingly reveal how domestic absorptions dominated foreign affairs.

In the almost three years between the outbreak of fighting and U.S. involvement, two broad lines of thought competed to define the American response to the conflict. On one side stood the picture of America as an entirely neutral arbiter unwilling to join the fray, a nation above the passions driving the belligerents to fight. In this scheme of things, which largely commanded the support of Wilson and the great majority of Americans, the United States was a peacemaker that would lead the contending powers away from the conflict and into a new era of harmony under law. Pitted against this view was the argument espoused by Theodore Roosevelt and a minority of nationalists or "realists": Imperial Germany posed a direct threat to the United States which must be met by involvement in the fighting. According to this idea, German success "would mean the overthrow of democracy in the world, the suppression of individual liberty, the setting up of evil ambitions, the subordination of the principles of right and justice to physical might directed by arbitrary will, and the turning back of the hands of human progress two centuries."[14]

These pacifist and "realist" views were different sides of the same progressive coin. To Wilson and most Americans, the objective was to lead the "civilized" world toward the goal they envisaged for the United States, an end to the economic, political, and social strife undermining human advance. The country, Wilson said on entering the White House, was on the threshold of a new age, a renaissance of American political, artistic, and social life. By the fall of 1914, after twenty months in office, Wilson was declaring his conviction that his administration had overcome the divisions of the past and restored the country's sense of self-mastery. ". . . The deep perplexities and dangerous ill-humors, [the] agitation which shook the very foundations of . . . political life, brought . . . business ideals into question," and condemned social standards—all were now, the President asserted, past. The future was to be a time of cooperation, new understanding, and shared purpose. Although Wilson would soon acknowledge by his own actions that this evaluation was too sanguine, his portrayal of what he hoped to achieve in America bore a striking resemblance to what he wished to build abroad. Similarly, in pressing the case for American involvement in the war, Roosevelt and his fellow "realists" were extending their fight against anti-democratic forces at home to even more ominous ones looming overseas. Unless America joined the Allies in checking the Kaiser's imperialistic autocracy, these interventionists declared, it would mean the end of democracy and freedom in the United States.[15]

America's shifting response to the war had far more to do

with progressive concerns than with realistic needs in foreign affairs. To be sure, from the start of the fighting, many Americans saw an Anglo-French victory over Germany as more compatible with their own selfish interests, but this was not what animated their response to the struggle. Instead, they wanted the United States to stay out of the war and promote an early peace settlement which would eliminate the causes of the fighting and create international harmony. If this were not possible, they intended unselfishly to fight autocratic Germany for the same end—universal freedom and justice under law. Though sincerely meant, these professions of altruism may be read as indirect expressions of unrelenting concern with American domestic ills: Faced with the reality of a world war that inevitably affected the United States, Americans unconsciously used the conflict to urge a negotiated settlement featuring what they wanted at home, that is, a harmonious social order free of debilitating economic and political strife; at the same time, they prepared for the possibility of taking part in the fighting by unconsciously turning the Germans into domestic foes of progressive advance.[16]

Wilson, though strongly preferring the first alternative, managed to keep a foot in both progressive camps. In 1914 he called upon Americans to be neutral in "thought as well as in deed," and in January 1915 he sent Colonel Edward House to Europe to work for a "just" peace settlement. It is striking that this initial effort to secure a "just and lasting peace" followed closely on the heels of Wilson's announcement that he had achieved his progressive goals in domestic affairs. Though House had pressed him from the start of the war to take up this international challenge, Wilson did not act on this advice until he felt he had gained his reform goals at home. The obvious implication is that Wilson saw his peace drive as an enlarged or international campaign for reform, which, indeed, it was. Wilson urged upon the belligerents not just an end to the fighting but general disarmament, an international peace-keeping body, and freedom of the seas to assure the future peace.[17]

By the spring of 1915, however, it was clear to Wilson and most other Americans that they could not yet put across such a peace program. Neither side in the fighting was ready to yield sufficient ground. Worse yet, German actions were compelling a crisis in relations with the United States. In May 1915 a submarine campaign culminated in the sinking of the *Lusitania,* a passenger liner carrying (though this was not generally known at the time) troops and munitions as well as civilians. The loss of over 1,100 lives, including 128 U.S. citizens, caused Americans to view the German government as indifferent to international law and human rights. When these actions were added to earlier suspicions about German militarism and ruthlessness—suspicions effectively encouraged by British propaganda through exaggerated reports of German savagery—a majority of Americans came to see Germany as the enemy of civilized advance. Though only a small number of Americans now concluded that Washington would have to fight Berlin, the thought of war with such an enemy was regarded as compatible with progressive values.

During the year after the *Lusitania* sinking, even Wilson, who was devoted to keeping America out of war and promoting a lasting peace, began to accept such a possibility. In the fall of 1915, he reversed his earlier opposition to military preparedness by asking Congress for a greatly enlarged army and navy, which, despite keen opposition from southern and midwestern pacifists, gained approval. At the same time he launched a new peace initiative which might compel the United States "to join the Allies and force the issue." He now agreed with House that German autocracy and American democracy were bound to clash and that the United States could not allow a military autocracy to dominate the world. In brief, Wilson renewed his efforts for "a reasonable peace settlement that would benefit all mankind." But if German obstinacy caused it to fail, he envisaged an idealistic appeal to Americans to join in a drive to end the war. His principal aim was to bring the belligerents to the peace table, but if this failed, he was ready to lead the country into the conflict. In either case, he expected to serve progressive goals, and he reasonably believed that most Americans would stand behind whatever he did.[18]

Wilson found ample support for his assumptions in the course of 1916. During the first four months of the year, confrontations with Germany over humane principles of international law rested on popular support. In February, an announcement that German submarines would attack armed merchant ships without warning led to congressional resolutions warning Americans against travel on such ships. Though advised that a failure to pass such legislation might lead to war with Germany, Wilson and a clear majority of the country opposed any curtailment of U.S. rights. Bowing before the German threat would be a "deliberate abdication of our hitherto proud position as spokesmen . . . for the law and the right," the President declared. It could mean the crumbling of "the whole fine fabric of international law." Americans largely agreed. "Whoever defends these resolutions defends German lawlessness against American rights and American honor," one newspaper announced. Both houses of Congress decisively defeated the resolutions.

Similarly, the country lined up behind Wilson in March and April, when he threatened to break relations with Germany over the sinking of the unarmed Channel steamer *Sussex.* In a note to the German government, which he paraphrased in a speech to the Congress, the President described America as "the responsible spokesman of the rights of humanity. . . . We owe it to a due regard for our own rights as a nation, to our sense of duty as a representative of the rights of neutrals the world over, and to a just conception of the rights of mankind to take this stand now with the utmost solemnity and firmness," he said. The issues at stake were profound: "the sacred and indisputable rules of international law and the universally recognized dictates of humanity." Although Wilson and the bulk of the country continued to wish otherwise, they were ready to fight Germany for the progressive principles they had struggled to advance at home: justice, law, and the larger social good. Wilson's action, the *New York Times* declared, was "eternally right."[19]

In the spring and summer of 1916, events combined to turn American attention away from the war and back to the domestic scene. In May, Berlin temporarily halted the slide toward war with the United States by promising not to sink merchant ships without prior visit and search. When the Germans honored this pledge over the next several months and the British simultaneously refused renewed suggestions for mediation by the United States, Americans devoted themselves to a new round of progressive reform and to the 1916 presidential campaign. In the spring and summer, for example, the administration steered through the Congress "the most sweeping and significant progressive legislation in the history of the country up to that time." While the necessity of luring "advanced" progressives into Wilson's camp may go far to explain this election year outburst, it is striking, nonetheless, that this explosion of reform energy came when the possibilities for attaching progressive hopes to foreign affairs were on the wane. It is also noteworthy that the chief emotional appeal of Wilson's campaign became his devotion to peace. "He kept us out of war" emerged as the President's principal campaign slogan. Invariably, however, it was coupled with his domestic reforms: "Peace and progressivism" became the keynotes of his successful campaign. In a word, the country voted for freedom from foreign concerns that would shift reform energies from domestic to international advances. To Democrats and progressives, Arthur Link believes, the election meant "another four years of peace and an intensification of the drive for social justice." Indeed, the election may be read as a mandate for an advance along the road toward a more just and harmonious social order.[20]

But this is just what Wilson and the country could not achieve. For all the many and significant reforms the administration had instituted in its first term, it had come nowhere near settling the great economic and social problems of an industrial America. Corporate power, labor strife, and urban blight remained almost as much a part of the national scene as before Wilson had taken office. In the weeks immediately after his reelection, for example, the President and the country faced the prospect of a nationwide railroad strike that could paralyze American economic life. The threatened strike posed the central dilemma that progressives wished to overcome: the power of organized capital and organized labor to injure the "unorganized public." "The central theme in Progressivism," Richard Hofstadter has written, "was this revolt against the industrial discipline: the Progressive movement was the complaint of the unorganized against the consequences of organization." Struggle as they might against this industrial discipline, the progressives, Hofstadter adds, "did not seriously propose to dismantle this society, forsake its material advantages, and return to a more primitive technology." The progressives, then, were reasonable men and women "whose fate it was to attempt, with great zeal and resourcefulness, a task of immense complexity and almost hopeless difficulties."[21]

Because many progressives understood this dilemma, it is not surprising that they found considerable appeal in channeling their reform energies into foreign affairs. Thus, when the election was over, Wilson resumed his efforts to end the fighting and eliminate the causes of future wars. The danger of being pushed into the fighting by developing events gave him good reason to act, but the impulse to play peacemaker probably stemmed also from this domestic impasse. In December, therefore, Wilson publicly asked the belligerents to define their war aims as a prelude to peace talks. When neither the Allies nor Germany showed themselves receptive to the President's lead, he announced his conception of a lasting settlement: a "peace without victory" which would neither produce humiliation nor create inequities among the belligerents. "I have said what everybody has been longing for but has thought impossible," Wilson declared. "Now it appears to be possible."[22]

Germany's announcement in January 1917, however, that it would begin an all-out submarine campaign compelled the United States to abandon the role of peacemaker and consider instead whether it should enter the war. Neither Wilson nor a majority of Americans were eager to join the fray. Having reached the conclusion during 1916 that the Allies as well as the Germans were fighting for conquest, they no longer saw a war against Germany as a well-defined contest between ruthless autocrats and defenders of civilized rights. In American eyes, both sides shared responsibility for the war and hoped to gain from it advantages that would willy-nilly create fresh tensions and lead to another struggle. In response to Germany's announcement, therefore, Wilson did not ask for a declaration of war or even condemn German "barbarism," as Secretary of State Lansing advised. Instead, the President reiterated his desire for peace and declared that Americans would refuse to "believe that they [the German people] are hostile to us unless and until we are obliged to believe it."

This did not take long. Revelations concerning German plans for an anti-American alliance with Mexico and submarine attacks on U.S. merchant ships during the next two months pushed the country toward war. When the provocations combined with the belief that "American belligerency now offered the surest hope for early peace and the reconstruction of the international community," Wilson and the country found strong reason to join the fighting. Nevertheless, they remained deeply divided about entering the conflict. Participation in the fighting, many liberals warned, would serve the country's moneyed interests and destroy its democracy. Wilson shared these fears, telling one confidant in March that involvement in the war would mean the collapse of democracy and law in the United States; war would bring an insistence on conformity, an end to tolerance, the Constitution, free speech, and the right of assembly. "... A state of war," he told a congressman at this time, "suspended the law, and legal and moral restraints being relaxed, there not only ensues an era of recklessness and crime, but also the disregard of commercial integrity and a saturnalia of exploitation, profiteering and robbery."

If these concerns held the country back from the fighting, they also served as a reason for going in. In depicting the triumph of reaction as an outcome to the struggle, Wilson and other progressives exaggerated the impact of the conflict on domestic life. War, it would have been more accurate to say, would assure the status quo or an end to possibilities, however slim, of gaining the larger progressive design. "Wilson had foreseen that the waging of war would require turning the management of affairs over to the interests the Progressives had been fighting," Richard Hofstadter has written, "—but this was hardly the change that he had imagined it to be, for only on limited issues and in superficial respects had the management of affairs ever been very far out of those hands." Involvement in the war unconsciously appealed to progressives as a way to fix blame for the failure of their crusade on forces outside themselves.

Ironically, it was also a way to sustain progressive hopes. Since war and not an unrealizable progressive vision defeated reform, the setback could be viewed as only temporary. Better yet, the war itself could be converted into a platform for a fresh crusade. As Wilson now asserted in his request to the Congress for a war declaration:

> ... our object ... is to vindicate the principles of peace and justice in the life of the world against selfish and autocratic power. ... We are now about to accept the gage

of battle with this natural foe of liberty. . . . We are glad
. . . to fight thus for the ultimate peace of the world and
for the liberation of its peoples . . . : for the rights of nations great and small and the privilege of men everywhere to choose their way of life and obedience. The
world must be made safe for democracy.

If the survival of democracy could be assured abroad, he might
have added, it surely could not fail at home. This, then, was to
be a war not only to make the world "safe for democracy" but
also to save the progressive faith. If the "interests," the organized forces of industrial life, remained at the center of power
in America after the conflict, the culprit was not a flawed
progressive vision, but the war. If progressives had doubts
about the viability of their democratic design, a universal
struggle for "the principles that gave . . . [America] birth and
happiness" promised a strong measure of relief.[23]

For most Americans, including Wilson, the war never principally focused on foreign affairs; substantive questions about international relations or the details of how the world would look
after the fighting were matters on which they did not care to
dwell. In their initial response to involvement in the conflict,
for example, few Americans envisioned the war as altering their
traditional relations with the rest of the world. Congressional
speeches on the resolution declaring war suggested that "no
legislator believed that the European war was of any consequence to Americans except as it affected their right to travel
unmolested upon the high seas." Furthermore, the great majority of the country entered the fighting without tangible war
aims. Beyond vague commitments to the idea that they were
fighting a selfless struggle to defend democracy against autocracy, most Americans had no specific goal they wished to see
come out of the war. "We enter the war not for dollars, not for

empire, not for conquest or hope of reward," a congressman asserted, "but only for the preservation of our modest and un-
doubted right to be free. . . . Could any nation enter a war so
completely without selfishness and without guile?" This emphasis on the country's altruism, on its lack of any tangible
reasons for fighting, was an honest expression of how most
Americans felt about the conflict, but it masked the psychological gain they wanted from it—the preservation of hope that
America might yet reclaim a harmonious social order in which
democracy and justice would flourish.[24]

Wilson's enunciation of peace aims during the war and
subsequent actions at the peace table consistently spoke to
these concerns. In January 1918, after Russia's revolutionists
had undermined the moral standing of the Allies by revealing
their secret "imperialistic" treaties, Wilson outlined America's
postwar goals in his memorable Fourteen Points. In three
speeches between February and September he added thirteen
points to his peace program. With the exception of specific references to self-determination for particular countries, his pronouncements were little more than vague "articles of faith"
around which all liberals could rally. Calling for open diplomacy, freedom of the seas, reduced economic barriers, arms
limitation, the adjustment of colonial claims with justice to
both subject peoples and ruling governments, and a general association of nations guaranteeing political independence and
territorial integrity to great and small nations alike, Wilson in-
timately linked progressive values to the postwar peace settlement. In effect, he told Americans that "they were undertaking
the same broad responsibilities for world order and world democracy that they had been expected . . . to assume for their
own institutions. The crusade for reform and for democratic
institutions, difficult as it was at home, was now to be projected
to the world scene."[25]

Americans, led by progressives of all persuasions, rallied at
once to Wilson's call. The President, one magazine declared,

had "articulated . . . the very conscience of the American people." His Fourteen Points and the association of nations, in particular, suggested a new harmonious world order of national self-fulfillment and democracy under law. More important, the country found fresh hope in Wilson's broad statement of post-war principles that the United States might yet remake itself in the progressive image; for most Americans the crusade abroad was an abstraction which counted for little beyond its relation to domestic affairs. In November 1918, for example, after Wilson had asked the electorate to support his leadership in the coming peace negotiations by electing a Democratic Congress, voters demonstrated a greater concern with immediate domestic problems by returning Republican majorities to both the House and the Senate.[26]

The outcome of the election forcefully reminded Wilson that only a progressive peace settlement which spoke to American domestic needs could find acceptance in the United States. Convinced that he alone could carry this off, he led the American delegation to Paris, where he saw himself fighting against the same reactionary forces he had confronted at home. The Americans were the "only disinterested people at the Peace Conference," Wilson told his advisers, and the Europeans with whom they had to deal "did not represent their own people." The President's presence at the peace table, Richard Hofstadter has written, "repeated with ironic variations the themes of American domestic Progressivism: for here was Wilson, the innocent in the presence of the interests, the reformer among such case-hardened 'bosses' of Europe as Lloyd George and Clemenceau, the spokesman of the small man, the voiceless and unrepresented masses, flinging his well-meaning program for the reform of the world into the teeth of a tradition of calculating diplomacy and an ageless history of division and cynicism and strife."[27]

Wilson also sensed that a peace settlement which put compromise agreements about concrete international problems ahead of progressive principles would neither win acceptance in the United States nor sustain hopes for further domestic advance. Consequently, he insisted that the first business of the conference be the League of Nations, which would stand at the beginning of the peace treaty as a promise of enduring cooperation against war. His insistence on settling the League issue before dealing with more immediate postwar decisions evoked complaints that he was an impractical visionary. Wilson "seems to see the world in abstractions," the writer Walter Weyl observed. "To him railroad cars are not railroad cars but a gray general thing called Transportation; people are not men and women, corporeal, gross, very human beings, but Humanity—Humanity very much in the abstract." General Tasker Bliss complained about American plans for the conference: "I am disquieted to see how hazy and vague our ideas are." But this was just what Wilson wanted. Instead of demoralizing tensions that would inevitably surface over specific political and economic questions, he wished first to emphasize the positive— a new world order embodied in a League. "The League of Nations means, if not the whole Treaty, at least the only part of the Treaty in which he was interested," David Lloyd George said of Wilson. It was the "key to the whole settlement," the President himself said.

In February 1919, after having won Allied agreement to a League, but before the outlines of a peace treaty with Germany were even in place, Wilson returned to the United States to press his case for the world body. More concerned about keeping alive the progressive spirit than about hammering out the details of a postwar settlement, the President wished to assure Americans that a new world order was now within reach. While some liberals in the country were already beyond convincing and some conservatives were already dead set against compromising American sovereignty by joining a League, a majority of the people remained sympathetic to the idea. Arguments that it would mean a continuation of the country's humanitarian crusade, and that its rejection would destroy idealism, seemed to strike a resonant chord. As long as the League could be presented as an abstraction confirming progressive virtues and involving no specific commitments to international affairs, the general public had little quarrel with taking a part. In March, as Wilson prepared to return to Paris, his critics could brand him an Alice in Wonderland urging a "League of Denationalized Nations," but he was confident that the "people" were still with him, and he was probably right.[28]

Back in Paris, however, Wilson weakened his appeal by compromising his progressive principles. To reach a settlement, he felt compelled to give ground on most of his Fourteen Points. Open covenants *openly arrived at,* freedom of the seas, self-determination, arms limitation, reduced economic barriers, a peace among equals or a "peace without victory"—all fell victim in one degree or another to the demands of his Allies. For Wilson this was the most trying period of his life. The struggle over the treaty compelled a painful confrontation with realistic limitations on progressive advance. The idealistic vision of a harmonious, liberal order at home and abroad now had to give ground to traditional concerns with power, security, and selfish advantage. Wilson, however, refused to accept these facts as evidence of progressivism's demise. The fault, he believed, was not with the progressive vision but with the cynical European statesmen and his own closest adviser, Colonel House, who fixed their eyes on immediate needs and could not take the long-term view.[29]

Despite the shortcomings of the treaty, Wilson believed that it contained enough of his progressive program to make it worthwhile. Consequently, in the sixteen months between his return from Paris in July 1919 and the November 1920 election he devoted himself to winning American approval of the treaty and the League. Traveling thousands of miles in a historic speaking effort that broke his health in September 1919, the President urged Americans to understand that his efforts in

France marked a fulfillment of progressive hopes that reactionaries must not be allowed to turn aside. "It liberates great peoples who have never before been able to find the way to liberty," Wilson announced at the start of this campaign. "It ends, once for all, an old and intolerable order. . . . It associates the free Governments of the world in a permanent league . . . to maintain peace by maintaining right and justice. It makes international law a reality. . . . It lays the basis . . . for every sort of international cooperation that will serve to cleanse the life of the world. . . . [It is] a great charter for a new order of world affairs." He had brought back a "just peace," he declared, "and now the great task is to preserve it" so that "when the long reckoning comes men may look back upon this generation of America and say, 'They were true to the vision which they saw at their birth.' "

In his struggle for popular support, Wilson called upon the same ethos of moral responsibility that had been the basis of the whole progressive movement. America had no choice but to accept the treaty and go into the League, he asserted. "The stage is set, the destiny disclosed. It has come about by no plan of our conceiving, but by the hand of God who led us into this way. We cannot turn back. We can only go forward, with lifted eyes and freshened spirit, to follow the vision. It was of this that we dreamed at our birth. America shall in truth show the way. The light streams upon the path ahead, and nowhere else." Not only the spiritual well-being but also the fundamental institutions of Americans were at stake in this argument. If the country rejected the treaty and the League, Wilson warned, it would compel future international strife and constant preparation for war—militarism that would definitively end social reform and democracy in the United States. The very things for which Americans had gone to war—democracy, justice and order, the rudiments of the progressive faith—would now be lost unless they participated in the peace. The appeal contained an unnoted irony: Progressive insistence on making foreign affairs an extension of domestic reform had now made liberalism abroad a requirement for further advance at home.[30]

Wilson's argument was not lost upon most Americans. The best evidence suggests that a majority of the country and the U.S. Senate wished to join the League. Indeed, even after the Senate had rejected the Versailles Treaty in November 1919, organized sentiment in the country remained "so strongly in favor of some kind of league that three months later the Senate was forced to reconsider its decision and resume the debate." At a time when the United States was experiencing high inflation, labor strife, and mass hysteria about radical subversion, the idea of a League that promised explicit international and implicit domestic harmony had irresistible appeal.[31]

Why, then, did Wilson fail to win Senate approval for the treaty and the League? Because, it may be reasonably suggested, he wanted it that way. Unconsciously aware that his claims for the League were unrealizable, that a new world social order and advance toward domestic harmony were out of reach, he preferred rejection of the treaty by senators whom he could then label killers of the progressive dream. Refusing to accept reservations that would have made little difference in the long-term functioning of the League and would have assured Senate passage, Wilson contributed mightily to the final result. As earlier, it was easier to blame the war and uncompromising foes of reform than to acknowledge that a small-town homogeneous America, where equal opportunity, democracy, and individualism flourished, was part of a bygone era which the country could no longer reclaim.[32]

But the nation would no longer accept Wilson's explanation of what had gone wrong. Although it continued to share his impulse to return to a less complicated, less divided America, it now rejected progressivism as the facilitator of that dream. In its nostalgia, it turned instead to Warren G. Harding, who promised "not heroism, but healing, not nostrums but normalcy."

4

Between the Wars: The Diplomacy of Hope and Fear

The greatest problem in civilization today is WAR. It is the paramount question of politics, morality and religion.

The Christian Century, November 27, 1924

To hell with Europe and the rest of those nations!

Senator Thomas Schall, Minnesota, 1935

For most of the twenty years after Theodore Roosevelt assumed the presidency in 1901, a coherent progressive mood dominated American public life. Greater democracy, law, justice, morality, and order were national articles of faith. By 1920–21, however, this idealistic surge had largely run its course. In place of a lofty vision of selfless Americans pursuing shared national goals, the country embraced special-interest politics: Cities vied with small towns, Protestants with Catholics, Drys with Wets, farmers with businessmen, laborers with corporations, fundamentalists with intellectuals, radicals with conservatives, and government with private enterprise. At the same time the country struggled with fears that traditional habits were in jeopardy from alien influences: Southern and Eastern European immigrants incapable of assimilation into American life; anarchism and bolshevism exported from Europe to the United States.

Still, this waning of idealism, pursuit of group interests, and xenophobia did not entirely kill off reform. Farmers, ethnic minorities centered in big cities, congressional liberals, and state and city officials sustained progressivism in the twenties and kept it alive until the Depression once more made reform the predominant national mood.[1]

These domestic crosscurrents largely determined U.S. actions abroad during the twenties and the thirties. Efforts for arms control and an end to war, which loomed large in American minds during these years, reflected not only a pacifist reaction to World War I but also enduring progressive hopes for unselfish commitments to general or "public" rather than to special interests. Progressive anxiety in the twenties about domestic social tensions destructive to democracy found some release in the drive to eliminate international conflict. Stymied in their fight against selfishness in the United States, progressives shifted their focus to the world scene, asking all governments to serve the common good by sacrificing national rights and power to wage war.

At the same time, group antagonisms in America gave rise to cynical nationalism in foreign affairs. The turn toward special-interest politics at home encouraged the belief already set in motion by the Versailles settlement that similar motives operated abroad. The European powers and the United States as well, postwar commentators said, had fought the war not for idealistic goals but for self-serving ones. Power, territorial aggrandizement, and economic self-interest were now viewed by Americans as the causes of the Great War and, more important, as enduring motives in world affairs. From here it was a small step to the conviction that the country had been duped into the war by self-serving Europeans, international bankers, and munitions makers. Perceiving a need to protect themselves from further exploitation, Americans now warmly endorsed economic nationalism and political isolation.

Other powerful currents reinforced the impulse to isolate

the United States from foreign affairs. The failure of progressivism to reverse the trend from individualism toward an organized society of concentrated power and wealth further eroded public confidence in the durability of traditional institutions. But unwilling to regard these changes in American life as the product of irreversible internal forces, middle-class citizens blamed influences coming from Europe. Given some credence by the mass movement of European immigrants to the United States between 1900 and 1920 and the growth of imported radical ideas, traditional America saw compelling reasons to close itself off from peoples and events abroad.

Because these domestic hopes and fears played so big a part in foreign policy, the pacifism, nationalism, and isolationism of the twenties and thirties were more abstractions than realistic responses to world affairs. The pacifist impulse to eliminate war, for example, was not aimed at any particular war or at any specific conflict which might involve the United States. Rather, it opposed war or conflict in the abstract. It was not potential bloodshed between Germany and France or Japan and the United States but clashing special interests in general that seemed to worry the pacifists. Similarly, the foreign interests and alien influences against which Americans had to protect themselves were perceived largely as hidden and sinister. It was those interests and dangers in the abstract rather than any actual outside influence in particular that made Americans eager to defend and close themselves off from external affairs.

As in earlier years, these domestic preoccupations were not a successful formula for dealing with foreign affairs. The progressive impulse to eliminate arms and war may have sustained hopes of easing social conflicts in the United States, but it did little to advance the cause of world peace. Moreover, independence from economic and political developments overseas may have satisfied cynical convictions about the state of world affairs and temporarily eased anxieties about preserving traditional institutions in America, but it did not make the nation more secure from subversion and attack. "What is dangerous to the world," one critic of pacifism in the twenties observed, "is not that nations should act reasonably, in accordance with their interests, but that they should act unreasonably, at the dictation of the reforming instinct, or of some megalomaniac dream."[2]

In the period immediately after World War I, Americans largely turned their backs on overseas concerns, especially events surrounding the war. "It is as if the war had never been," the novelist Robert Herrick observed in 1921. "Three years after the bloodiest conflict known to mankind . . . one may go to almost any theatre . . . one may buy almost any magazine or book on the stalls, and except for an occasional remote allusion to happenings in the years of interregnum it is impossible to guess that anything momentous had happened to the world, to life itself since 1914." One historian has written: "By 1920 publishers were warning authors not to send them manuscripts about the war—people would not hear of it. When at last they were willing to think about it at all, they thought of it as a mistake, and they were ready to read books about the folly of war."[3]

Yet in the midst of this apathy a small group of progressives remained true to their vision of a just and peaceful world under law. In the 1920s a handful of clergymen, women, attorneys, intellectuals, and political radicals led a passionate crusade to reduce arms, adjudicate international disputes, and eliminate war. Unlike most progressives who abandoned general-interest for special-interest politics during the decade, these men and women continued to push for broad moral goals that could serve all mankind. What apparently set them off from other reformers was the fact that they were chiefly middle-class urban dwellers with rural or small-town roots. They were as comfortable in great cities as they were in the countryside. Because the cultural antagonisms of the twenties did not engage them, they were able to stay above the special-interest battles of the day and continue the fight for national and international advance.[4]

They had at least one other trait in common. They believed that the country's involvement in the war had caused special-interest politics to replace shared national goals or the "public" interest. In their view, involvement in Europe's conflicts had aroused tensions among ethnic groups in America and unsettled social stability. "How can we prevent dissension and hatred among our own inhabitants of foreign origin when this country interferes on foreign ground between the races from which they spring?" Elihu Root asked. The restoration of the reform mood and further advance toward progressive goals, peace advocates believed, now depended upon international reforms which would do away with selfish nationalism and war. The war demonstrated, the philosopher John Dewey wrote in 1920, that "our internal policies, our problems of domestic politics, are entangled with foreign questions and invaded by foreign issues." If Americans could persuade Europeans to cleanse the processes of international diplomacy by outlawing war, it would bring "a great revival of liberal confidence and interest." In *The Fight for Peace,* a major history of the peace movement published in 1930, the prominent pacifist writer Devere Allen describes international harmony or the elimination of war and domestic social reform as two facets of the same movement. The point was perhaps best put by the National Council for Prevention of War when it declared, " 'America First'—In the Crusade for a Warless World." The historian Charles DeBenedetti concludes: ". . . What was remarkable about postwar progressive peaceseekers was . . . their capacity to minimize the points of incompatibility between their quest for international peace and their guiding Americanism. Captained by liberal reformers, Protestant and feminist peace groups pursued their reform in postwar America by stressing the national value of the peace cause."[5]

The extent of the pacifist appeal was also remarkable. In

the interwar years some fifty peace societies led by about 100 individuals working through a maze of groups as diverse as the Socialist party and the United States Chamber of Commerce reached out to between 45,000,000 and 60,000,000 Americans. In January 1927, for example, the National Committee on the Cause and Cure of War distributed 430,000 pieces of antiwar literature. In one year alone, 1932, it sent out more than 2,600,-000 pieces of mail urging reform of a maladjusted social order to preserve peace. Reflecting mass guilt about American participation in the war, a widespread desire for reduced military spending, fear of another conflict, and, perhaps most of all, hope for renewed social harmony, peace advocates crystallized and vocalized general sentiment in the country against armaments and war.[6]

Dramatic evidence of this mood appeared in the first half of 1921, when public pressure for naval arms limitation forced the Harding administration to call the Washington Arms Limitation Conference. "What appeared impossible in November 1920," the historian Roger Dingman writes, "seemed desirable only a month later, and by November 1921, statesmen, admirals, and ordinary citizens thought a naval limitation agreement was both urgent and attainable." The single most important factor in this transformation of attitude, Dingman points out, was not economic necessity or the demands of strategy and weapons technology but domestic politics. As late as his inauguration in March 1921, Harding saw little reason to satisfy demands for a naval arms conference. Though Senator William Borah of Idaho had stirred some interest in the issue with a congressional resolution in December, national economic problems led by unemployment and inflation seemed far more pressing concerns to the public. During the spring of 1921, however, public interest in Borah's proposal grew at an astonishing rate. Led by women's organizations and churches, which staged mass meetings on Easter Sunday, organized a National Disarmament Week in May, and designated June 5 as Disarmament Sunday, some 6,000,000 Americans flooded Washington with petitions demanding arms reduction. ". . . The surge of hope and faith that swelled up in the nation," Robert Osgood writes, "had assumed the proportions of a mammoth revival meeting." Against a backdrop of economic dislocation, political repression of radicals, and rising social tensions among conflicting groups, pacifist promises of ending war and healing social ills by disarmament were an attractive panacea millions of Americans could not resist.[7]

The Washington Conference produced three major treaties—the Four-, Five-, and Nine-Power agreements—which principally spoke to enduring progressive hopes among Americans for social harmony and order or the triumph of public over special interest politics. Focusing on the great powers' rivalry in Asia, the treaties identified means of reducing tensions and preventing wars. The Four-Power agreement committed America, Britain, Japan, and France to respect one another's rights in the Pacific and to confer should any dispute arise about those rights or should any outside force threaten them. The Five-Power Treaty, which included Italy, consisted of a ten-year prohibition against building capital ships, set a ratio of capital ship tonnage among the five powers of $5:5:3:1.75:1.75$, and restrained the signatories from building any new fortifications or naval bases in the Pacific. The Nine-Power Treaty pledged all the nations at the Washington Conference to support the Open Door principle and respect the sovereignty, independence, and territorial and administrative integrity of China.

Viewed in terms of international politics, these agreements were an attempt to ease the danger of a future explosion by great power accommodation. In return for accepting inferior naval power, Japan insisted on freezing construction of Anglo-American bases which could threaten it. In exchange for giving up a twenty-year-old alliance with Britain, Tokyo received pledges in the Four-Power Treaty to consult about threats to any of their interests. As a concession for agreeing to remain relatively weak in capital ships, France was left free to build as many cruisers, destroyers, and submarines as it believed necessary to its defense. The Washington settlement, a later writer notes, "did not supplant the competition for national power; it simply set a pattern for moderating and regularizing that competition. It did not transform the basic relations among nations; it registered existing facts about those relations."

Yet it was just this assumption of fundamental change that great numbers of Americans took away from the successful Washington talks. From the opening day of the conference, when Secretary of State Charles Evans Hughes startled the delegates by calling for prompt disarmament in specific categories of ships, numerous Americans saw the United States permanently turning the rest of the world away from war. By the close of the meeting they were convinced, as Hughes told them, that they were "taking perhaps the greatest forward step in history to establish the reign of peace." They envisioned a reconstructed world and a new epoch now in store for international relations. The treaties were seen not as a triumph *of* power politics but as a triumph *over* power politics.[8]

That so many Americans blindly subscribed to this assumption revealed less about their naïveté toward world affairs than about their anxiety over current domestic tensions and their continuing progressive dreams of recapturing a harmonious past. Seeing the Washington agreements as an abandonment of selfish interest for the sake of universal good, Americans turned the world community into a kind of orderly middle-class utopia, where political and social harmony won out over national or group rivalry. Contemporary comments on the treaties as promoting goodwill, friendly dealings, harmony, and permanent peace suggest that Americans were describing not international relations in the twenties but a nineteenth-century small-town social order progressives had wished to reclaim. Indeed, the response to the Washington agreements was as pure an expression of the old progressive mood as one could find after World War I.

Only the sense of responsibility or the commitment to what the progressives had described as civic participation was in fact absent. Though the treaties imposed no substantive obligations on any of the signatories to assure their fulfillment, the provision for consultation in the Four-Power agreement was enough to arouse fears of an "entangling alliance" or of civic participation on the world scene Americans were now rejecting at home. A superfluous reservation that there was no "commitment to armed force, no alliance, no obligation to join in any defense," however, allowed the treaty to squeeze through the Senate by four votes.[9]

This impulse to convert international agreements into triumphs of progressive hopes found a logical culmination in the Kellogg-Briand Pact of 1928 outlawing war. Dating from at least 1918, when Salmon O. Levinson, a wealthy Chicago attorney, began publicizing the idea, prohibiting war was a striking example of the progressive faith in reform legalism or in the power of public opinion and law to abolish pernicious social institutions and bring order out of chaos. Despite a Senate resolution introduced by William Borah in 1923 to make war a public crime under the law of nations, nothing came of the proposal until 1927. In the spring of that year, in hopes of adding to a series of bilateral nonaggression pacts aimed at encircling Germany, French Foreign Minister Aristide Briand proposed a Franco-American agreement outlawing war. Though the proposal was backed by prominent American internationalists eager to encourage renewed United States interest in collective security, mass attraction to the scheme did not appear until the fall.[10]

The catalyst for this interest was a combination of domestic and international tensions arousing fears of social collapse. In August 1927, after six years of intense debate about the case of Nicola Sacco and Bartolomeo Vanzetti, two alien anarchists, the state of Massachusetts executed them for murders allegedly committed during a 1920 robbery. Arguing that the court and all the forces of upper-class respectability in America had condemned the two men to death less on the merits of the evidence than because of their political beliefs and Italian origins, critics regarded the executions as an act of class reprisal which split the nation into warring camps. Coming on the heels of the 1924 National Origins Act restricting the "new" immigration from Southern and Eastern Europe, the split at the 1924 Democratic party convention over whether to condemn the Ku Klux Klan, and the 1925 Scopes trial pitting the city against the country, Christians against Christians, and scientists against fundamentalists, the suggestion of class war in America did not seem farfetched. At the same time, rumors of foreign war fed by Anglo-Russian tensions, aggressive Italian maneuvering in the Mediterranean, and conflicts among the new Balkan states made Europe appear closer to war than at any time since November 1918. Equally disturbing to Americans, a Geneva conference called by President Coolidge to restrain a growing arms race in cruisers, destroyers, and submarines collapsed after only six weeks with nothing to show for its efforts but heightened tension between Britain and the United States.[11]

In these circumstances, the idea of outlawing war quieted mass anxiety about the dangers of domestic and foreign strife. Led by "Pacifists and . . . Earnest Christians," who gathered 2,000,000 signatures on petitions, a "tidal wave of public sentiment" pressed the Coolidge administration to join other nations in making war illegal. In response, Secretary of State Frank B. Kellogg proposed that Briand's suggestion be converted into a multilateral renunciation of war. Despite Kellogg's insistence on excluding wars of self-defense, fifteen nations signed a pact in Paris on August 27, 1928, renouncing war as an instrument of national policy. Acclaimed as "superb," "magnificent," and "a greater hope for peaceful relations than . . . ever before given to the world," the treaty evoked widespread enthusiasm in the United States and won Senate approval by a lopsided 85 to 1 vote.

Rational calculation cannot explain the appeal of the pact. It was "a letter to Santa Claus," "a New Year's resolution," or an "international kiss" not "worth a postage stamp," as numerous commentators at the time emphasized. "There is no evidence, even in religion, to prove that the world can outlaw war any more than it can outlaw the weather," one of them said. The exclusion of defensive wars alone made the agreement worthless, others pointed out. Wars of self-defense were "as limitless as the imagination" and covered "almost any war that has occurred in the last century." But none of this registered on the mass of Americans, whom Senator Carter Glass of Virginia saw taking psychological comfort from the treaty. Indeed, carrying no obligations except to abstain from aggressive war, the pact reflected enduring progressive hopes that "the aroused and sustained public opinion of the people" alone could assure universal harmony under law.[12]

This progressive commitment to harmony and general interest politics also registered forcefully on policy toward Latin America between the wars. Washington's high-handed insistence on order and stability and military interventions to compel them before 1920 now gave way to a more benign approach, emphasizing negotiation, nonintervention, and kinship among equals. Undoubtedly, the demise of German sea power at the end of World War I eased earlier concerns about American security in the Caribbean and allowed Washington to be less assertive about its interests in the area. But this alone is insufficient to explain the dramatic shift in attitude beginning in the twenties. Rather, it rested largely on a change in public mood from a preoccupation with national security and tutelary democracy to an insistence on self-determination and friendly dealings. It was based on the same vision of cooperation and shared interests motivating the Washington treaties and the Kellogg-Briand Pact. Unlike these agreements, however, a

Good Neighbor policy in Latin America, where the United States remained predominant, could hold together and more or less sustain mass nostalgia for social harmony under law.[13]

Mexico is a case in point. In 1925, after Plutarco E. Calles had become president of Mexico, the Mexican Congress enacted laws denying alien landowners the protection of their own governments and making oil deposits the "inalienable" property of the nation. The petroleum law set up strict regulations for concessionaires, with which they had to comply by January 1, 1927. Major American oil companies, refusing to accept the new restrictions, denounced Calles as a Bolshevik who was opening the way to Communist control of the hemisphere. When the Calles government also began enforcing anti-Catholic provisions in the Mexican Constitution, confiscating church property and forbidding religious instruction in private schools, and began as well to aid revolution in Nicaragua, demands for intervention in Mexico arose in the United States. But this was a distinctly minority sentiment. Reflecting a more broadly held view in the country, the U.S. Senate, led by progressives like Borah and George Norris of Nebraska, gave unanimous approval to a resolution urging the settlement of all disputes with Mexico by arbitration. In response to this mood, President Coolidge appointed Dwight W. Morrow, a wealthy attorney, as ambassador to Mexico with the instruction "to keep us out of war." True to his charge, Morrow skillfully cultivated good relations with the Mexicans, and reached accommodation with them on every outstanding problem.[14]

Similarly, in dealings with Nicaragua, public pressure in the United States for conciliation rather than force compelled the Coolidge administration to back away from an aggressive policy. In 1925, Coolidge ended a thirteen-year occupation of Nicaragua by withdrawing American marines. In less than a year, however, Nicaragua's reversion to the sort of anarchy that had brought intervention in the first place moved Washington to send in a new force of marines. The government's action provoked a storm of criticism in the United States. "The expressions from all parts of the country which have reached Washington, and been given to the public in the newspapers," the *New York Times* observed in January 1927, "show that this country is at present in the mood to insist upon reasonable compromise, methods of conciliation, submission to arbitration—all to be tried out honestly before there is any talk of the appeal to the ultimate reason of kings." Military responses to Latin American problems were out of date. There was "a swelling demand that some other way be found," and "a steady pressure from public sentiment" to make use of it.

Again, as with Mexico, Coolidge and Kellogg responded with a conciliatory policy. They sent Henry L. Stimson, Taft's secretary of war and Herbert Hoover's future secretary of state, to Managua to negotiate a settlement among the warring Nicaraguan factions. Stimson satisfied sentiment in the United States by largely halting the civil war and creating conditions for the eventual withdrawal of American marines.[15]

Intervention in Nicaragua in the twenties was an exception to a new rule. Whereas the United States had intervened militarily twenty times in Caribbean countries between 1898 and 1920, it did so only twice in the interwar years, in Honduras and Nicaragua. Secretary Hughes gave voice to this policy in 1923: "Our interest does not lie in controlling foreign peoples. . . . Our interest is in having prosperous, peaceful, and law abiding neighbors with whom we can cooperate to mutual advantage." By incremental steps in the twenties and thirties, Republican and Democratic administrations alike gave form to this enduring progressive vision of harmony under law, the Good Neighbor policy.

In 1923, Hughes signed a Pan-American treaty which provided that controversies between American nations not settled by diplomacy or brought under arbitration would be sent to a commission of inquiry before any military action should take place. Further, in 1928, Under Secretary of State J. Reuben

Clark declared in a memorandum that Roosevelt's Corollary of 1904 justifying interventions in Latin America had no validity under the Monroe Doctrine. Clark's memorandum, however, did not directly repudiate the practice of intervention. This repudiation occurred at the Montevideo and Buenos Aires conferences of 1933 and 1936, when the Franklin Roosevelt administration subscribed to the principle that no state has the right to intervene in the internal or external affairs of another. Roosevelt gave substance to this commitment when he signed a treaty abrogating the Platt Amendment, thereby abolishing the U.S. right to intervene in Cuba; ended the United States's twenty-year occupation of Haiti; and negotiated a treaty with Panama abolishing the right held since 1903 to intervene unilaterally and take unlimited control of Panamanian territory. In sum, through the sixteen years after Wilson left office and liberalism gave way to reaction, depression, and eventually a new reform mood under the New Deal, the progressive ideal of like-minded people working for a larger social good endured in inter-American relations—a standing, symbolic assurance to millions in the United States that a harmonious nineteenth-century culture had not entirely disappeared.[16]

American diplomacy in the twenties and thirties seems patently inconsistent. On the one hand, the country took the lead in urging a strife-ridden world to give up arms and selflessly pledge itself to peace for the good of mankind. On the other, it fostered international rivalry and world economic ills by selfishly pursuing policies of economic nationalism. Though outwardly contradictory, these impulses were rooted in a common concern: anxiety over group conflict and special-interest politics in the United States. In the twenties Americans hoped they could cure the disease of clashing interests at home by first eliminating them abroad. At the same time, they fell prey to fears that group rivalry would not disappear and that the world without mirrored the world within, as the Versailles settlement and renewed national conflicts seemed to make clear. This gave rise to a general belief that only a strict defense of the national economic interest could preserve the country from exploitation at alien hands.

Historians have seen the sources of this economic nationalism in other things: ignorance of how domestic prosperity depended on economic and financial cooperation with other states; a calculated drive to ensure an American share of markets, raw materials, and investment opportunities around the globe; and a preoccupation with preserving bountiful domestic markets from foreign competition. These explanations are not mutually exclusive; each contributes something to our understanding of America's postwar economic nationalism. Parochialism, willful efforts to assure economic gains abroad, and determination to reap the benefits of home markets—all, to one degree or another, influenced U.S. economic policy after the war. But none of these interpretations satisfactorily explains the change in mood from Wilson's idealistic appeals for international economic cooperation to the uncompromising defense of every American advantage in world economic affairs. The triumph of special over general interest politics or the erosion of progressive hopes for a moral, homogeneous society in the face of domestic economic, religious, racial, and geographic conflicts was more important in changing America's economic outlook toward the world.[17]

War debts in the twenties and thirties are illustrative. A combination of wartime and immediate postwar foreign loans had put the Allied powers $10.3 billion in debt to the United States by 1920. Arguing that the money should be considered America's contribution to the war, which others had made in blood, and that insistence on repayment would wreak havoc on the world economy, the Allies pressed the United States to cancel the debts. Were Washington to adopt this policy, they declared, it would allow them to scale down German reparations and speed the economic recovery of Europe.

No U.S. officeholder who valued his political life would consent to this idea. A number of American leaders accepted the wisdom of what the Europeans said, but none of them felt free to advocate cancellation openly. Indeed, though actually agreeing in the twenties to reduce Allied indebtedness by approximately 43 percent, government leaders would never admit that they had allowed partial cancellation of the debts. Even when it became transparently clear in the thirties that the Allies would default on their obligations, the Roosevelt administration refused to defy popular feeling by declaring debt payments at an end. Throughout the interwar years the war debts were seen as something of a sacred cow that could be tampered with only at great political risk.

At least one historian believes that government officials "created and nurtured, rather than followed," this anti-cancellation sentiment. "If politicians thought they heard strong opposition to debt repudiation," writes Joan Hoff Wilson, "it was because they were tuned in to nationalist business opinion. . . ." In fact, Wilson argues, public opinion in the United States was largely uninformed and indifferent to the issue. It was "too technical and complex for most businessmen, let alone the man in the street, to understand." Moreover, "the ease with which the downward scaling of debts was accepted without mass outcries against cancellation . . . either confirms this basic lack of understanding or implies a potential malleability or outright indifference of the public on this issue."[18]

Wilson's analysis is revealing. She is undoubtedly right that most Americans understood next to nothing about the complex debts. Yet this did not necessarily imply malleability or outright indifference to the issue. It is difficult to believe that a generation of politicians in both the congressional and executive branches of government would so uniformly misread the mass mood. The fact that Americans generally knew little

about the debts and accepted their reduction without significant complaint suggests not indifference to the issue but that it
had become a surrogate for other concerns. It was not debts per
se that concerned Americans, but rather what they stood for in
American minds. To cancel them was to act selflessly in a selfish world. During the early years of the century, when
progressive zeal was at its height, it is entirely conceivable that
Americans might have fixed on this as a noble deed. But in the
postwar era, in a society and world dominated by clashing
forces intent on defending group, corporate, and national interests with little regard for the general good, debt cancellation
seemed self-destructive and naive. Statesmen could repackage
the debts in almost any form they pleased, but cancellation
would have challenged the prevailing belief that human affairs
were governed by the war of all against all. It was not, then, a
rational estimate of what would be lost by cancellation, but a
climate of opinion describing the world in strictly self-serving
terms, that made for insistence on repayment.

The same influence went far to determine U.S. tariff policy
in the twenties and thirties. Between 1913 and 1921, under the
sway of Wilsonian internationalism, which preached the expansion of American commerce through reciprocal elimination
of world economic barriers, tariffs took a clear downward turn.
The Underwood Tariff Act of 1913, for example, lowered rates
by some 25 percent and placed a host of important products on
the free list. In the closing days of the Wilson administration,
moreover, when farm interests pushed the Congress into ap-
proving higher tariffs on agricultural produce, the President
vetoed the measure, maintaining that it would not relieve the
postwar economic distress of farmers. With Wilson's departure,
however, economic nationalism gained the upper hand. The
Harding administration enacted the Fordney-McCumber Tariff Act of 1922, which pushed rates to levels not reached before
in American history.[19]

Traditional Republican and business attachment to high

tariffs does not adequately explain this sharp turn toward protection. Unlike earlier times, the business community was deeply divided over the issue. Import-export companies joined hands with large manufacturing establishments to oppose the "hysterical" drive of medium-sized manufacturers and agricultural producers for unprecedented tariff increases. For the first time in American history, one senator remarked, the representatives of "great big business" were asking for lower rates, while the spokesmen of "small business" were demanding "excessively high rates." Joan Hoff Wilson observes that "On paper, the two sets of opponents appeared somewhat evenly matched." In fact, however, the smaller manufacturers dominated the proceedings. Though larger industries voiced the rational concern that the nation's new status as an international creditor and exporter of like amounts of factory and farm goods made traditionally high American duties obsolete, they were out of step with the national mood. The prevailing belief throughout the country was in the need to preserve the American market for the American producer.

The Depression, beginning in 1929, deepened this mood and helped spawn the even higher Hawley-Smoot Tariff schedules of 1930. Influenced by the domestic and international struggles of the 1920s, Americans could not conceive of a cooperative world in which the injured nations joined to overcome the economic dislocations of the time. Consequently, in spite of warnings from nearly every reputable economist in the United States that higher duties would "injure the great majority of our citizens" by impeding intergovernmental debt collections, stifling trade, aggravating unemployment, and deepening the depression, the country endorsed the tariff as a way to protect itself from cheap imports and preserve its standard of living. As events shortly demonstrated, there was little rational basis for this assumption. Instead of contributing to American well-being, the Hawley-Smoot Tariff added to international and domestic economic decline. But rational calculation probably had little to do with this measure. More important in making so economically unsound a tariff possible was the prevailing conviction that in public affairs groups and nations must cover up, not open up. The belief, moreover, that the Depression stemmed from forces abroad against which the United States had to insulate itself also gave a "protective" tariff an irresistible symbolic appeal.[20]

These crosscurrents were so strong in the United States that even the more flexible and internationalist Roosevelt administration was unable to reverse American tariff policy significantly. Despite impulses in this direction led by Secretary of State Cordell Hull—a fervent economic internationalist who described the tariff as the "king of evils"—the administration succumbed to the prevailing protectionist mentality. During the Hundred Days, for example, though the President made gestures toward initiating a reciprocal trade policy, the Agricultural Adjustment Act and the National Industrial Recovery Act, central parts of the New Deal recovery program, included protectionist features to shelter American agricultural and industrial output from foreign competition. Moreover, despite considerable rhetoric about cooperation at a World Economic Conference in London to promote international recovery, Roosevelt felt compelled to serve America's economic advance by torpedoing the talks. In retrospect, historians have seen Roosevelt's action as excessive, suggesting that for all his internationalist talk he had entered into the nationalistic mood of the time. Like many of his countrymen, who took satisfaction in his uncompromising defense of the national interest, FDR enjoyed the thought that the United States would not come away a loser from this international conference.

Roosevelt's ultimate resolution of the tariff issue rested on the same attitude. Though the Congress passed a Reciprocal Trade Law in 1934, ostensibly opening the way to freer trade, the administration of the act reflected an enduring nationalism in the United States. The trade agreements negotiated under the law in the 1930s "did less to revive world trade by increasing imports and reducing America's credit balance than to expand American exports, which increased enough in this period almost to double America's favorable balance of trade. . . . The reciprocal trade program chiefly served American rather than world economic interests." And in so doing, it reflected the central belief in America in the interwar years that human affairs in general, and economic relations in particular, rested on the pursuit of selfish interest. Foreign economic policy between the wars demonstrated that an industrial nation beset by social strife had eclipsed the progressive vision of a harmonious nineteenth-century social order as the dominant image in the American mind.[21]

If Americans recognized social tension or domestic strife as the governing fact of national life in the twenties and thirties, they rejected suggestions that this was a permanent condition brought on by long-term economic and social changes in the United States. Instead, they blamed the loss of an earlier national harmony on alien forces destructive to traditional habits. It was not something native to America but rather unassimilated foreign influences that accounted for progressivism's failure to reach its largest goals or for the continuing vulnerability of the country's political and social customs to modern currents. These fears were not wholly irrational. The more than 15,000,000 immigrants who came to America in the first twenty years of the century significantly transformed national life, leaving native Americans with "a vague uneasy fear of being overwhelmed from within. . . ." At the same time the successful Bolshevik uprising in Russia, engineered by a small fraction of the population, and the spread of revolution across Europe and of strikes and bombings across America aroused some understandable concern that a handful of determined radicals might touch off an uprising in the United States.

But the fear of a foreign-controlled revolution in America soon passed all reasonable bounds. Although there was clearly no danger of a successful upheaval, and labor walkouts were caused by genuine grievances, millions of Americans felt menaced by alien radicals, and enthusiastically supported arbitrary arrests and deportations. In the winter of 1919–20, when Attorney General A. Mitchell Palmer committed wholesale violations of civil liberties by seizing innocent people, holding them incommunicado, denying them counsel, and subjecting them to kangaroo courts, the country applauded his actions. When he overreached himself in the spring of 1920, however, by falsely predicting an attempt to overturn the U.S. government, the nation lost its enthusiasm for the Red Scare. The hysteria over a supposedly looming, alien-dominated revolution disappeared as quickly as it had begun.[22]

Nonetheless, strong feelings of xenophobia remained, as evidenced by the growth of the Ku Klux Klan and the passage of the National Origins Act in the 1920s. Between 1920 and 1924 the Klan grew from a small anti-black Deep South organization of some 5,000 members to a national society of 3,000,-000 centered in the Southwest, Midwest, and Far West. Its members were chiefly lower-middle-class native white Protestants who feared the "big cities" with their "foreign" influences and habits so at odds with the "American way of life." Klan members celebrated the Constitution and practiced what William Leuchtenburg has called "a kind of magical nativism," a form of activity in which they tried to re-create the total situation in which their ancestors had lived. To preserve the older, more homogeneous America they revered, Klansmen plumped for an immigration law which would keep America for Americans by preventing the Nordic race from being swamped. They thereby reflected not simply a longing for the restoration of their influence in the country but the mass belief that American troubles resulted from contacts with foreign ideas and peoples. By the early twenties the image of a pure America now sadly contaminated by involvement with foreigners had had a strong impact on popular thought.

This general attitude expressed itself in a drive for an immigration statute barring any further entry to the Alpine, Mediterranean, and Semitic peoples who had recently come to America in such great numbers. A continued flood of such aliens to our shores, one restrictionist proponent declared, would create a race of hybrid Americans "as worthless and futile as the good-for-nothing mongrels of Central America and Southeastern Europe." In response to this xenophobia the Congress passed the National Origins Act of 1924, forbidding all Oriental immigration and sharply limiting the "new" immigration from Southern and Eastern Europe. The act, commented one newspaper, guaranteed that America's future would remain in the hands of the American people. Within a year's time, an immigration official was reporting that virtually all immigrants coming through Ellis Island "now looked exactly like Americans."

This nativist upsurge, this fear that insidious alien influences were endangering America's unique institutions, was the central force behind the isolationist impulse in the country's foreign policy between the wars. Though this mood did not remain constant, but alternately rose and fell in intensity, it nevertheless determined the nation's principal reactions to events abroad during the interwar years. Two major expressions of this nativism/isolationism were the refusal to recognize the Soviet government in Russia in the twenties and the American rejection of all political ties to the League of Nations.

The nonrecognition policy toward the Soviets rested on the belief that Russia was not a civilized nation—that is. not one that paid its debts, honored agreements, and renounced international revolution. As the historian Christopher Lasch has explained, it was a widely held view that the United States "could have relations only with a regime which shared its own attitudes and assumptions about the world."[23]

The resistance to joining the innocuous World Court is an even more telling example. An autonomous judicial arm of the League, the Permanent Court of International Justice, as it was formally called, embodied the American ideal of the rule of law. Its establishment grew out of the idealistic assumption that a world court could settle international disputes and prevent wars. In practice, however, the Court had almost no power: It could take jurisdiction in a dispute only when requested by all the parties, and it lacked the authority to enforce a decision even when disputants did let it rule on a controversy. But because it at least symbolized a commitment to so thoroughly progressive a concept as the adjudication of international conflict, the Court commanded considerable support in the United States: Both political parties repeatedly endorsed American participation, and all three Republican administrations in the twenties proposed adherence to its protocols. Yet despite these considerable influences in its behalf, the country remained outside the Court. The effective deterrent to participation was always the suggestion that joining would mean involvement with the League, and foreign control and contamination of American affairs. "Let America once get into this League Court House with its trap doors and its panel walls and its false ceilings and its collapsible stairways and its packed bench," an isolationist newspaper warned, "and she will find that she is involved, and she can not get out." The one time the Senate did vote adherence to the Court, in 1926, it was on the condition that it would never render an advisory opinion on a dispute involving the United States without America's prior consent. The Court's unwillingness to concede its small symbolic power compelled resistance to this humiliating demand, preventing American entrance in the twenties.[24]

The advent of a Democratic administration under an ostensibly internationalist President revived the issue in 1933. Though convinced that widespread sentiment for joining the Court existed in the country, Roosevelt believed that an attempt to achieve this goal in 1933 and 1934 would delay essential recovery measures. Such a proposal would have antagonized progressive Republican senators convinced that involvement threatened destruction of American sovereignty. In January 1935, however, with a poll of the Senate showing more than a two-thirds majority in favor, Roosevelt pressed the case for the Court. His request touched off a nativist response out of all proportion to the issue. Since membership in the Court meant no more than a symbolic endorsement of world peace, the opposition came less from realistic fears of the body than from nativist hysteria about foreign influences destroying the "American way of life." The radio priest Father Charles Coughlin urged: "Every solid American who loves democracy" should stand foursquare with Court opponents "to keep America safe for Americans and not the hunting ground of international plutocrats." Once the Court rendered "advisory opinions in which the United States is interested," Senator Hiram Johnson warned, "the whole fabric we have built up since we were a nation goes crumbling to the ground." And Senator Homer T. Bone of Washington declared: "I am a believer in democracy and will have nothing to do with the poisonous European mess. I believe in being kind to people who have the smallpox such as Mussolini and Hitler, but not in going inside their houses." These irrational fears struck a resonant chord in the country and the Senate, where an initial group of ten opposing senators grew to thirty-six. With only fifty-two senators voting aye, the proposal fell seven votes short of the required two-thirds.[25]

What is perhaps most remarkable about the question of joining the World Court is not that it went down to defeat but that it kept coming up for consideration in the twenties and the first half of the thirties. It suggests that the nativist impulse fueling the isolationism of these years was not a fixed influence but varied in its hold on the public imagination. Down to 1924 nativist feelings were intense, but between 1925 and 1934 they lost some of their grip on the public. In the late twenties, John

Higham points out, "a billowing prosperity washed over and helped to smooth the emotional turmoil of the preceding years. . . . Furthermore, . . . a democratic balance-wheel, working deep inside the national culture, partially counteracted the nativist movements. . . . The nation's traditional values undoubtedly exercised a quiet brake on xenophobia." Finally, there was the fact that the nation "relapsed into a general indifference toward all big problems, international and internal alike." It went on "a moral holiday," counting its material blessings—a chicken in every pot, a car in every garage—and reassuring itself that "It Ain't Gonna Rain No More." Although the economic collapse beginning in 1929 replaced the indifference to domestic problems and the mood of optimism with demands for economic remedies and renewed fears about the durability of American institutions, nativist fears of foreign dangers remained distinctly in the background. The intense concern with domestic difficulties left almost no room for mass attention to external affairs or alien threats. This does not mean that Hoover and Roosevelt were free to cast aside isolationism and follow an activist course in foreign affairs from 1929 to 1934. But they did have more leeway in these years than Hoover's Republican predecessors had had in the early twenties or Roosevelt after 1934.[26]

The response to the Manchurian crisis of 1931–32 is one example. In September 1931 an alleged act of Chinese sabotage on the Japanese-controlled South Manchurian Railway moved Japanese forces to overrun much of South Manchuria in violation of the League Covenant, the Nine-Power Treaty of 1922, and the Kellogg-Briand Pact. While it thoroughly disapproved of the Japanese action, the Hoover administration replied equivocally to the crisis. On the one hand, mindful of the little patience the public would show in the midst of a depression for so remote a problem as fighting in Manchuria, Washington refused overtures to align itself directly with possible League action. On the other hand, the government reversed the Harding-Coolidge policy of shunning official ties to the League by agreeing to have a representative sit with its council during discussions of the Sino-Japanese dispute. Moreover, in January 1932, after the League had refused to do more than investigate the incident and Japan had defied international opinion by continuing its aggression, the Hoover administration announced its refusal to recognize the legality of any situation brought about by violations of the Open Door or the Kellogg-Briand Pact. Though no more than a moral condemnation of aggression, it represented a challenge to Japan which stirred isolationist fears of involvement in a pointless war. "The American people," the Philadelphia *Record* asserted, "don't give a hoot in a rain barrel who controls North China." While it hardly committed America to fight or join other nations in a meaningful action, the Hoover-Stimson policy was more than that which the intense isolationist feelings of the early twenties and later thirties would have allowed.[27]

Roosevelt also found at least some room to maneuver in foreign affairs during his first two years in office. With only a small group of bankers, businessmen, and idealists paying much attention to foreign relations during this time, he felt free to take some modest internationalist steps: an endorsement of the Hoover-Stimson nonrecognition doctrine; the appointment of Cordell Hull, a Wilsonian internationalist, as secretary of state; invitations to foreign leaders for personal talks; a public declaration at the Geneva Disarmament Conference of 1932–34 that the United States would support collective efforts against war; a request, which he soon abandoned, for a discriminatory arms embargo punishing aggressors; the recognition of the Soviet Union; public support for the League of Nations as "a prop in the world peace structure"; and the request to the Senate to join the World Court. None of these actions, of course, seriously challenged the prevailing antagonism in the United States to international political commitments or collective security, and they were balanced by a vigorous economic nationalism. Yet, compared to what happened immediately after 1934, Roosevelt's initial foreign actions seem relatively bold.

The World Court defeat in January 1935 signaled something of a turning point in American foreign relations. The struggle reawakened the isolationist feelings or xenophobia which had been so palpable in the early twenties. It was not involvement in the Court, but the rising prospect of another European war, coupled with new departures in domestic affairs, that scared Americans and produced the warnings against foreign dangers to national institutions. However conservative and popular, Roosevelt's New Deal measures also excited concern that something radical was happening in the United States which would produce basic changes in American economic and political habits. The Depression and the New Deal remedies created the feeling that domestic institutions were in a delicate condition and could not survive involvement in another foreign war. The mass of Americans feared that if the country were drawn into a new European power struggle, the virus of totalitarianism would infect its weakened democratic institutions and bring dictatorship to the United States.[28]

As the historian Manfred Jonas has stated, isolationism in the thirties was a "general American sentiment," cutting across all sections of the country and political attitudes. ". . . Men from New York and California, from Idaho and Texas, men whose political creeds ranged from the socialism of Norman Thomas to the conservative Republicanism of Herbert Hoover, made common cause in the field of foreign policy because they believed in unilateralism and feared the effects of war on the United States." Liberals and conservatives alike saw involvement in war as a prelude to a dictatorship. "We must treat war as a contagious disease," a Kansas American Legion commander announced. "We must isolate those who have it and refrain from all intercourse with them."[29]

The manifestations of this attitude are well known: the neutrality laws of 1935–37 barring meaningful American support to victims of attack as well as aggressors; rejection of League overtures for joint sanctions punishing Italy's invasion of Ethiopia; indifference and neutrality toward the existing Republican government and the Fascist rebels in Spain's Civil War; passive acceptance of Japanese aggression in China, including an attack on the American gunboat *Panay;* acquiescence in German reoccupation of the Rhineland and annexations of Austria and Czechoslovakia's Sudetenland; narrowly defeated demands for a national referendum on any congressional declaration of war; and the failure of neutrality revision in the summer of 1939, or the rejection of pleas to allow Anglo-French arms purchases from the United States should Hitler drive them into a war.

No single episode during this time, however, better demonstrates the nature of American isolationism than FDR's quarantine speech of October 5, 1937. An attempt to educate the public to the fact that the United States could not isolate itself entirely from foreign problems or remain secure in a lawless world, the speech was an internationalist appeal presented in isolationist terms. While proposing that neutral nations join in some nonbelligerent fashion to punish aggression, it emphasized the idea that foreign dangers threatened American institutions and that nations needed to quarantine aggressors. "The present reign of terror and international lawlessness," Roosevelt warned in his address, had "reached a stage where the very foundations of civilization are seriously threatened." Contact with lawless nations, in short, might destroy civilized traditions. The remedy was to "quarantine" the "epidemic of world lawlessness." Elaborating on this metaphor, FDR declared: "When an epidemic of physical disease starts to spread, the community approves and joins in a quarantine of the patients in order to protect the health of the community against the spread of the disease. ... There must be positive endeavors to preserve peace," he concluded. "America hates war. America hopes for peace. Therefore, America actively engages in the search for peace."

The initial public response to the speech was very positive.

Newspapers, peace groups, and White House mail almost uniformly backed the President's remarks. By condemning aggression, particularly the unrestrained bombing of civilians, which the Japanese had committed at Nanking in September 1937, the address provided a release for widespread public anger toward Japan. But its appeal came more from Roosevelt's suggestion that the civilized nations would "quarantine," "isolate," or overcome aggressors by peaceful means. In a word, his proposal was highly popular because it struck all the isolationist chords: Foreign dangers threatened the foundations of American life; to survive, America needed to quarantine itself from the contagion of international disease; and Roosevelt would do this not through self-defeating political involvements and war but by peaceful means. Popular support for the President's idea, however, quickly waned. Lacking the means or anything more than conventional political or military steps to satisfy the expectations he had aroused through his speech, Roosevelt could not sustain the initial enthusiasm prompted by the quarantine idea.[30]

At the same time that Americans wished to isolate themselves from foreign troubles threatening to disrupt domestic affairs, they also reverted to a belief in America as the world's last best hope. While the New Deal excited fears about the durability of national habits, it simultaneously spawned a new nationalism, a regard for the country's economic and political traditions as capable of outlasting the Depression and appealing to people around the world. Inspiring a fresh sense of shared national purpose and confidence in American customs as superior to anything existing abroad, Roosevelt's New Deal laid the groundwork for a new round of Missionary Diplomacy, or a new crusade to save the world from itself.

In 1936 and 1937, well before this mood found full expression in World War II, it manifested itself in Roosevelt's rhetoric and approach to Latin American relations. During the 1936 presidential campaign, for example, FDR publicly declared that he saw people in other lands who, having grown too weary to carry on the fight for freedom, "had yielded their democracy. . . . Only our success," he said, "can stir their ancient hope. They begin to know that here in America we are waging a great and successful war . . . for the survival of democracy. We are fighting to save a great and precious form of government for ourselves and for the world." To the Pan-American Conference in Buenos Aires in December he proclaimed that "Democracy is still the hope of the world. If we in our generation can continue its successful application in the Americas, it will spread and supersede other methods by which men are governed." Greeted by huge crowds in South America shouting, *"Viva la democracia,"* Roosevelt attributed their enthusiasm to the belief that he had "made democracy function and keep abreast of the time and that as a system of government it is, therefore, to be preferred to Fascism or Communism." Others outside the United States shared his perception. "You have made yourself the trustee for those in every country who seek to mend the evils of our condition by reasoned experiment within the framework of the existing social system," John Maynard Keynes, the noted economist, had publicly advised him in December 1933. "If you fail, rational change will be gravely prejudiced throughout the world, leaving orthodoxy and revolution to fight it out." Under Roosevelt's leadership, a Montevideo newspaper asserted, the United States had again become "the victorious emblem around which may rally the multitude thirsting for social justice and human fraternity."[31]

The interwar years in American foreign relations had been a time of lingering hopes and powerful fears. The vision of a peaceful, democratic world that Wilson had enunciated during World War I did not entirely lose its grip on the American imagination in the twenties and the thirties. But it survived in weakened form, overshadowed by fears of foreign exploitation and alien influences which could contaminate and destroy shaky American institutions. In the thirties, when domestic affairs saw so much change, isolationists played effectively on these shadowy dangers and threats. Once the Second World War began, however, and the national focus shifted from internal to external dangers, the realities of what the struggle meant to American survival combined with the renewed self-confidence in national institutions to challenge abstract isolationist concerns. At the same time, however, this upbeat feeling about the state of the nation encouraged resistance to involvement in the fighting. Feeling little need to affirm their faith in democracy by fastening it onto others abroad, Americans were reluctant to see the conflict as a struggle for freedom requiring their participation in combat. A contest between these impulses became the dominant fact of American life in the twenty-seven months after Hitler invaded Poland. But the Japanese attack on Pearl Harbor on December 7, 1941, broke this emotional deadlock and opened the way to a new round of internationalism in the United States which, as before, rested more on feelings about domestic affairs than realities overseas.

5

World War II: E Pluribus Unum

With God's help, we will lift Shanghai up and up, ever up, until
it is just like Kansas City.

Senator Kenneth Wherry of Nebraska, 1940

There are now, during the war, common purposes in the minds
of men living as far apart as the citizens of Great Britain and the
Free Commonwealth of Nations, the Americans, the Russians,
and the Chinese.

Wendell L. Willkie, *One World* (1943)

The Second World War compelled Americans to focus on foreign affairs. A struggle chiefly between constitutional, parlia-
mentary systems and totalitarian powers, the war, especially
after the fall of France in June 1940 and the Pearl Harbor attack in December 1941, forced even the most doctrinaire isolationist to confront the dangers to national survival. Yet however much foreign events determined the U.S. response to the
international crisis of 1939–45, prevailing convictions about
domestic affairs continued largely to shape American thinking
about the world outside.

Between the start of the fighting in September 1939 and
Pearl Harbor, the mass of Americans wished to avoid involvement in the war.* Their opposition had more to do with feel-

* The advent of public opinion polls in the 1930s allows one to speak more
confidently about the state of mass feeling.

ings about conditions in the United States than with developments abroad. A minority of the country which thought of itself as isolationist opposed American belligerency out of fear that a war would collapse traditional institutions and replace democracy with totalitarianism of the left or the right. It also rejected the idea that the war posed a threat to American security or represented more than a traditional European power struggle jeopardizing democratic survival everywhere.

While sharing isolationist beliefs, a majority of Americans were much more ambivalent about them. Unlike the isolationists, the bulk of Americans were confident that democracy in the United States could survive an extended conflict. With the Depression essentially over, the New Deal generally considered a great success, and no controversial domestic changes imminent, fears of internal collapse so prevalent in the thirties largely waned. Indeed, by 1939–40 most Americans were more confident about the durability of national institutions than at any time since the 1870s. The New Deal, in the words of one commentator, had put "a new face upon the social and political life" of the country. More than at any time since the late nineteenth century Americans had a sense of membership in a national community, a sense of belonging and participation in something larger than themselves. Moreover, a majority of them had greater qualms about foreign threats to the nation's security than the isolationists had. By the middle of 1940 most Americans feared an eventual Nazi attack on the Western Hemisphere and believed that a German victory over Britain and France endangered democracy in the United States.

All this made Americans ready to give Hitler's opponents substantial aid. But in the twenty-seven months before Pearl Harbor it was always aid short of war. For at the same time the country took its distance from the isolationists, it continued to find some appeal in their ideas. The repressive actions of the Wilson administration during World War I, the shattered confidence in national habits provoked by the Depression, the extraordinary growth of executive power under the New Deal were all too recent for Americans to be indifferent to isolationist warnings about the loss of democracy in war. Furthermore, memories of the "unjust" Versailles settlement and Hitler's inability to conquer Britain created doubts in American minds as to whether or not this was more than a traditional European power struggle in which Germany had no intention of striking at the United States. Also, in a paradox peculiar to this period, the restoration of confidence in national institutions worked both to make the country face the war with greater self-assurance and to restrain it from going in. By contrast with the progressives, who had wished to impose American institutions upon peoples abroad as a test of whether democracy could still work at home, the New Deal generation of 1940 had little need to reassure itself about domestic traditions by mounting moral crusades overseas.

Once the country got into the war, however, the national mood quickly changed. Antagonistic feelings toward Germany, Japan, and Italy, which had existed in more or less muted form before Pearl Harbor, now expressed themselves fully, and the conflict took on many of the qualities of an all-out crusade. Indeed, the progressive, humanitarian side of the New Deal, which had taken second place to the practical, unsentimental economic reforms of the thirties, now gained the upper hand. The idealism of the sort which had had progressives singing "Onward, Christian Soldiers" and doing away with evil now overshadowed the detached New Dealers' preference for making things work. Yet the idealism of World War II was strikingly different from that of World War I. Like the generation of 1917-19, Americans in the years 1941-45 wanted to do away with war and assure the future of democracy. Still, there was something less shrill, less intense, and more realistic about mass feeling during the Second World War. The country favored establishing a new world body and hoped for an extended period of postwar peace, but it did not assume that this was "a war to end all wars." It hoped to see the spread and triumph of democracy, but less because other peoples perceived it as a morally superior system than because it was a more effective one. Indeed, Americans mistakenly assumed during the war that Russia and China were becoming more like the United States and that after their defeat Germany and Japan would refashion themselves along U.S. lines. Again, as in the progressive era, these hopes rested principally on feelings about domestic rather than foreign affairs. But they were now less the product of uncertain dreams or insistent fears about internal conditions than of convictions that the country's institutions worked and that, as Roosevelt said in 1936, "the very air of America is exhilarating."[1]

For more than two years after Hitler had engulfed Europe and the Middle East in war, most Americans agonized over the best response to the fighting. The isolationists had no such problem. Held fast by domestic concerns, they could not see clearly or think realistically about developments overseas. Despite internal Nazi repression and repeated acts of aggression culminating in the attacks on Poland, Denmark, Norway, Belgium, and Holland, isolationists viewed the war as "the same old struggle for advantage between the 'haves' and the 'have-nots.' ... A struggle in which democracies and dictators, aggressors and potential victims, treaty upholders and treaty violators, are so inextricably mixed up that it would tax the powers of a Solomon to discover where right and justice lie." Isolationists perceived little difference between Axis fascism, Russian communism, and British imperialism. Senator D. Worth Clark of Idaho described the British Empire as the outstanding example of aggression in the history of the world, while Senator Gerald Nye of North Dakota called it "the very acme of reaction, imperialism and exploitation." In 1941 the novelist Theodore Dreiser said, "The British Empire is not a democracy and never has been." He urged detachment from "a European war that has . . . no more to do with the problem of democracy or civilization in Europe or the world than it has to do with the state of the inhabitants of Mars, if any."[2]

Similarly, despite the effectiveness of Hitler's blitzkrieg tactics, which demonstrated the capacity of a modern state to attack across great distances, isolationists continued to assume that, as in earlier times, America remained impregnable to attack. "Save for the vaporings of disgruntled renegades and sensational journalists," one isolationist wrote in the fall of 1940, "there is no evidence that the totalitarians even remotely contemplate any onslaught against us." With an adequate defense, another said at the time, "America can become as secure as though Germany were located on the moon." During the debate on the lend-lease bill in February 1941, a congressman declared himself "free from any fear that it is within the range of possibility that the United States of America can be invaded by any single nation or combination of nations in Europe, or Asia, or both." And Senator William Bulow of South Dakota, speaking in opposition to lend-lease, proclaimed that "If I were as certain of a place in Heaven as I am that Herr Hitler will never invade, or attempt to invade the United States, I would feel very safe; I would feel just as if I were already in God's pocket."[3]

It was difficult for isolationists to understand how most Americans could hold views about the war that were so different from their own. "Sometimes as I watch and listen to others, intelligent, conscientious, and forceful, as they work themselves into fevers over what they allege to be the grave emergency confronting this country of ours," Senator Nye said in August 1940, "I come up wondering if I'm 'all there,' if I have lost my reason, if I ever had the power of reasoning well." Though he would not admit it, Nye feared that there was something highly unrealistic about isolationist thinking. Unlike most Americans, the isolationists were so fearful of how involvement in war would affect U.S. institutions that they could not make a rational assessment of what was happening overseas. Indeed, the central, constant refrain of the isolationists on the war was the danger to democracy not from standing aloof but from getting involved. "Nothing would be so destructive of democratic government as war," Senator Robert Taft of Ohio warned shortly after Hitler invaded Poland. ". . . A completely socialized form of life [destroying] the liberty and freedom heretofore regarded as characteristic of America" would follow from involvement in the conflict. "The method of modern totalitarian warfare is self-defeating," Socialist party leader Norman Thomas told FDR. "War itself is the only victor. Each particular war begets its more deadly successors. Intolerance, dictatorship, brutality are its inevitable accompaniments and they live on even when exhaustion temporarily stills the guns."

Isolationists of the left and the right shared the fear that "an all-out war abroad" meant "the liquidation of political democracy, of Congress, the Supreme Court, private enterprise, the banks, free press, and free speech; . . . witch hunts, forced labor, fixed prices, rationing, astronomical debts, and the rest." Unconvinced that the New Deal had solved the country's ills and fearful that a war would put an insupportable burden upon domestic institutions, isolationists were too preoccupied with the dangers from within to credit those from without. "Possessed of such fears," historian Manfred Jonas writes, "the isolationists were largely immune to world events."[4]

By contrast, the majority of Americans, who had largely lost these fears, were ready to risk war to help defeat Berlin. From the very start of the conflict, mass opinion largely rejected isolationist assertions that there was little to choose between the Axis and the Allies. In the fall of 1939, 82 percent of Americans blamed Germany for the war, and 83 percent hoped for an Anglo-French victory. By December only 10.5 percent of people surveyed regarded the war as simply another manifestation of Europe's endless conflicts. Moreover, the bulk felt themselves directly threatened by Hitler's victories over Poland and the Western European states, especially France. The day after Warsaw surrendered, 63 percent of respondents in a poll saw a German victory in Europe eventually leading to an attack on the United States. Following the fall of France, the same number predicted an immediate Axis move against the Western Hemisphere, while 42.5 percent anticipated a prompt assault on the United States. By September 1940, 53 percent of Americans believed it more important to help Britain defeat Hitler than to stay out of war. The number rose to 68 percent by January 1941 and remained nearly constant for the rest of the year.[5]

This national mood was reflected in the country's steady move toward greater backing for the Allies. Repeal of the arms embargo in November 1939, the destroyer-bases deal and the first peacetime draft in September 1940, lend-lease in March 1941, the occupation of Iceland and economic sanctions against Japan in July, Roosevelt's Atlantic Conference with Churchill in August, escorting cargo ships in the Atlantic in September, and the transport of lend-lease goods in American vessels to Britain in November were substantive expressions of majority belief that the national survival was at stake in the war.[6]

At the same time the country clung to hopes that it could stay out of the fighting. In the fall of 1939, for example, when 80 percent expressed partiality for the Allies and between 50 and 60 percent favored aid to Britain and France, an overwhelming majority of Americans did not want to enter the war. Two years later, when some 70 percent accepted the need to overcome Hitler, even if it meant war, a like majority continued to oppose direct participation in the conflict. Mindful of mass ambivalence throughout this period, Roosevelt tried to balance the country's desire to stay out of war with its contradictory impulse to assure the defeat of Nazi power. His solution was not to intensify the conflict by choosing one aim over the other but rather to weave the two together; the surest road to peace, he repeatedly told the nation during this time, was material aid to the Allies. His whole program of support from 1939 to 1941 rested on the false hope that it would keep the country out of war.[7]

Roosevelt understood that however realistic most Americans had become about overseas events, they had not entirely shed isolationist attitudes or parochialism about foreign affairs. In the summer of 1941, for example, he used his Atlantic Conference with Churchill to enunciate "principles relating to the civilization of the world." Convinced that "a great many" Americans had not yet fully awakened to the Nazi danger, he hoped to educate his countrymen to what was at stake in the struggle and make them more willing to fight. Moreover, in the fall of 1941, Roosevelt tried to persuade the country that the Soviet Union, to which he was trying to extend lend-lease aid, shared an American concern for religious freedom. Although he knew that freedom of religion did not exist in Russia and that he could grant land-lease help simply on grounds of strict expediency, he felt that Soviet identification with this democratic principle would ultimately make it easier to bring the United States into the war. Indeed, believing that only a stark contrast between freedom and totalitarianism would provide for Americans the emotional wherewithal they needed to fight, he wished to associate the Russians with Anglo-American ideals as fully as he could, and disarm lingering suspicions that the conflict was simply another traditional European war.

Similarly, FDR realized that isolationist fears of domestic dislocation in a war also continued to have some hold on the public imagination. The destroyer-bases deal, for instance, evoked complaints that he had arbitrarily "committed an act of war" and become "America's first dictator." Furthermore, a survey in November 1941 showed a majority of Americans convinced "that the sun will never shine as bright after the storm as it did before." Despite expectations of military victory, between 60 and 70 percent of the country expected to work harder for less money, pay higher prices, and suffer higher unemployment after a war than before.[8]

But no isolationist argument appealed more to Americans than the admonition against reforming foreign peoples and habits through war. Remembering the failure of Wilson's crusade, feeling little need to reassure themselves about the durability of national institutions by preaching their acceptance abroad, Americans saw good sense in isolationist contentions that the United States lacked "the power to force peace on Europe and Asia, to assure the establishment of democratic and pacific governments there, or to provide the social and economic underwriting necessary to the perdurance of such governments." The *American Mercury* warned its readers in December 1940: "The greatest and most irretrievable error into which American liberalism could fall today would be to be lured into supporting another crusade . . . prompted by a general dislike of the totalitarian idea and by the pathetic illusion that all the broken pieces of Europe, Asia and Africa could be neatly put back in place by such a war." Circulating its message through a poem, "The War—'Over There' 1917–1940," the America First Committee told the country:

> *"Over there," there's mud, and shedding of blood,*
> *And tongues confusing and strange,*
> *So why lend a hand to an alien band*
> *Whose dreams we can never change?*[9]

Though the majority of Americans were considerably more realistic than the isolationists and saw the need for a major U.S. role in the destruction of nazism, they shared enough of the isolationists' thinking to resist the logical conclusion that the country would have to enter the war. Moreover, the revival of general confidence in the superiority and distinctiveness of U.S. institutions weakened the need to export the American way of life and reinforced the impulse to steer clear of the fighting. The shock of Japan's surprise attack on Pearl Harbor, however, broke the remaining isolationist hold on the mass mind and opened the way to another crusade in which Americans once more made world affairs an extension of domestic beliefs.

During the almost four years Americans fought in World War II, they held a nearly constant picture in their minds of postwar international cooperation guided by a new league. It was hoped that World War II would assure the triumph of Wilsonian universalism or collective security. Like-minded people and states, nations great and small, were to band together in a new organization which would eliminate the need for traditional alliances and spheres of influence in which the strong dominated the weak. Free peoples, joined in a United Nations Organization, were now to guarantee each other's security. In *One World,* a book that sold over one million copies in 1943, Wendell Willkie approvingly quoted Chiang Kai-shek's advice that "we must advance from the narrow idea of exclusive alliances and regional blocs, which in the end make for bigger and better wars, to effective organization of world unity. Unless real cooperation replaces both isolationism and imperialism . . . , there will be no lasting security. . . ." *The Time for Decision,* a 1944 book by Sumner Welles, FDR's former Under Secretary of State, won a large national audience by echoing these ideas. By the closing months of the European war in early 1945, between 80 and 90 percent of Americans supported involvement in a new world league, with 83 percent saying that such participation was "very important" and eight out of ten favoring the commitment of United States forces to help keep the peace. Reflecting the strength of this universalist impulse, 88 percent of Americans wanted all countries fighting the Axis to participate in a postwar force which, 76 percent believed, should police all nations, including the United States. Similarly, 82 percent were willing to continue food rationing for five years after the war to help feed other peoples, while 75 percent were prepared to accept that part of the U.S. Army remain overseas to help keep order after the fighting ended.[10]

On the surface, this universalism seems like a triumph of naïve hope over experience: in the midst of the greatest power struggle among nations in history, Americans were projecting a vision in which universal principles won out over selfish national interest. The noted journalist Walter Lippmann attacked the whole idea in a book entitled *U.S. War Aims,* published in 1944. (Its sales, it should be noted, lagged well behind those of the Willkie and Welles books.) The Wilsonian idea, Lippmann complained, was a series of unrealistic moral strictures which "forbid national states to do the things which they have always done to defend their interests and to preserve their integrity." The principal difficulty with universalism, he explained, was "the error of forgetting that we are men and of thinking that we are gods. We are not gods. . . . We are mere mortals with limited power and little universal wisdom." Advised by an American internationalist that the world was now ready for the "more perfect union" the Americans had achieved in 1789, Lippmann replied: "We must not substitute for the world as it is an imaginary world such as eighteenth century America. We must begin with this world, making as just an estimate as we can of the actual and potential connections and conflicts among nations, and then seek the principles of order which apply to it." This sort of globalism was not only naïve, Lippmann believed, but also dangerous. Whereas traditional spheres of influence would give the great powers a sense of security, this revived Wilsonianism would provoke international tensions over fringe areas and lead to another war.[11]

Although most Americans warmly subscribed to the universalist vision, they were not as naïve as Lippmann believed. At the same time that they looked forward to a league fostering international justice and peace, they were skeptical that this would actually come to pass. Asked in the summer of 1943 whether major wars in the future were avoidable, only a quarter of the population believed this possible, while close to 60 percent thought there would "always be wars" and that the United States would participate in another conflict sometime in the next fifty years. In the spring of 1945, as many as 38 percent of Americans thought that the country would fight another world war within twenty-five years. Even after the United Nations had become a reality later that summer, three out of five Americans continued to doubt the ability of a world body permanently to preserve the peace. A universal league also appealed to the mass of Americans because it seemed likely to serve the national interest. "We went to war," the opinion analyst Jerome Bruner wrote in 1944, "because our security demanded it. To us this war is a crusade to regain that security and the freedom it gives us." The American impulse toward universalism, he also concluded, rests on "expediency," the belief that U.S. self-interest demands postwar cooperation in world affairs.[12]

For all this, as Lippmann then and others later complained, Americans favored an idealistic system of world order that could not guarantee peace and justice in either the long or the short run. Part of the attraction to this scheme was a clearly enunciated guilt over having failed to follow Wilson's lead after World War I. "In our disillusionment after the last war," Roosevelt told the country in January 1945, "we gave up the hope of achieving a better peace because we had not the courage to fulfill our responsibilities in an admittedly imperfect world. We must not let that happen again, or we shall follow the same tragic road again—the road to a third world war." A 1944 film biography of Wilson helped crystallize this sentiment. A sentimental, nostalgic portrait of a long-suffering President betrayed by a vindictive Senate, the movie was a highly effective "hymn to internationalism." Audiences came away from the theater, interviewers in New York reported, expressing "a warm enthusiasm for a league of nations ideal."[13]

More important, however, in predisposing the country to this Wilsonian revival were its feelings about domestic affairs. Throughout the war, despite the drama of events abroad, Americans continued to think first and foremost about internal conditions. "To the average American," Bruner wrote in an analysis of wartime opinion, "the domestic and international are far from equivalent in either personal significance or interest. In spite of the years of war, the events and problems which beset the world beyond our boundaries are of secondary interest to the man in the street. To him, the payoff is what happens right here at home—and what is likely to happen." Opinion polls in the fall of 1943 illustrated the point: asked to name the greatest problem facing the nation in the future, 58 percent said "jobs," and only 13 percent thought "lasting peace." "Which interest you more—" another survey asked, *"international* problems (like a new league of nations and an international police force) OR *domestic* problems (like full employment and production)?" Only 16 percent answered "international" problems, while 53 percent said that "domestic" issues were their greatest concern.[14]

Specific inquiries confirmed these results. Asked in January 1942 if they had heard of the Atlantic Charter, 77 percent of a cross section of Americans said no. Of the 23 percent who claimed some recollection of the pronouncement issuing from FDR's dramatic meeting with Churchill five months before, only 4 percent could name one or more of the charter's eight provisions. Similarly, in 1943 almost 80 percent of the public favored a postwar international police force, but most Americans had "no very clear idea" of how it would work. Like vaccination against smallpox, however, it seemed to be a good thing. In March 1945, moreover, private State Department polls showed that only 30 percent of the country knew that the highly publicized Dumbarton Oaks Conference of six months before had developed plans for an international organization. Americans were involved in a total war reaching around the globe, but their attention largely remained fixed on what was and would be happening inside the United States.[15]

Hence, when Americans prescribed a cure for postwar ills abroad, they based it largely on their experience at home. The New Deal and the war had created a strong sense of national unity or shared purpose the country now hoped could become the basis for international affairs. During the thirties the United States underwent a "consolidation of transportation, communications, and mass media, resulting in a country-wide standardization" that affected "everything from manufacturing codes and farming practices to soap operas. Homogenization of such regional distinctions as language, dress and custom proceeded rapidly, a result not only of technological advances but also of federal application of national policies and programs to local areas." Film, radio, and journalism contributed to this development, producing "more and more standardization in American tastes and attitudes. People in every part of the country—in cities, towns, and rural areas—eventually saw the same motion pictures, heard many of the same radio programs, and read the same magazines and the same syndicated material in newspapers." By the mid-1940s, Americans were "talking alike, dressing alike, and perhaps thinking alike as never before." In religion, education, literature, and historical scholarship as well, the impulse was toward shared values and a national sense of purpose.[16]

The thirties and the forties also witnessed a push in the United States for a "federation or commonwealth of nationalities." The objective was "to recognize the diversity of national strains in America and to seek to create a harmony among them." The hope was that from the many varieties of peoples in America, one would emerge. The New Deal era, the historian Richard Weiss asserts, "saw the emergence of an ethnically diverse intelligentsia that held to cosmopolitan values. Their ideal ... society was one in which national, racial, or ethnic backgrounds did not count for or against people. As one prominent academic expressed it, 'I should like to live in a world in which all people regarded men as individuals, good or bad, able or mediocre, interesting or dull, but not as New Englanders, or Middle Westerners, Irish or Germans, or Italians or Jews, except for the bland interest in origins that men have always had.' " Wendell Willkie expressed a similar view in *One World:*

> Our nation is composed of no one race, faith, or cultural heritage. It is a grouping of some thirty peoples possessing varying religious concepts, philosophies, and historical backgrounds. They are linked together by their confidence in our democratic institutions as expressed in the Declaration of Independence and guaranteed by the Constitution. . . . Our success thus far as a nation is not because we have built great cities and big factories and cultivated vast areas, but because we have . . . learned to use our diversities.

America had reached a high level of civilization, Willkie believed, because of "the ability of peoples of varying beliefs and of different racial extractions to live side by side ... with common understanding, respect, and helpfulness."[17]

These ideas were central to American universalism during World War II. Americans hoped that, as in the United States, people from all over the globe would work together for the common good. If technology had gone far to create a unified America, its citizens believed that this was also true of the world. "There are no distant points in the world any longer," Wendell Willkie wrote. ". . . The myriad millions of human beings of the Far East are as close to us as Los Angeles is to New York by the fastest trains. . . . In the future what concerns them must concern us, almost as much as the problems of the people of California concern the people of New York." At the same time that technology shortened the distances and differences between the farthest reaches of the globe, America's ability to link many various peoples together suggested that it could also happen abroad. Indeed, the capacity of so many different peoples to work together in the war demonstrated to Americans that this objective was within reach. It was simply now a matter of finding the right machinery or building a workable league to assure the desired result. "When you fly around the world in forty-nine days," Willkie said in his enormously popular book, "you learn that the world has become small not only on the map, but also in the minds of men. All around the world, there are some ideas which millions and millions of men hold in common, almost as much as if they lived in the same town." Buoyed by a renewed sense of shared purpose and harmony in the United States, Americans assumed that the same state of affairs could take hold abroad; one America could now become one world.[18]

Most Americans agreed that universal harmony after the war rested principally on Soviet-American cooperation. Without an accommodation between the two strongest victors in the war, a United Nations Organization and world peace would soon collapse. Convincing themselves that this would come to pass required considerable mental gymnastics. Asked in 1939 which they would prefer if they had to choose between communism and fascism, a majority of Americans picked the latter. Moreover, throughout the war Americans remained hostile to a Communist ideology which seemed to be thoroughly at odds with traditions of private enterprise and free choice. During the fighting, a handful of American writers warned the country against wishful thinking; a wartime alliance serving mutual interests in defeating Hitler was fine, they argued, but it should not obscure distasteful realities about the USSR. According to wartime polls asking whether Russia could be trusted to cooperate after the fighting, some 20 percent of the country consistently said no. Another 45 percent vacillated between optimism and pessimism or had no opinion.

Yet 35 percent of the nation unswervingly believed in postwar cooperation with Russia, with another 20 percent hopeful that this would occur. In the midst of an all-out struggle in which the Soviet Union bore the brunt of the suffering and sacrificed millions of lives in the common cause against Hitler, it was difficult to resist the idea that Soviet-American collaboration would continue indefinitely. In a surge of wartime euphoria American opinion molders of the left, right, and center preached this conclusion. In books and articles reaching millions of people, leaders as different as Henry Wallace, Joseph E. Davies, Wendell Willkie, Henry Luce, and Herbert Hoover forecast the likelihood of lasting friendship with the USSR.[19]

They all agreed that Russia was becoming more and more like the United States. In perhaps the most famous wartime expression of this view, *Life* magazine, a Luce publication, announced in March 1943 that the Russians were "one hell of a people ... [who] to a remarkable degree ... look like Americans, dress like Americans and think like Americans." The NKVD was "a national police similar to the FBI." More than a year later, in April 1944, the *New York Times* declared it no misrepresentation "to say that Marxian thinking in Soviet Russia is out. The capitalist system, better described as the competitive system, is back." Other commentators described Russia as no longer "Communistic," pointing to a steady movement away from a "narrow Marxian ideology in the direction of ideas that we can call, in very broad terms, democratic." In the summer of 1943, conservative Congressman John Rankin of Mississippi described communism as so unpopular in the Soviet Union that Russians were running it out of the country. Herbert Hoover told the 1944 Republican convention that

Russia was no longer truly Communist. Will Russia cooperate with the other great powers after the war to create a stable world? the editors of *Life* asked former Ambassador Joseph Davies. "They will do exactly what we would do, if in their shoes," Davies replied.[20]

As with his appeal for postwar universalism, no one articulated the general wartime mood toward Russia better than Willkie in *One World*. His trip to the Soviet Union in the fall of 1942 showed him that there were many more similarities between the United States and Russia than he had previously understood. The grain crops running to the horizon reminded one of Texas; the irrigated valley near Tashkent looked like Southern California; the stately manors along the Volga were like the great houses on the banks of the Hudson. A visit to the small stone house of a collective-farm manager evoked memories of a prosperous farmhouse in the United States. There was "a hearty hospitality, with much laughing good humor," and the manager's wife urging Willkie "to eat as I have been urged many times in Indiana farmhouses." Yakutsk in Siberia was like a western town in America a generation ago. It reminded Willkie of "our own early and expanding days—especially the hearty, simple tastes, the not too subtle attitudes of mind, the tremendous vitality." It was like "Elwood [Indiana] when I was a boy." The leader of the Republic of Yakutsk was a thirty-seven-year-old go-getter who "talked like a California real-estate salesman" and once more reminded Willkie of earlier days in America when men were "chiefly interested in getting things done." Above all, the American visitor found a democratic Russia, where the country was fighting a people's war and men and women enjoyed equality of opportunity and a chance to improve their lives. Stalin, their leader, was "a simple man, with no affectations or poses. . . . If you continue to educate the Russian people," Willkie told him, ". . . you'll educate yourself out of a job." Stalin was highly amused.

Roosevelt encouraged this view of Soviet-American ties after the Teheran Conference in December 1943. "I got along fine with Marshal Stalin," he told the nation in a fireside chat. ". . . I believe he is truly representative of the heart and soul of Russia; and I believe that we are going to get along very well with him and the Russian people—very well indeed." What were "your personal impressions of Marshal Stalin?" a reporter asked the President after Teheran. "We had many excellent talks," Roosevelt replied, which would "make for excellent relations in the future." Another reporter asked, "What type would you call him? Is he dour?" The President answered: "I would call him something like me . . . a realist."[21]

What explains these wartime illusions about Soviet Russia? Awareness of the fact that many Russians were dying in a cause with which Americans could thoroughly identify is part of the answer. With Russians giving their lives in a struggle that directly served U.S. national survival, it was easy for Americans to lose sight of differences between the two countries. Yet this alone seems inadequate to explain the extent to which educated people fell into this mood. Wartime polls indicated that a favorable attitude toward Russia was much more common among well-educated, prosperous Americans than among less-educated, low-income groups. This suggests that well-off Americans who identified most strongly with the country found it easy to imagine that the whole world wished to be like them or that the rest of the world was naturally drawn to imitate what existed in the United States. A Russia abandoning communism for capitalism and democracy made transparent good sense to those convinced that their nation was a model which peoples all over the globe would wish to emulate. Henry Luce expressed the idea perfectly in a 1942 *Life* article:

Because America alone among the nations of the earth was founded on ideas which transcend class and caste and racial and occupational differences, America alone can provide the pattern for the future. Because America stands for a system wherein many groups, however diverse, are united under a system of laws and faiths that enables them to live peacefully together, American experience is the key to the future. . . . America must be the elder brother of the nations in the brotherhood of man.[22]

The American impulse to regard the national experience as an irresistible model for other peoples and governments applied to China as well. The Nationalist regime running China during World War II was a corrupt, ruthless dictatorship devoted chiefly to its own survival. Militarily ineffective, politically repressive, and economically corrupt, Chiang Kai-shek's government offered limited resistance to the Japanese, killed and imprisoned opponents of Nationalist rule, and put the personal gain of its leaders above the economic well-being of China's masses. The Chinese Army, General Joseph Stilwell privately reported in 1943, "is generally in desperate condition, underfed, unpaid, untrained, neglected, and rotten with corruption." Reporting on a 1943 famine in Honan Province, the journalist Theodore H. White described dying peasants exploited by an indifferent government:

They were dying on the roads, in the mountains, by the railway stations, in their mud huts, in the fields. And as they died, the government continued to wring from them the last possible ounce of tax. . . . The government in county after county was demanding of the peasant more . . . grain than he had raised. . . . No excuses were allowed; peasants who were eating elm bark and dried leaves had to haul their last sack of seed grain to the tax collector's office.[23]

Americans, hearing little of this during the war, gave free rein to fantasies of a stable, reliable China determined to become just like the United States. It was America's favorite ally. Untainted by Russian communism or British imperialism, a victim rather than a practitioner of power politics, China above all was seen as a natural democratic partner. In 1942 more than 80 percent of those questioned in a national poll expected China to cooperate with the United States during and after the war. Asked in May 1942 whether Stalin, Chiang, or Churchill had the most support from his people, 23 percent of Americans chose Chiang, 24 percent selected Churchill, and 30 percent picked Stalin. According to a poll taken in 1944, 63 percent of the country wanted China to be one of the nations having the greatest say in a future international organization.

Out of a desire for wartime unity and because of wishful thinking, American leaders encouraged these illusions. Henry Luce repeatedly featured Generalissimo and Madame Chiang on the cover of *Time*. The people of China, President Roosevelt said publicly in 1943, "have been, in thought and in objective, closer to us Americans than almost any other peoples in the world—the same great ideals. China in the last—less than half a century has become one of the great democracies of the world." Chiang Kai-shek, "both as a man and as a leader, is bigger even than his legendary reputation," declared Wendell Willkie in *One World.* "Quiet" and "soft-spoken," he gave the impression of being a "scholar." Though China was now in a "tutelary stage," Willkie also said, its people were "being educated into new habits of living and thinking designed to make them good citizens of a complete democracy, with electoral rights, at a later time." He found evidence of this change in the fact that China's "farmers" were eagerly fighting for their freedom in a "people's war." Its armies were "tough, fighting organizations of men who know both what they are fighting for and how to fight for it. . . . Even the sons of those of high estate enlist as privates in the army. . . ."[24]

Distortions of the record by publicists and political leaders certainly contributed to wartime delusions, but they do not fully explain why so many Americans embraced the image of an effective, democratic China. Again, as with Russia, Chinese losses against an enemy directly threatening the United States encouraged Americans to think of the Chinese as being like themselves. By fighting America's battles, the Chinese became almost honorary U.S. citizens. Equally as important, the traditional picture of American regard for Chinese well-being, of Sino-American friendship, strengthened the belief in a China tied to and becoming an East Asian United States. Everywhere he went in China Willkie found an unspoken hope that America would remain China's friend. ". . . China was not an alien country, full of strange customs, but a warm-hearted, hospitable land filled with friends of America." The fruit of this friendship, Willkie advised his countrymen, was a China growing more and more like us. As had been true a generation before in America, China had a vast unsettled frontier. "The opening up of this new China compares only, in modern history, with the opening up of our own West. We know the struggle of those people. We know the hope. And in some significant measure we know what the fulfillment can be. The economic aim of the leaders of modern China is to develop their country much as we developed ours." Above all, they wanted freedom for themselves and for all the people of Asia.[25]

When Madame Chiang visited the United States in 1942–43, she aroused an outpouring of admiration and welcome unseen in the country since Lindbergh had flown the Atlantic. A speech to Congress "enraptured" her audience, moving one congressman to the verge of tears and captivating the rest with her "perfect English." Educated in the United States, thoroughly westernized in thought and speech, she "conveyed to the average American a sense of China's similarity to [Americans] rather than a sense of difference." Her visit, a British observer noted, "consolidated the American obsession for

China." Convinced that people everywhere were naturally drawn to their superior values and management of domestic affairs, Americans assumed that the Russians and the Chinese consciously wished to become just like them. This, Henry Luce predicted in a 1941 issue of *Life,* was to be "The American Century." Despite almost fifty years as a world power, Americans still had difficulty distinguishing between foreign and domestic affairs.[26]

In 1943, as the Allies gained the upper hand in the fighting, Americans began arguing about how to deal with their enemies after the war. Germany particularly caused debate. One school of thought, led by Secretary of the Treasury Henry Morgenthau, Jr., and supported by FDR, argued the case for repression: The Germans were a naturally aggressive people who must be firmly held in check; left to its own devices, Germany would inevitably spawn another Hitler and a future war. By contrast, State Department planners believed in the possibility of rehabilitation: Hitler was more the product of a punitive Versailles Treaty than of any fatal flaw in the German character; a generous settlement aimed at bringing out the best in the German people could lead to a democratic Germany ready for peaceful cooperation with other European states.

In the summer of 1944, as the Allied invasion of Europe raised hopes that the war against Germany would end before the close of the year, Roosevelt endorsed plans for a repressive settlement. "We have got to be tough with Germany, and I mean the German people, not just the Nazis," FDR told Morgenthau in August; "we either have to castrate the German people or you have got to treat them in such a manner so they can't just go on reproducing people who want to continue the way they have in the past." It was not just a few Nazi leaders but the whole German people whom Roosevelt blamed for the war. Consequently, at the Quebec Conference with Churchill in September, Roosevelt endorsed the Morgenthau Plan for turning Germany "into a country primarily agricultural and pastoral in character." The objective was to dismantle German industry—in Morgenthau's words, to "take every mine, every mill and factory and wreck it. . . . Steel, coal, everything. Just close it down." For the President, this was not simply a vindictive plan for punishing Germany but a way to allay Soviet fears of U.S. intentions. By proving to Moscow that America meant to hold down German might, FDR hoped to promote long-term cooperation with the USSR.[27]

But the bulk of Americans did not share the President's desire for a repressive peace, and Roosevelt had to backtrack from the Morgenthau Plan. Shortly after the Quebec Conference, leaks to the press about Morgenthau's ideas on Germany evoked an overwhelmingly negative public response. Americans feared that news of this scheme was stiffening German resistance on the western front. More important, there was a fundamental aversion to a harsh peace which would punish the German masses. As Jerome Bruner demonstrated in his wartime analysis of public feelings, between 70 and 80 percent of Americans felt that they were fighting against the German government, not the German people, who had been misled into the war by Hitler and the Nazis. Unlike World War I, when Americans stopped playing German music and struck the German language from school curricula, they did not now "hate" their enemies. "In this war," Bruner pointed out, "sauerkraut is still sauerkraut, and no move has been started to 'abolish' kindergartens. Our enduring hatred has been reserved for enemy leaders, not people." Consequently, at the end of the war a majority of Americans wanted a "humane" occupation of Germany in which its people were treated with kindness and consideration. Likewise, two-thirds of the American public favored keeping Germany intact under a new government. And most important, a series of polls in 1944–45 showed that some 60 percent believed that Germany could rehabilitate itself and become "a good nation" ready for membership in a new world league.[28]

As a result of public feeling and practical considerations, the government chose a program of rehabilitation over repression. In February 1945 Roosevelt agreed to follow the State Department's recommendation for "assimilation—on a basis of equality—of a reformed, peaceful and economically non-aggressive Germany into a liberal system of world trade." Though FDR had also given sanction to a modified program of repression or a less severe policy of "planned chaos" in a final memo on Germany in March, Truman decisively turned in the direction of rehabilitation after the end of the war in May. The impracticality of destroying German industrial capacity, which could help restore Europe to economic and political health, became transparent to thoughtful Americans at the close of the fighting. Also, the desire for a democratic, cooperative Germany aligned with the West against a potentially hostile Russia made irresistible good sense. Echoing the wartime convictions of most Americans, Secretary of War Henry Stimson told Truman in May:

> Punish her war criminals in full measure. Deprive her permanently of her weapons. . . . Guard her governmental action until the Nazi-educated generation has passed from the stage. . . . But do not deprive her of the means of building up ultimately a contented Germany interested in following non-militaristic methods of civilization. . . . It is to the interest of the whole world that they [the Germans] should not be driven by stress of hardship into a non-democratic and necessarily predatory habit of life.[29]

Wartime attitudes toward the Japanese, evidenced by the internment of more than 100,000 Japanese-Americans, were less generous. Whereas 18 percent of Americans expressed hatred toward the German people in 1942, 28 percent said they hated the Japanese. Moreover, when news of Japanese atrocities against American prisoners of war became known in 1943–44, anger in the United States increased. The impulse to view the war in the Pacific as a fight principally against the Japanese government rather than its people fell from 63 percent of Americans in 1942 to 43 percent in 1944. While 29 percent in 1942 saw themselves in a struggle against both Japan's government and people, the number two years later had risen to 51 percent. Yet, as with Germany, the hope that the Japanese would eventually adopt democratic institutions and reject militarism made Americans want to treat them humanely. "Do you feel our chief enemy is the Japanese people as a whole or the Japanese government?" pollsters asked in June 1944. Only 11 percent named the Japanese people, with 55 percent picking the government. In December, an opinion survey showed that only 20 percent of the country wanted "definite punitive action" against the Japanese people after the war, with this number falling to 14 percent on the eve of Japan's surrender. Within a week after the war ended, just 3 percent put exclusive blame for the Pacific fighting on the Japanese people as a whole.[30]

This attitude found embodiment in U.S. postwar planning for Japan. In July 1945 a proclamation demanding Japan's surrender insisted on the elimination "for all time [of] the authority and influence of those who have deceived and misled the people of Japan into embarking on world conquest." Assurances were offered that the Japanese would not "be enslaved as a race or destroyed as a nation." But the government would have to "remove all obstacles to the revival and strengthening of democratic tendencies among the Japanese people. Freedom of speech, of religion, and of thought, as well as respect for the fundamental human rights shall be established." After these conditions had been met and "a peacefully inclined and responsible government" had been democratically elected, the occupation of Japan would come to an end. In a definitive statement of post-surrender policy on September 6, the Truman administration reiterated these points: The eventual establishment of a Japanese government was to result from the "freely expressed will of the people," with the regime to conform as closely as possible "to principles of democratic self-government." Moreover, the Japanese people were to "be encouraged to develop a desire for individual liberties and respect for fundamental human rights, particularly the freedoms of religion, assembly, speech, and the press." Japan's economy was also to be democratized as much as possible. In brief, the Japanese were "to become familiar with the history, institutions, culture, and the accomplishments of the United States" and, by so doing, turn themselves into a "New Deal"–style democracy.[31]

That Americans held such feelings about their enemies reveals more about their wartime self-image than about their knowledge or understanding of Germany and Japan. American instincts here were of course sound. For both moralistic and self-interested reasons, the United States did well to turn two of the world's most powerful nations into self-reliant, cooperative, democratic states. But the motives for doing it included more than these traditional influences on foreign policy; the actions were less the product of calculated thought about high-minded ideals and selfish need than of mass mood or emotions. Most Americans during the war knew little about Germany and less about Japan. Ideas about the two countries derived more from stereotypes than from hard facts about their past and current affairs. "Probably never has a modern nation fought an enemy about which she knew so little as we do of Japan," Bruner wrote in 1944.

With little information about their enemies and little forethought about the realities of postwar international affairs, Americans designed occupation policies which expressed their current feelings about themselves or conditions in the United States. During World War I, for example, when citizens lived with continuing anxieties about the state of domestic affairs, they were intolerant of alien influences and "hated" their German enemy. They drove a distinguished conductor from the podium of a great symphony orchestra because he was German and, by "common consent," banned the playing of Wagner's music. Moreover, the war was fought as a crusade to convert the world to the American way of life, a frenzied effort on America's part to reassure itself about democracy at home by insisting on its acceptance abroad. During World War II, however, when Germany and Japan committed "bestial atrocities," a list "unique in the history of evil," Americans were less emotional about their enemies and less evangelistic about converting them to their political customs.[32] This more relaxed attitude largely rested on positive feelings about the state of domestic affairs. United, free, victorious over the Depression, and moving toward victory in the war, a majority of Americans expected their enemies to adopt American habits after defeat. Unlike the Russians and the Chinese, whom Americans saw freely moving in this direction, the Germans and the Japanese would need supervision. But the outcome in all cases was to be the same: Russians, Chinese, Germans, and Japanese alike were to embrace what many in the United States now viewed as the universally compelling tenets of American life.

The fact that these mass feelings went so far to shape thinking about world affairs has undermined Roosevelt's historical reputation as a wartime leader. To be sure, historians see FDR as an architect of victory in World War II, but they find little to praise beyond that: His wartime dealings with Russia, China, and France, and his advocacy of a new world body and an end to colonial empires, have evoked complaints, on the one hand, of superficiality and naïveté and, on the other, of excessive timidity in confronting his countrymen with the realities of world affairs. Whether blaming him for being too idealistic or too fearful of public opposition to act openly on his realistic perceptions of overseas events, critics of FDR's wartime diplomacy agree that he had the opportunity to push matters either in another direction or farther than he did. In the judgment of both sets of critics, Roosevelt failed to use fully the influence at his command.[33]

These views make too much of the President's personal shortcomings and too little of the constraints under which he had to work in foreign affairs. There is, of course, merit to the arguments that FDR was naïve about other peoples and leaders and that he hid postwar realities from public view to forestall an isolationist revival. This still leaves the fact that he faced limitations at home and abroad which he could not realistically ignore. Abraham Lincoln, Roosevelt once told someone impatient for presidential action, "was a sad man because he couldn't get it all at once. And nobody can. . . . You cannot, just by shouting from the housetops, get what you want all the time."[34]

This, the wartime mood in America suggests, was particularly true of any shift from traditional universalism to realism or a reliance on power politics. Roosevelt himself was more skeptical than he indicated publicly of the universalist vision of nations everywhere, great and small, culturally and racially diverse, politically and economically at odds, cooperating through a new league. While he spoke repeatedly during the war of an end to spheres of influence and balance-of-power politics, of Soviet-American friendship, of a democratic, great power China, of freedom for former colonies, and of a United Nations organized to assure the peace, his private comments and actions suggest that he thought more in terms of *Realpolitik* than he would publicly concede.

His attitudes toward Russia and postwar bases are cases in point. Privately, he was less certain of postwar Soviet-American cooperation than he professed to be publicly. In September 1944, for example, he secretly agreed with Churchill that the

United States and Britain would develop atomic energy for their exclusive military and commercial purposes after the war and that the Russians were not to share in this. Though three weeks before this agreement he encouraged the Danish physicist Niels Bohr to believe that he favored international control of atomic energy or sharing the secret of atomic power with the Soviets, Roosevelt had no intention of doing it in the immediate future. By his agreement with Churchill, he hoped to shore up British power and guard against Soviet domination of the Balkans and possibly all Europe. At the same time he wished to signal Moscow through Bohr, who had ties to Russian scientists, that he was ready to entertain a Soviet role in ultimate control of atomic power, or that postwar cooperation on other issues could be a prelude to shared control of the bomb. Similarly, while Roosevelt publicly described the Yalta agreements of February 1945 as "the beginnings of a permanent structure of peace," he was not so sure in private. "I didn't say the result was good," he told a State Department adviser. "I said it was the best I could do." To his longtime aide and speech writer Samuel I. Rosenman, he expressed "doubt whether, when the chips were down, Stalin would be able to carry out and deliver what he had agreed to."[35]

On postwar bases as well, Roosevelt was reluctant openly to acknowledge what he intended. During the war he repeatedly spoke of a system of international trusteeships for colonies and mandates detached from their ruling countries after the fighting. Publicly he described plans for three or four of the United Nations to share responsibility for subject peoples until they were ready for self-rule. At the same time, he saw a trusteeship system allowing the United States to establish long-term naval and air bases at strategic points in the Pacific and elsewhere without confronting traditional American antagonism to power politics. Because the annexation of Pacific islands, or even exclusive U.S. responsibility through mandates granted by a world body, seemed likely to provoke domestic opposition,

Roosevelt envisaged a system of collective rule for the benefit of emerging nations so as effectively to deemphasize American military control. In 1945, for example, when his military chiefs pressed him for full U.S. sovereignty over some former League mandates and detached enemy territory, FDR resisted, saying that it could encourage a scramble for national control of "dependent" areas all over the world and discourage American readiness to participate in postwar international affairs. While he sincerely hoped that a trusteeship system would lead to independence for former colonies, Roosevelt also wanted this idealistic approach to mask his concern with power.[36]

In refusing to acknowledge openly that spheres of influence and power politics would dominate postwar international affairs, the President recognized something about the national mood to which later critics have given too little weight. The universalist impulse in America was an expression of strongly held feelings which no leader, however strong his grip on the public mind, could readily change. Predictions of postwar international harmony and of vastly different peoples and systems imitating U.S. institutions were the products not of rational thought or close attention to the external world but of ingrained parochialism or blind conviction that everyone wanted to follow the American lead. For all the apparent danger to survival from World War II, Americans still could not see the world for what it was or substantially free themselves from thinking about the globe in domestic terms. Supported by Allies that carried a heavy burden of the fighting, relatively unscathed in a war that cost the Russians fifty times the number of lives lost by the United States, Americans remained largely insulated from the hard facts of foreign affairs. Only the onset of the Cold War, in which America for the first time shouldered principal responsibility for Western security, forced the country to confront more directly the painful realities of international life.

6

Cold War Parochialism:
The Truman Years

If our society ... is to retain its vitality, [we must] ... change
ourselves from an exclusive to a receptive nation in psychology
and in practice. ... There is no salvation for America in a frame
of mind that tries to shut out its world environment.

George F. Kennan,
Realities of American Foreign Policy (1954)

In 1906, when that quintessential American, William Jennings
Bryan, visited Constantinople on a world tour, he impressed his
hosts in the U.S. Embassy as having only the barest acquaint-
ance with anything other than "American political psychology." His questions about Turkey, the diplomat Lewis Einstein
recalled, would not have taxed the powers of a ten-year-old.
Seeing Bryan off at the station, Einstein remarked that he
would have an interesting journey through the Balkans. "What
are the Balkans?" asked the future secretary of state.[1]

Whereas numerous Americans as late as World War II continued to share Bryan's ignorance of the outside world, this
changed rapidly after 1945. The return home of millions of
Americans thrown into wartime contact with places as remote
as Tunisia and New Guinea and postwar responsibilities as the
world's premier power made them more aware of the foreign
scene. "Talk about Europe is in every household now," a
small-town Indiana housewife remarked in 1947. Burdened

with the defense of the "free world," touched in countless ways by the rise of a "military-industrial complex" charged with securing U.S. interests abroad, Americans could no longer turn their backs on world affairs. In the prewar era, when Americans spoke of "empire," they usually meant the Caribbean. After the war the term expressed a worldwide concern. Previously unknown or little-known places like Iran, Korea, Yugoslavia, Vietnam, Quemoy, and Matsu became everyday topics of discussion in the United States.[2]

A greater realism about overseas affairs now complemented this growing awareness of other peoples and lands. After World War II Americans heard repeated injunctions against excessive emotionalism, moralism, or idealism in responding to the world beyond their shores. Nations have no permanent friends or enemies, only interests, foreign policy specialists urged their fellow Americans to understand. Power and self-interest, not international law or moral good, were the persistent ingredients of international life. These injunctions did not fall on deaf ears. In the year after the war ended in the Pacific, for example, most Americans, who were normally indifferent to overseas events, accepted the need to challenge Soviet actions abroad. Taking their knowledge "by a sort of intellectual osmosis from the headlines and their favourite wireless commentators," British observers in the United States reported, "ordinary" Americans encouraged an "uncertain and reluctant administration" to confront Soviet expansion.[3]

At the same time that the mass of Americans were responding more rationally to overseas events, they still thought about the world in traditional legalistic-moralistic terms. They continued to invest exaggerated hopes in international law and selfless moral action as models of conduct superior to the pursuit of national self-interest in foreign relations. In his famous work *American Diplomacy,* published in 1951, George Kennan counseled against the perpetuation of this "legalistic-moralistic approach to international problems," which he saw running "like a red skein through our foreign policy of the last fifty years." Instead, he urged Americans to recognize that "our own national interest is all that we are really capable of knowing and understanding" and that the pursuit of decent, constructive national purposes "can never fail to be conducive to a better world."[4]

Beyond this, Kennan also saw that Americans continued to make foreign affairs an extension of immediate domestic concerns. ". . . We run the risk," he warned the nation in 1954,

> of becoming essentially a provincial nation, an eddy in the current of world thought, unable to receive stimulus and inspiration from without and unable to impart it to others. . . . In the intellectual sense as in the demographic sense, we are either a cosmopolitan nation, part of the world stream of thought and feeling, or we are nothing at all. Smaller nations, weaker nations . . . might be able to get away with exclusiveness and provincialism. . . . Americans cannot. . . . Thus the first dictate of progress toward a better world is . . . that America must become more receptive and more outgoing.

Kennan was referring to the fact that what Americans experienced at home in the postwar years continued to frame their response to developments abroad. This is not to say that domestic crosscurrents, as was often the case before 1945, largely determined American reactions to external events. After World War II foreign pressures substantially shaped Truman's specific answers to overseas challenges. Nevertheless, shifting attitudes toward domestic events still had a significant impact on what the United States did abroad. The source of this impulse was enduring tension over the nature of American life. The wartime sense of shared national purpose had created false hopes that the New Deal and the war had somehow resolved the long-standing conflict between the old individualism and the new organized machine culture. In the Truman years the country vacillated between the reality of this tension and dreams of restoring the national harmony of World War II. These feelings encouraged Americans, on the one hand, to see themselves as locked in a life-and-death struggle with Communist power and, on the other, to cling to visions of sustained cooperation abroad. Although mass inclination to make foreign policy an extension of domestic preoccupations no longer dominated American thinking about international relations after 1945, national mood continued to influence the reaction to external affairs.[5]

For eighteen months after Japan had surrendered in September 1945 Americans struggled to square the emerging reality of internal and external tension with wartime visions of long-term unity at home and abroad. The year and a half between the close of World War II and Truman's Doctrine in March 1947 was one of the most difficult and confusing periods in U.S. diplomatic history. Reflecting swiftly changing domestic and foreign currents, Americans gyrated between hopes of peaceful cooperation and fears of all-out strife. Internal and external contradictions, prosperity and disarray at home, conflict and compromise abroad, made uncertainty the keynote of the time.

Postwar developments took Americans by surprise. Instead of a cooperative national effort to overcome a new round of economic difficulties, the country experienced inflation, strikes, and special-interest conflicts reminiscent of the twenties. Internationally, instead of Big Four cooperation assuring reconstruction and peace through the UN, the major powers found themselves at cross purposes in Europe, Asia, and the Middle East. Though Americans did not ignore these realities, demanding actions at home and abroad that would settle labor disputes, restrain price increases, and check Russian expansion, they clung to hopes that domestic and foreign strife would go away if shortsighted leaders acted in more sensible ways.

To most Americans, postwar domestic turmoil was the product not of major economic readjustments but of selfish actions on the part of special interests and ineffective leadership on the part of the Truman administration. But conditions made labor-industrial conflict and higher prices nearly impossible to stop. At the close of the fighting, the need for a forty-eight-hour workweek abruptly ended and laborers found themselves with smaller paychecks. With unions clamoring for higher pay to compensate for reduced hours, and industry denying that it could raise wages without increasing prices, strikes became the inevitable order of the day. In 1946 alone, more than 115,000,000 man-days of work were lost to work stoppages by about 4,600,000 laborers. When Truman blamed some of the walkouts on men "who place their private interests above the welfare of the nation," it encouraged the belief that less selfish attitudes by management and labor would have prevented such conflicts. Similarly, the rush of higher prices after the war impressed most Americans as more the result of human greed and Truman's mismanagement than of economic forces beyond rational control—the possession by citizens of billions of dollars in wartime savings, combined with a scarcity of the consumer goods for which they were clamoring. In 1945–46, the President himself contributed to the false hope that a new round of economic and social harmony could occur by his public criticism of Congress, labor, and industry for not pulling together.[6]

For most Americans, hopes of unity at home continued to translate into visions of friendly dealings abroad. Although foreign developments in the immediate postwar months did not escape mass attention, the focus of national concern remained on domestic affairs. Asked in October 1945, for example, to identify the most important problems facing the country in the next year, 98 percent of the people in a sample poll mentioned jobs, strikes, reconversion, wages, and food shortages, while only 12 percent cited peace, demobilization, or the atomic bomb. With internal problems foremost on American minds, feelings about them colored national thinking about the external world. At the same time that the public struggled with internal tensions and hoped the general harmony of the New Deal and war years might yet be reclaimed, Americans mixed a growing anti-Soviet mood with yearnings for joint efforts to keep the peace.[7]

The response in the United States to the major international developments between the spring of 1945 and the beginning of 1947 illustrates the point. Difficulties with Russia in the closing weeks of the European war started a slow but steady erosion in American confidence that Moscow meant to cooperate with the United States after the fighting. By the middle of May 1945, 38 percent of a poll, the highest percentage since March 1942, doubted Soviet interest in postwar friendship with America. Explicit references to the possibility of war with Russia now became daily occurrences in the American press. Yet if Russia's actions in Eastern Europe reduced its "enormous store of goodwill" in the United States, they also evoked assertions that the Soviets were doing no more than defending their self-interest against a hostile America. In a radio broadcast on May 22, for example, former Under Secretary of State Sumner Welles complained that "in five short weeks since the death of President Roosevelt the policy which he so painstakingly carried out has been changed. Our Government now appears to the Russians as the spearhead of an apparent bloc of the western nations opposed to the Soviet Union."[8]

Although Americans now increasingly questioned Soviet attachment to a universalist or collective-security design for assuring national security, they favored further efforts to realize that idealistic dream. Reflecting their mood, Truman sent Harry Hopkins, a principal architect of FDR's pro-Russian policy, to Moscow in May. The objective, as Hopkins shortly indicated to Stalin, was nothing less than preserving Roosevelt's policy, which assumed that "both the United States and the Soviet Union had worldwide interests." Because Stalin was accommodating on every point except Poland, Truman felt free to tell a press conference in June that "if we keep our heads and be patient, we will arrive at a conclusion; because the Russians are just as anxious to get along with us as we are with them." The fact that the Soviets remained committed to sphere-of-influence diplomacy was now swept under the rug. Walter Lippmann urged Americans to understand that accommodation with Russia depended on recognizing its domination of Eastern Europe, but most people refused to hear. Still hopeful that the country could achieve harmony at home and abroad, they continued to reject elementary facts about Soviet intentions in international affairs.[9]

But these realities kept pressing in on Americans. At the Potsdam Conference among Churchill, Stalin, and Truman in July, the Russians refused to budge on Eastern Europe. When the President pressed for free elections in Rumania, Hungary, and Bulgaria in accord with the Yalta agreements, Stalin replied that they had democratic governments closer to their peoples than the one set up in Italy by Britain and the United States. Truman's insistence that this was not true, and Churchill's contention that British representatives in Rumania were cut off from communication with national political leaders evoked the reply "All fairy tales." At an impasse, the Big Three left the issue for later discussion by their foreign ministers. Even though there was no reason for Truman to think that the Soviets would back down on Eastern Europe, he told the American people in August that Rumania, Hungary, and Bulgaria "are not to be the spheres of influence of any one power." His private reasoning is revealing. He would ultimately be able to deal with the Soviet dictator, he thought, because Stalin was "as near like Tom Pendergast [the Missouri political boss] as any man I know." The President intended to approach the problem of dealing with Russia by following the example of the typical Middle American "who believed without contradiction in loving his neighbor and steadily watching him at the same time." In short, we could get along with Russia the way Americans got along with each other in the United States. There was an even more direct tie in Truman's mind between Soviet-American accommodation and social harmony at home. The reason for the Russians' current aggressiveness, the President said on the way home from Potsdam, was their expectation of a postwar depression and disorder in the United States. The point was clear to Truman: An economically healthy and united America would encourage Russia to get along with it.[10]

A foreign ministers' conference in London in September 1945 challenged this hope. Though Secretary of State James F. Byrnes believed that American control of atomic power would make the Soviets more amenable to pressure for free elections in the Balkans, he was disappointed. At the close of the talks he complained that satisfactory relations with Russia had evaporated with the end of the war. No longer dependent on America for supplies, the Russians "were taking an aggressive attitude and stand on political and territorial questions." The fact that fundamental differences existed between the United States and the USSR now became obvious to most Americans. Yet when Truman responded to these developments by publicly suggesting exclusive U.S. control of the atomic bomb, newspapers and leading liberals in the country sharply attacked this proposal. The public at large was painfully torn over whether America alone or the international community should exercise control. A poll at the end of October showed 71 percent of Americans in favor of holding onto the secret of the bomb. Subsequent surveys in November and December, however, registered a majority preference for turning the United Nations into "a kind of world government" with the power to inhibit the use of atom bombs.[11]

This craving for a unified America leading a harmonious world also continued to shape thinking about China. In the immediate postwar period Americans remained hopeful that China might still evolve into an East Asian United States. There was even less reason for them to assume this than to believe that Russia would abandon an Eastern European sphere of control or that the United Nations would oversee the use of atomic power; yet, in spite of civil war and chaos in China, Americans held to hopes of Nationalist-Communist cooperation leading to democracy and stability. If the Chinese could not do this on their own, Americans hoped to arrange it for them. Why was China falling apart? Patrick J. Hurley asked when announcing his resignation as ambassador in November 1945. Because subversive Foreign Service officers had counseled the Chinese Communists to resist pressure for an accommodation with Chiang Kai-shek. What stood in the way of a unified China were not unbridgeable differences between Communists and Nationalists, but procommunist American diplomats who wished "to keep China divided against herself."

Though the administration rejected Hurley's charges, it accepted the proposition that the United States could make a decisive difference in China's civil conflict. Truman sent General George C. Marshall to Chungking to mediate differences between the two sides and "develop a united and democratic China." Indications of a willingness on both sides to consider a compromise; an apparent degree of Soviet support for coalition rule; and a desire to block Russian control in Manchuria, all encouraged the Truman administration, and Americans generally, to accept this impossible task. But at bottom, what drew Americans into this hopeless enterprise was the enduring parochial vision of a grateful China intent on imitating a stable, democratic America.[12]

No such wishful picture of an ally evolving along U.S. lines could be sustained even temporarily in the case of Russia. Developments in the winter of 1945–46 persuaded an increasing number of Americans that Moscow was less interested in self-determination and collective security than in unlimited expansion which threatened the survival of the United States. In September 1945 Soviet fulfillment of a pledge to fight Japan encouraged 54 percent of Americans to express confidence in postwar Russian intentions. By the end of February 1946, however, the number had fallen to 35 percent. Several events beyond continuing Soviet domination of Poland and the Balkans contributed to this mood. On February 9 Stalin gave a public address in which he darkly hinted at an eventual war between capitalist and Communist states. *Time* described the speech as "the most warlike pronouncement uttered by any top-rank statesman since V-J Day." A week later, news of a Canadian spy ring working to steal atom bomb secrets for Moscow created a sensation. When Americans coupled these matters with stories of Soviet determination to keep troops in Iran and Manchuria, antagonism to Communist Russia became widespread.

Subsequent developments added to this feeling. In his famous "long telegram" of February 22, 1946, George Kennan, then chargé d'affaires in Moscow, provided persuasive justification for the growing belief in Washington that the USSR saw no room for compromise with the West and aimed by external and internal means to overturn democratic institutions. The Truman administration shortly gave public voice to this concern in a widely publicized speech by Secretary Byrnes. Firmly declaring American intentions to defend the United Nations Charter against aggression, Byrnes said, in the words of one reporter, "what the country wanted and was waiting to hear." Less than a week later, President Truman tacitly endorsed this policy by his presence during a speech by Winston Churchill in Fulton, Missouri, in which the former prime minister proclaimed that "From Stettin in the Baltic to Trieste in the Adriatic, an iron curtain has descended across the Continent." The Soviets did not want war, Churchill said, but they did want "the fruits of war and the indefinite expansion of their power and doctrines." Demonstrations of American strength, coupled with a "fraternal association of the English-speaking peoples," were Churchill's answer to the Soviet threat. In the spring of 1946, when the Truman administration acted on this tough talk by pushing the Soviets into a troop withdrawal from northern Iran, the public warmly supported the President's policy. By the second half of 1946, opinion polls showed that almost two-thirds of the American people saw the Soviet Union as aiming to dominate as much of the world as possible.[13]

At the same time that Americans accepted the reality of a Soviet threat, they remained hopeful that these difficulties would go away. A generally upbeat mood about domestic affairs continued to make the country sanguine about overseas concerns as well. "A spectacular fact emerged" in the postwar period, historian Eric Goldman points out: "[The] America that was settling was not so much settling down as it was settling upward. The high hopes of V-J [Day] were, at least in one important respect, being realized. Whatever the ravages of inflation, the masses of ordinary Americans were living at a higher material standard than their groups had ever known and with a much greater sense of status in the community." This was "an era in the national life when, for all minority groups, for all lower-status Americans, the social and economic walls were coming tumbling down." Fears of a postwar depression were now forgotten. "Apart from the serious shortages of meat and housing," Robert J. Donovan, the journalist and Truman biographer, writes, "the economy was booming in the fall of 1946. Full employment had arrived in fact. . . . Out of a labor force of 60 million, 58 million Americans had jobs." To be sure, there were grievances and discontents aplenty in the society, and these would surface forcefully in the election of 1946, but in the year after the war had ended in the Pacific the country remained relatively hopeful about the world within and without.[14]

This general optimism about domestic conditions registered on foreign policy in several ways. At a Moscow foreign ministers' conference in December 1945, Secretary Byrnes accepted a series of symbolic concessions by the Soviets for the sake of agreement. Byrnes's "main purpose," George Kennan lamented, "is to achieve some sort of an agreement, he doesn't much care what. The realities behind this agreement, since they concern only such people as Koreans, Rumanians, and Iranians, about whom he knows nothing, do not concern him. He wants an agreement for its political effect at home." Or, perhaps more to the point, he was intent on expressing the enduring hopes which at least half the country continued to hold for good relations with Russia.[15]

Similarly, Churchill's "iron curtain" speech in March 1946 aroused as much opposition as support. American liberals complained that his "fraternal association" would destroy the United Nations by excluding non-English-speaking peoples from a major role in world affairs. "Winnie, Winnie, go away, UNO is here to stay!" pickets shouted when the British statesman gave another speech in New York City. However sympathetic the administration was to Churchill's proposal for an alliance against Russia, it saw too much opposition in the United States to his ideas to uphold them openly. He was not ready to endorse Churchill's remarks, Truman wrote privately a week after the speech. "Your presence on the stage at Fulton . . . has led to some speculation that you endorse the principles of Mr. Churchill's speech," a reporter told the President. "I didn't know that would be in Mr. Churchill's speech," Truman untruthfully replied. The President "reacted coldly to Churchill's suggestion of an Anglo-American partnership that would tie the United States to a declining, nearly bankrupt England," Walter LaFeber points out. ". . . Throughout 1946 . . . Truman never publicly condemned Soviet policy."[16]

He not only avoided open condemnation of Russia but also felt compelled to continue efforts at accommodation, especially over atomic power. By early 1946, while the administration was now more concerned to assure American security than to find a workable scheme for international control, it went forward nevertheless with plans to put a proposal before the United Nations in June. Since the government viewed the Soviets as certain to reject any plan that did not offer them the secret of the bomb and its unrestricted use, the Baruch Plan, as the proposal was called, was little more than a gesture. It urged control of atomic energy through an international agency dominated by the United States. The plan was predictably rejected by the Russians, but to the American people, by and large, it seemed to satisfy their wishes for continuing efforts toward global cooperation. Depicted by the press as a U.S. offer to give up its atomic bombs and reveal its nuclear technology upon adoption of international controls, the Baruch Plan impressed most Americans as "a noble and plausible way to avert a nuclear war."[17]

This desire for a universalist approach to atomic power reflected a fundamental impulse toward a pacific or nonmilitary solution of all world problems. Despite the development of a "get tough" mood toward Russia in 1946, the country insisted on the reduction of American military forces. Servicemen and their families were understandably in the forefront of this movement. Shortly after the war had ended in the Pacific, congressmen came under intense pressure from their constituents to "bring the boys home." Wives deluged congressional offices with baby pictures and baby shoes, while servicemen sent home mail inscribed with the legend "No Boats No Votes," implying retaliation in the 1946 congressional elections unless the administration speeded up demobilization. In January, after Truman had explained the slow pace of demobilization as the result of the need to build a firm foundation for the future peace of the world, riots erupted at American military bases overseas.

The pressure to reduce the armed forces came from more

than special interest groups. It also grew out of the continuing general belief in harmony at home and abroad. Although the Congress agreed in the spring of 1946 to extend the Selective Service Act for another year, for example, it refused to grant the President's request for the introduction of Universal Military Training. Consequently, in the one year after June 1945 the armed forces fell from 12,000,000 to 3,000,000 troops and slipped to only 1,500,000 men by the following year. "Do you think the present disagreements between Russia and the United States are serious enough to go to war about. . . ?" pollsters asked the public in October 1946. Seventy-three percent of the respondents said no.[18]

Despite growing tension with Russia throughout 1945 and 1946, Americans continued to desire a postwar accommodation with Moscow. "It is our hope," an administration assessment of relations with the Soviets stated at the time, "that they [the Russians] will change their minds and work out with us a fair and equitable settlement when they realize that we are too strong to be beaten and too determined to be frightened." As long as the country thought that the general domestic unity, the national cohesiveness of the New Deal and war years, could be preserved, it clung to hopes of resolving difficulties abroad.[19]

In the six months between September 1946 and March 1947, wartime visions of peacetime harmony at home and abroad largely disappeared. In the fall and winter, an intensification of domestic tensions plaguing the country since the close of the fighting set the mood for a more determined confrontation of overseas threats. In September, after Secretary of Commerce and former Vice-President Henry A. Wallace had attacked the administration's "get tough with Russia" policy, Truman reluctantly fired him. Most Americans saw the President's action as evidence that he was moving to the right. Because Wallace was the leader of the liberal wing of the Democratic party and the last major holdover from FDR's Cabinet, his departure suggested that "the New Deal, as a driving force, is dead within the Truman administration." Whereas 44 percent of a national sample in early 1946 saw the President following "left" policies, only 19 percent thought this the case in the following year. Truman's shift to the right set off "a dynamite charge under liberal unity" and badly split the Democratic party.[20]

The congressional elections in the fall of 1946 underscored and deepened this sense of renewed division in the country. During the campaign the Republicans played effectively on the frustrations of the previous year and a half with inflation, strikes, and shortages, particularly of meat in the summer and fall of 1946. When Truman gave in to pressure to increase meat supplies by pulling off price controls, liberal critics complained that any special interest could now feel free to "dislocate the economy of the entire country, or impair the health of the people, or jeopardize the life and safety of the community" until its demands were met. Antagonizing both conservatives and liberals by first maintaining and then removing controls on meat, the administration also took a beating on the subject of Communist subversion. Encouraging fears of Communist infiltration of the government, the Army, labor unions, and universities, Republicans and anticommunists generally weakened the country's confidence in itself and reawakened mass anxiety about the durability of national institutions. ". . . Only the batblind can fail to be aware of the Communist invasion of our country," Francis Cardinal Spellman, archbishop of New York, wrote in November. FBI Director J. Edgar Hoover warned publicly that at least 100,000 Communists were at work in the United States, putting their imprint on newspapers, magazines, books, radio, movies, churches, schools, colleges, and even fraternal orders. Replying positively to the Republican campaign slogan "Had enough?," voters ended sixteen years of Democratic majorities in both houses, giving the Republicans a six-seat advantage in the Senate and a fifty-eight-seat margin in the House. The turnabout, a columnist pointed out, threatened to bring "back an atmosphere you had forgotten or never thought possible. . . . Victories fought and won years ago were suddenly in doubt. Everything was debatable again."[21]

This mood of division and confrontation gained further momentum in the winter, when Truman decisively thwarted a coal miners' strike, Republican senators challenged liberal nominees to head the TVA and the new Atomic Energy Commission, and General George Marshall's mediation in China collapsed. In November and December the President, in an action FDR had never dared, even in wartime, directly opposed John L. Lewis's decision to strike. With the federal courts backing him, Truman handed Lewis and the UMW a dramatic defeat. At the same time, Truman and the Republican-controlled Senate came to blows over the President's recommendations of men described as "extreme Left-wingers" to run the TVA and AEC. Although he managed to push his nominees through the Senate, the episode gave the country a foretaste of the conflicts he would have with the Eightieth Congress. Furthermore, in January 1947, Marshall returned to the United States, where he acknowledged that his efforts at mediation had failed and that China was caught between Kuomintang reactionaries and Communist ideologues who put the interests of their parties above those of the people and the nation. The outbreak of full-scale civil war in China, where Americans had such high hopes of a united democratic nation similar to their own, further jolted their confidence in their ability to avert conflict and to put in order their own affairs.[22]

The growing sense of separation and vulnerability at home now registered forcefully on foreign affairs. In February 1947 the British government informed Washington that internal economic problems would shortly compel a suspension of economic and military aid to Greece and Turkey which would make them vulnerable to Communist control. Perceiving this as a threat not only to the Middle East but also to pro-Western governments in Europe and ultimately to the United States, the Truman administration appealed to Congress for $400,-000,000 to replace the lost aid. In an appearance before a joint session on March 12, the President described the issue as an ideological conflict between two ways of life—freedom and totalitarianism. "This is no more," he said, "than a frank recognition that totalitarian regimes imposed upon free peoples, by direct or indirect aggression, undermine the foundations of international peace and hence the security of the United States. . . . It must be," he asserted, "the policy of the United States to support free people who are resisting attempted subjugation by armed minorities or by outside pressures."

Historians have generally regarded the Truman Doctrine as an attempt to frighten the public or "bring people up to the realization that the war isn't over by any means." This was unquestionably part of the administration's intent, but the speech may also be viewed as an expression of an existing mood or a general attitude in the United States. A White House official sensed this at the time when he objected to the sweeping universalist tone of the address. "There has been no overt action in the immediate past by the U.S.S.R. which serves as an adequate pretext for [an] 'All-out' speech," the official complained. "The situation in Greece is relatively 'abstract'; there have been other instances—Iran, for example—where the occasion more adequately justified such a speech and there will be other occasions—I fear—in the future." Similarly, Walter Lippmann objected to a "global policy" which aimed at aiding "free peoples everywhere." He thought it "better to address the Soviet Union directly" and adopt "a precise Middle Eastern policy. . . . A vague global policy, which sounds like the tocsin of an ideological crusade, has no limits. It cannot be controlled. Its effects cannot be predicted. Everyone everywhere will read into it his own fears and hopes. . . ."[23]

But it was just this that appealed to so many Americans. Instead of speaking directly to the confrontation with Russia in the Middle East, the doctrine addressed the issues of division and danger in the abstract. Moreover, it responded to American fears that strife within the United States weakened its ability to resist Communist subversion. By announcing that the nation would support free peoples threatened with totalitarian subjugation, Truman principally encouraged Americans to feel that he would stand forth against both unwitting and self-conscious domestic forces endangering freedom at home. Of course, the country perceived and felt the need for a stand against dangers abroad, but it was the conflicts and threats at home that gave greater meaning to this menace overseas. In November 1946, for example, when pollsters asked Americans what they viewed as the "main causes of wars," 81 percent spoke of "greed," "selfishness," and "jealousy," while only 10 percent mentioned "bad diplomacy," "power politics," "secret treaties," and "armaments." In other words, war, like the conflict with the Soviet Union, was best understood in terms of personal and group motives operating in the United States rather than as the result of more remote institutional forces common to international affairs.[24]

On March 21, nine days after he had spoken to the Congress about Greece and Turkey, Truman issued an executive order setting in motion loyalty investigations of employees in the executive branch of government. His action further demonstrated the extent to which fears of domestic division and subversion had captured the public imagination. The President himself had little concern about internal dangers. "People are very much wrought up about the Communist 'bugaboo,'" he wrote in February 1947, "but I am of the opinion that the country is perfectly safe so far as Communism is concerned—we have far too many sane people. . . . I don't believe there will ever come a time when anyone will really want to overturn it." He felt compelled, nevertheless, to adopt a program against "infiltration of disloyal persons" into the ranks of the government. Though Truman had qualms about introducing a program which established a new system of preventive law and violated traditions of due process, he recognized that it was extremely good politics. When coupled with his actions toward John L. Lewis and the Near East, it produced a sizable rise in his popularity in the spring of 1947. Americans—viewing the world scene in apocalyptic terms or as a vast and fundamental conflict between different ways of thinking and acting—now made Arnold Toynbee's *Study of History*, a scholarly analysis of the rise and fall of twenty-six civilizations, an unlikely best seller, and took comfort in strong measures against enemies at home and abroad.[25]

At the same time they could not shed their hopes for a peaceful coming together. Truman recognized this in June 1947, when he vetoed the Taft-Hartley Act, which sharply inhibited the powers of labor unions. The measure, he warned, "contains seeds of discord which would plague this nation for years to come"; it would "adversely affect our national unity." Passing the law over the President's veto, the Congress, by this and other actions, made Americans long for a return to the mood of wartime harmony. "Should the United States continue to try to get Russia to cooperate with us in setting up a world organization or should we go ahead with other nations . . . and leave out Russia. . . ?" pollsters asked in May 1947. By a two-to-one margin, 62 to 31 percent, Americans preferred further efforts at agreement. In September as many as 85 percent of a sample poll declared themselves in favor of the UN; 83 percent wanted a world conference to work out plans to make the organization stronger; 82 percent believed it "very important" that the UN succeed; and 56 percent were ready to see it turned into "a world government with power to control the armed forces of all nations, including the United States."[26]

The continuing desire for universal harmony also expressed itself in the Marshall Plan. In the spring of 1947, with European economic recovery proceeding far more slowly than had been expected and U.S. officials fearful that this might drive all

Europe into the Soviet camp and reduce American trade, the Truman administration outlined plans for a recovery program. It stated its proposal, however, not, like the Truman Doctrine, in the language of anticommunism but as a scheme for restoring *all* Europe to economic health. "Our policy is directed not against any country or doctrine," Marshall declared, "but against hunger, poverty, desperation, and chaos."

> Its purpose should be the revival of a working economy in the world so as to permit the emergence of political and social conditions in which free institutions can exist. . . . Any government that is willing to assist in the task of recovery will find full cooperation . . . on the part of the United States Government. . . . It would be neither fitting nor efficacious for this Government to undertake to draw up unilaterally a program designed to place Europe on its feet economically. . . . The initiative . . . must come from Europe. . . . The program should be a joint one, agreed to by a number, if not all [*sic*], European nations.

The plan was framed in such a way as to "make it quite impossible for the Soviet Union to accept," but the enduring universalism in the United States dictated that it be asked nevertheless. Moreover, though the plan aimed to make West Germany an integral part of a Western alliance, it also gave lip service to the idea of a unified Germany serving neither a Western nor an Eastern bloc.[27]

The tension in the country in 1947 between combative fears and universalist hopes partly expressed itself in a debate between George Kennan and Walter Lippmann over foreign affairs. In July, Kennan published an article in *Foreign Affairs* under the pseudonym "X." In it, he explained Soviet behavior not as the product of rational security needs shaped by

Russian history but as the expression of a messianic Marxist-Leninist ideology and a paranoid sense of insecurity. Committed to an inexorable drive for world power, the Soviets could only be "contained by the adroit and vigilant application of counterforce at a series of constantly shifting geographical and political points." In a series of articles, which eventually appeared as a book, Lippmann disputed Kennan's analysis as a misreading of Russian intentions. Describing their conduct as the product more of Russian history than of Marxist ideology, Lippmann saw the Soviets as open to a political settlement in Europe that would defuse the Cold War. "For a diplomat to think that rival and unfriendly powers cannot be brought to a settlement," he declared, "is to forget what diplomacy is all about." While the Kennan-Lippmann debate probably never reached more than 15 percent of the population, it neatly reflected the clashing impulses in the country between divisive fears and conciliatory hopes.[28]

This debate reached an abrupt end in the winter of 1947–48, when events at home and abroad persuaded the mass of Americans that conflict rather than harmony would be the order of the day. Between October and February the Democratic party coalition built by Roosevelt largely fell apart. Objecting to Truman's endorsement of a major civil rights program aimed at easing the palpable racism experienced by black Americans, southerners denounced the President and prepared to bolt the national Democratic party. At the same time Henry Wallace announced his intention to run for President as an independent candidate, describing the Democrats as the party of war and depression and the Republicans as hopeless. After fifteen years of Democratic dominance, the national political scene was in general disarray.[29]

This reality strongly influenced the American response to dramatic developments abroad. In late February the Soviet Union turned a multiparty government in Czechoslovakia into a Communist-dominated state, where Eduard Beneš, a founding father of the Czech state, lost his power and Jan Masaryk, the foreign minister and American-educated son of Czechoslovakia's first president, died under mysterious circumstances. An intense reaction, characterized by despair, rage, and loathing for Communists, swept the United States. Americans discussed the possibility of war, and Truman successfully appealed to a joint session of Congress for a renewed draft and appropriations for the Marshall Plan. He also praised the decision of five Western European nations to sign a collective defense agreement, the Brussels Pact, and promised full support. During the next three and a half months the administration took further steps to meet the Soviet "threat." Announcing through the Vandenberg Resolution that it would associate itself with the sort of collective security arrangement embodied in the Brussels Pact, it signaled its readiness for a military alliance with Western Europe. The administration also declared its intention to create an independent West German state. When Stalin then shut off all surface traffic into West Berlin, Truman's answer was a round-the-clock airlift.[30]

America's tough reaction to these developments was understandable up to a point. Czechoslovakia enjoyed a special regard in the United States as a friendly democratic state which, as with Hitler in 1938, a totalitarian power was swallowing. (The Czechs originally wanted to participate in the Marshall Plan but were forced by the Soviets to back off.) Moreover, Soviet actions in Germany suggested that the Russians intended to expand their sphere of control and that the United States needed to stand its ground or face the loss of Western Europe. Still, some Americans at the time sensibly concluded that the Prague coup and Soviet pressure on Berlin were "defensive reactions" to the Marshall Plan and the organization of a West German state, and that American behavior represented an unnecessary overreaction. They pointed, for example, to the fact that the U.S. government had regarded Czechoslovakia as a Soviet satellite since 1946. There was, Kennan later wrote, "nothing unexpected, nothing out of the ordinary, in any of the Communist behavior— . . . the Czech coup, and the Berlin blockade—that caused so much alarm in Western capitals. . . . Washington's reactions were deeply subjective, influenced more by domestic-political moods and institutional interests than by any theoretical considerations of our international position." A Chicago reporter at the time made a similar point:

> Cold fear is gripping people hereabouts. . . . Fear of what? Most people don't know exactly. It's not fear of Russia alone. For most think we could rub Joe's nose in the dirt. It's not fear of communism in this country. Few think there are enough Commies here to put it over. It's not fear of the atom bomb. For most think we still possess a monopoly. . . . But all winter, confidence in peace has been oozing away. With the Czech coup, it practically vanished.

If objective external dangers cannot explain America's more militant foreign policy in early 1948, perhaps the troubled domestic climate can. Beset by sharp conflicts at home, Americans could think only in terms of aggression and war abroad.[31]

Developments during the rest of the year continued to encourage a militant approach to foreign affairs. The presidential campaign of 1948 was one of the most contentious in American political history. Setting the tone by attacking Wallace and his "communist supporters" on the left and the "do-nothing, good-for-nothing" Congress on the right, Truman characterized the struggle as one between special interests and "the people," in which he had to give the opposition "hell" if he and the national interest were going to win. Coupled with the continuing crisis over Berlin, these domestic developments helped give rise to NATO, the first formal military alliance in United States history. As Kennan astutely noted at the time, no realistic need existed for such an undertaking. "The Russians had no idea of using regular military strength against us," he has written. He could not regard such a pact "as the main answer to the Russian effort to achieve domination over Western Europe. . . ." The "best bet was still the struggle for economic recovery and internal political stability. Intensive rearmament represented an uneconomical and regrettable diversion of . . . effort—a diversion that not only threatened to proceed at the cost of economic recovery but also encouraged the impression that war was inevitable and thus distracted attention from the most important tasks." But an America assailed by passionate divisions at home could not rationally judge the need for essentially nonmilitary solutions to problems abroad. In a climate of national recrimination, Americans committed themselves to unprecedented military ties overseas.[32]

The domestic crosscurrents which played a significant part in shaping general American policy toward Europe and the Middle East in Truman's first four years now partly set the nation's course in East Asia during his second term. The Marshall Plan, NATO, and greater Western European stability in 1949 allowed President and country to focus more of their attention on less stable East Asian affairs. During 1948 and the first half of 1949, as the Chinese Communists achieved the destruction of Nationalist rule and took complete control of mainland China, the administration backed away from any significant military intervention in the civil war. At a time when the country's mood was drawing it into the NATO alliance, why did it shun involvement in China? For one, because military commitments in Europe were made to deter a war, while involvement in China seemed likely to draw the United States into a full-scale struggle against the USSR. Having no experience with limited war, Americans could not imagine anything in China but an all-out conflict, which they wished to avoid. Further, in 1947 and 1948 the House Foreign Affairs and the Senate Foreign

Relations committees, which spoke for the Congress on international policy, opposed involvement in the fighting. Also, a significant group of China experts in the United States, who opposed intervention and threatened to provoke a public debate, discouraged policy-makers from taking America into the war.[33]

Finally, the administration's self-image as a progressive force at home also deterred involvement. During and after the 1948 presidential campaign, for example, Truman pictured himself as championing the people in their struggle with special interests. He emerged from the election of 1948, one commentator remarked, "as a kind of Andrew Jackson character, a plain man of the people against those who would exploit them." By his electoral victory, another commentator observed, Truman had "made himself the successor to Roosevelt." Now described as a progressive leader committed to serving the interests of all the people and restoring the harmonious mood of the New Deal years, Truman put a liberal domestic program before the Congress in 1949 which some said signaled the start of FDR's fifth term. "Every segment of our population and every individual," the President declared, "has a right to expect from our Government a fair deal."[34]

The administration's liberalism carried over to its dealings with China. Its rationale for not trying to save Chiang's Nationalists and the country from Communist rule was reminiscent of what Truman said during his 1948 campaign. Chiang's regime, a liberal newspaper declared, "has been interested primarily in maintaining a corrupt bureaucracy and a static social and economic system which serves landlords and warlords rather than people." The President privately described Chiang's government as a group of "grafters and crooks" who had no interest in the hungry Chinese masses. In the *China White Paper*, published by the State Department in August 1949, Secretary of State Dean Acheson depicted it as having "sunk into corruption" under reactionaries who had lost the confidence of "the mass of the Chinese people." The Nationalist defeat resulted from the fact that "its troops had lost the will to fight, and its Government had lost popular support." Though Acheson had nothing good to say about the Communists in the *White Paper,* representing them as serving the interests of Soviet Russia, not those of the Chinese people, by January 1950 he and Truman declared both their neutrality should the Communists try to seize Formosa and their desire to align the United States with progressive forces in Asia. "Throughout our history," Acheson said in a speech before the National Press Club on January 12,

> the attitude of Americans toward the peoples of Asia had been an interest in them not as pawns in the strategy of power or as subjects for economic exploitation, but simply as people. . . . The outstanding factor in the interest of the American people in Asia . . . was that over the years it had been parallel and not contrary to the interest of the peoples of Asia. In China, the Philippines, India, Pakistan, Indonesia, and Korea it had strongly, even emotionally, supported people working out their own destinies free of foreign control.[35]

Acheson's view that American interest in Asian peoples coincided with Asian ideas expressed the traditional liberal parochialism toward that continent, but it was now overwhelmed by a form of right-wing parochialism describing China's fall to communism as the product of betrayal within the United States. Between 1948 and 1950 a series of sensational charges against eleven Communist leaders, as well as against Judith Coplon of the Justice Department, Alger Hiss and Owen Lattimore, formerly of the State Department, and atomic spies Julius and Ethel Rosenberg, helped create an atmosphere in which many people believed that reverses abroad, like the Soviet detonation of an atom bomb and the Communist victory in China, were the result of subversion in the United States. "The reason why we find ourselves in a position of impotency in international affairs," Senator Joseph McCarthy announced in February 1950, "is not because our only powerful potential enemy has sent men to invade our shores, but rather because of the traitorous actions of those who have been treated so well by this Nation. . . . In my opinion the State Department, which is one of the most important governmental departments, is thoroughly infested with Communists."[36]

Though sensible Americans dismissed such allegations as unsupportable and accepted the administration's conclusion that China had not been "lost" but had simply gone its own way, many in the United States, for reasons having little to do with China, found McCarthy's assertion irresistible. Of the 84 percent who had heard of McCarthy's charges against the State Department, 39 percent thought they would be beneficial, while only 29 percent saw them as harmful, with the remaining 16 percent holding no opinion. There is no question but that the interest in and appeal of McCarthy's allegations registered forcefully on the administration. By June 1950 it was clear to Truman and his advisers that "the attack of the primitives," as Acheson called it, was playing a part in reducing public approval for the President's performance to its lowest level since April 1948.[37]

In these circumstances, McCarthy's irrational explanation for how China had been "lost" influenced Truman to fight the Korean War. On June 24, 1950, apparently in response to American indications that the United States would not use military force to defend South Korea, North Korea launched an attack across the thirty-eighth parallel. Truman, who held the reins of decision tightly in his hands, quickly decided to defend South Korea with U.S. armed forces. The most important consideration in his mind, according to close studies of his decision, was the historical parallel he saw with the 1930s, when Japanese, Italian, and German aggression led to World War II. "Refusal to repel the North Korean aggression," the President and his advisers agreed, "would be nothing but 'appeasement.'

And appeasement, as history has shown, would ultimately lead to war." The government's decision had little to do with Korea, a State Department official later said. It "was in the process of being made for an entire generation since Manchuria."

At the same time that the lesson of the 1930s decided Truman to go into Korea, the political capital Republicans in general and "primitives" in particular would gain from the "loss" of Korea must have played on his mind. The President himself never acknowledged this as a central concern, and he even rebuked one State Department official who suggested that it should be. But it is inconceivable that a politician as astute as Harry Truman would have blotted out of his mind the political repercussions in the United States from a North Korean conquest of the South. This is not to say that the President cynically calculated the cost in congressional seats in the fall election and then let partisan advantage be his guide. There was something more fundamental at stake—namely, allowing the ruthless McCarthyites a chance to extend their hold on the public imagination. Instinctively understanding how destructive this would be to the country's well-being, Truman took comfort from the thought that a defense of South Korea would not only avert World War III but also strengthen the hand of reasonable men in the United States. Lost in this rationalization, however, was the fact that a wildly irrational charge about American influence on China's internal affairs had helped bring about a major change in policy toward Korea.[38]

Parochial assumptions also centrally influenced the crucial wartime decision to cross the thirty-eighth parallel and unify Korea. At the start of the fighting, the United States described its military effort as "solely for the purpose of restoring the Republic of Korea to its status prior to the invasion from the north." By September 1950, however, as United Nations forces drove the North Korean Army above the thirty-eighth parallel and opened the way to military unification of the whole peninsula, the Truman administration had authorized military operations north of the parallel up to the Yalu River. This decision was based on the mistaken assumption that Communist China would see no threat to its security from such action and would not intervene. Despite private and public warnings to the contrary from Peking, American leaders, including Truman, Acheson, and General Douglas MacArthur, refused to take the Chinese at their word.

U.S. officials assumed that China's Communist leaders looked at the world in the same way they did. From Washington's perspective, the Chinese had nothing to fear from the United States, but a great deal to worry about with Russia. ". . . I give the people in Peking credit," said Acheson in September 1950,

> for being intelligent enough to see what is happening to them. Why they should want to further their own dismemberment and destruction by getting at cross purposes with all the free nations of the world who are inherently their friends and have always been friends of the Chinese as against this imperialism coming down from the Soviet Union I cannot see. And since there is nothing in it for them, I don't see why they should yield to what is undoubtedly pressure from the Communist movement to get into the Korean war.

By statements of this kind, the American government expected to reassure Peking of its intentions—namely, to repel aggression and create a free and united Korea which would in no way threaten China. The latter's intervention in the Korean War was "completely unjustified," Acheson said later. "Repeatedly, and from the very beginning of the action, it had been made clear that the sole mission of the United Nations forces was to repel the aggressors and to restore to the people of Korea their independence."[39]

At the same time, in a more oblique way, the mood in the United States encouraged the administration to see a unified Korea as the appropriate goal of the war. A prelude to Washington's decision was an upsurge of harmony and shared purpose at home. Involvement in the Korean War worked a dramatic change in the national mood from recrimination over internal subversion and foreign defeat to widespread, enthusiastic support for the President's bold action. Never in twenty years as a reporter had Joseph C. Harsch, Washington bureau chief of the *Christian Science Monitor,* "felt such a sense of relief and unity pass through the city." James Reston of the *New York Times* saw the decision to meet Communist aggression in Korea producing "a transformation in the spirit of the United States Government." Democrats and Republicans alike applauded the President's stand, and White House mail ran ten to one in favor of his action. The New York *Herald Tribune,* a leading Republican paper, described Truman's decision as "a basic contribution toward genuine peace in our disturbed and distracted world." When even isolationist Senator Robert Taft joined the chorus of applause, Truman's press secretary, Charles Ross, exclaimed: "My God! Bob Taft has joined the U.N. and the U.S." This burst of spontaneous unity expressed not only the normal pulling together in time of war but also a national surge of hope that facing down the Communists in Korea might ultimately stave off the horrors of World War III.[40]

This feeling at home now projected itself onto Koreans abroad. The "ephemeral separation of Korea . . . was so volatile," the American ambassador to the UN declared in October, ". . . nobody recognizes it. Let us not, at this critical hour and on this grave event, erect such a boundary. Rather, let us get up standards and means, principles and policies, according to the Charter, by which all Koreans can hereafter live in peace among themselves and their neighbors." As with so much else in the history of American foreign policy, the decision to cross the parallel and unify Korea rested on extraneous considerations. This possibly "most critical decision of the Korean War," Walter Millis has written, was the product of "blurred and fuzzy processes." It was made in the "worst way, for confused reasons, on deficient intelligence and with an inadequate appreciation of the risks." Blinded by mistaken assumptions about China and moved by possibly unconscious convictions that domestic unity would somehow translate into a unified, independent, democratic Korea, Americans refused to see that the conquest and attachment of North Korea to the South promised Chinese intervention in the war.[41]

If parochial absorptions influenced the decision to unify Korea, they now also deterred America from ending the war. In the last two years of its term the Truman administration struggled with the question of how to settle the Korean fighting. Once the Chinese Communists had committed large forces to the conflict, the U.S. government had to decide whether to return to its original goal of simply defending South Korea or to aim for unification and the defeat of China in a wider war. Since the latter goal risked alienating the European allies, tying down large forces in Asia, weakening American power in Europe, and provoking World War III, the administration decided to make Korea a "limited war." In response, General MacArthur and Republican critics in the United States advocated the defeat of China or an "Asia First" strategy in which there would be no "appeasement of communism" and "no substitute for victory."[42]

For reasons that had less to do with Korea than with domestic affairs, MacArthur's appeal struck a resonant chord with the public. Of course, the stalemate in Korea beginning in 1951 frustrated Americans and created a certain amount of hostility toward Truman and his political supporters. But, as a number of analysts agree, the war was more a catalyst for the expression of personal and cultural discontents brewing in the United States since the 1930s than a full-blown reason for the resentments and accusations that registered so forcefully on public questions in the closing months of Truman's presidency. Most important, for purposes of this discussion, this mood or climate of feeling in the country inhibited the administration from negotiating a settlement in Korea and beginning a rapprochement with Communist China. The attack of the "primitives," the political scientist John Spanier shows, was not powerful enough to compel a wider war, but it was "sufficiently strong to place American diplomacy in a domestic political straitjacket which foreclosed negotiations as a means to end hostilities. . . ." President Truman, Walter Lippmann later wrote, "was not able to make peace, because politically he was too weak at home. He was not able to make war because the risks were too great. This dilemma of Truman's was resolved by the election of Eisenhower. . . . President Eisenhower signed an armistice which accepted the partition of Korea and a peace without victory because, being himself the victorious commander in World War II and a Republican, he could not be attacked as an appeaser."[43]

The almost eight years of Truman's presidency were among the most tumultuous in American history. During this time the traditions of relative free security and military and political isolation came to a decisive end. Unprecedented involvements in Europe, the Near East, and Asia projected U.S. power to every corner of the globe and compelled economic, military, and political commitments few Americans foresaw as late as 1945. Yet in the midst of this revolutionary change, at least one thing remained largely intact: mass mood, dominated by an impulse to invest foreign issues with domestic meanings or to make external actions symbolic extensions of internal concerns, continued to set the broad outlines of what the country did abroad. However bold Truman was in foreign affairs, his policies were essentially expressions of general national sentiment, to which he was highly sensitive. Although this did not always result in unrealistic measures, it drove the country into a number of ill-advised actions which a more direct response to external conditions might have forestalled. As before 1945, domestic preoccupations remained an imperfect and even dangerous way to meet demanding challenges overseas.

7

Cold War Orthodoxy:
Eisenhower and Dulles

Forces of good and evil are massed and armed and opposed as
rarely before in history. Freedom is pitted against slavery, light-
ness against dark.

Dwight D. Eisenhower, January 1953

[Soviet communism] believes that human beings are nothing
more than somewhat superior animals ... and that the best kind
of a world ... is organized as a well-managed farm.... I do not
see how, as long as Soviet communism holds those views, ...
there can be any permanent reconciliation.... This is an irrec-
oncilable conflict.

John Foster Dulles, January 1953

The renewed sense of national unity and order the New Deal
and the war gave the nation largely disappeared in the seven
years after 1945. By 1952, beset by McCarthyism and the Korean War, the country once more felt divided and in need of a
fresh respite, a quieter time in which agreements overshadowed
differences, accepted standards held more appeal than change,
and private absorptions pushed aside public questions. The
consequence was a new period of general harmony in which the
nation self-consciously emphasized similarities and, as in
World War II, persuaded itself that divisions over fundamental
values were at an end. The painful quest of earlier years to reclaim a simpler, homogeneous life now became an insistence on

conformity as the national style. "Togetherness" and "belongingness" became national catchwords, while William H. Whyte Jr.'s *The Organization Man,* describing the triumph of "an organization ethic" over traditional individualism, became a best seller. Americans in the fifties, for example, burned "controversial" books and devoted themselves to a religious revival characterized by an unthinking faith in shared assumptions. Adding the words "under God" to the pledge of allegiance and making the phrase "In God We Trust" mandatory on all United States currency, Americans gained "a spiritual lift in a busy day" by dialing a prayer, read books like *The Power of Prayer on Plants,* and made "Vaya con Dios," "I Believe," and "Big Fellow in the Sky" musical hits of the decade.

The change, sociologist David Riesman argued at the time, was the product of a fundamental shift in America from a frontier society of economic scarcity to an industrial one of abundance, a country in which consumption replaced work and production as the primary focus of people's lives. This, in turn, he said, caused a shift in American character from "inner-directed" to "other-directed," from an emphasis on individualism to a preoccupation with group identity.

Americans now lived and worked in a society congealed into large units. Whereas in 1900, 60 percent of the country's 76,000,000 people lived in rural areas, by 1960, 70 percent of the nation resided in cities with a total population of 126,000,-000. In 1960 only 16 percent of the American labor force was self-employed, 20 percent less than the proportion of such workers in 1900. By the late fifties 38 percent of Americans were working for organizations with more than 500 employees, while 18,000,000 laborers, about 30 percent of the work force, belonged to unions. Government at the federal, state, and local level grew at a dizzying pace during these years; so did most other social institutions. In 1941, for example, only two American universities had more than 20,000 students; by the 1960s the number had reached thirty-nine.

These developments, Riesman also maintained, did not make for satisfaction among Americans. "It is my tentative conclusion," he wrote in 1949, "that the feeling of helplessness of modern man results from both the vastly enhanced power of the social group and the incorporation of its authority into his very character. . . . The point is that the individual is psychologically dependent on others for clues to the meaning of life." Great numbers of Americans, he added, had turned over their lives "to others in exchange for an agenda, a program for getting through the day." In some, this makes for maladjustment; in others, for "wan conformity." This malaise echoed the discontent of the progressive era, when middle-class Americans had struggled ineffectively against modernizing trends. By the 1950s, however, middle America had outwardly given up this battle and settled into subdued conformity.

But this was only a surface reality. Behind the façade of bland acceptance, great numbers of Americans seethed with tension and anxiety over their "relationships to people, to production and consumption. . . ." Instead of rebelling against their condition, however, they sought ways to rationalize it, to persuade themselves that they had no choice but to accept conformity or "other direction" as the only possible style of life. And in this, foreign affairs in the 1950s played a significant part.

At first glance, foreign policy seemed little more than a reflection of the conformity in the United States. While overseas actions dramatically showed the effects of this mood, they also served to rationalize and reinforce it. "Modern man," Riesman pointed out, "feels helpless, and justifies this feeling by looking at the frightening world around him. Like a hypochondriac, he uses the undeniable threat of real danger to rationalize an even greater anxiety than a balanced view might warrant." In other words, "relatively unconscious of his anxiety" about his dependency, the other-directed American blamed his sense of dread on an exaggerated Communist threat which was described in apocalyptic terms.

At the same time this Communist danger eased tensions Americans felt about the shift from an inner-directed to an other-directed perspective. A predilection for seeing a Communist menace where there was none, or less than alleged, encouraged unity, patriotism, and conformity—the belief that individualism was largely out of date and that an organization ethic was now essential to the survival of the United States. Both the continuity and the contrast with the progressive era are striking. Whereas the progressives used foreign affairs as a way to raise hopes that earlier nineteenth-century habits might reclaim their hold on the United States, middle America in the fifties, having largely abandoned this impulse, used overseas concerns to validate the need for conformity in American life. This is not to say that rhetoric about individualism had disappeared: conservatives continued to make effective appeals in the 1950s to the tradition of individual freedom—but usually with the qualification that in order to preserve personal liberties, Americans would *all* have to stand together against communism.[1]

Dwight David Eisenhower was the ideal man to preside over this national mood. Affable, benign, a seemingly apolitical figure who had never cast a ballot until the age of fifty-eight, he was the least controversial figure in American politics since Calvin Coolidge. Having faithfully served in major military posts under Roosevelt and Truman, he ran as a moderate Republican intent on taking America along "that straight road down the middle." After he had won the presidency twice by wide margins, his direction of national affairs, in the words of contemporary commentators, was a case of "the bland leading the bland" and "mastery in the service of drift."

This culture of conformity—of orthodoxy—put its stamp

on foreign affairs. As in domestic life, Americans found only one way to look at the outside world: as a contest between darkness and light, oppression and freedom, evil and good, in which one side or the other must eventually win. "Rollback," "liberation," "massive retaliation"—all suggested the apocalyptic nature of the struggle in which the country felt itself involved. The Republican party platform of 1952 promised to replace "the negative, futile and immoral policy of 'containment' " with the "contagious, liberating influences which are inherent in freedom." Soviet tyranny "is attempting to make all humankind its chattel," Eisenhower warned during the campaign. Though much of this talk may be written off as predictable election-year rhetoric, the moralistic tone and impulse to see matters in all-encompassing terms accurately reflected the national mood.

Whether on the campaign trail or in Washington, Eisenhower and Secretary of State John Foster Dulles continued to think and speak in sweeping ways. "Foreign policy must be clear, consistent, and confident," the President declared in his first State of the Union message. It "must be a coherent global policy. The freedom we cherish and defend in Europe and in the Americas is no different from the freedom that is imperiled in Asia." And he was reported to have said at a press conference in the spring of 1953 that "The world happened to be round and it had no end and he didn't see how you could discuss the problem, the great basic problems of today, which were so largely philosophical in character, without thinking in global terms."[2]

Throughout the fifties, this Eisenhower-Dulles orthodoxy persisted virtually unchanged. Though the administration never followed through on "liberation" or practiced a more flexible strategy than simple "massive retaliation," even agreeing to consort with the enemy by attending summit conferences, it never broke with conventional assumptions about the "Communist threat" and showed itself less responsive to external realities than one might have expected from leaders as familiar with the world as Eisenhower and Dulles. The reverses of the late forties and early fifties in foreign affairs, the Communist victory in China, the Soviet detonation of an atom bomb, the failure to defeat the Chinese forces and unify Korea—all made for frustrations and fears that help explain the single-minded approach to meeting the Communist challenge. But by the mid- and late fifties these reverses no longer seemed sufficient to account for this enduring Eisenhower orthodoxy. Instead, one needs to consider the possibility that throughout his term, policy toward the outside world had as much to do with the mood at home as with events overseas. Indeed, the national impulse to conform, to mute differences, to stand together without dissent seems to have reflected itself and found reinforcement in the ways Eisenhower and Dulles responded to world affairs.

Policy toward Europe in general and Russia in particular well illustrates the point. During their first term, Eisenhower-Dulles diplomacy in Europe reads like a morality play, in which the administration preached endless sermons on the virtues of banding together against godless communism intent on world domination. The first goal of his government, Eisenhower recorded in his memoirs, was to prevent divisions in the NATO alliance such as Communist propaganda had been encouraging. To this end, he sent Dulles to Europe to remind the allies of "the basic truth that only in collective security was there any real future in the free world." The Russian people as well were given a message on the virtues of universal "togetherness" under God. In March 1953, as Stalin lay dying of a stroke, Eisenhower publicly declared that "the thoughts of America go out to all the peoples of the U.S.S.R. . . . They are the children of the same God who is the Father of all peoples everywhere. . . . The prayer of us Americans continues to be that the Almighty will watch over the people of that vast country and bring them, in His wisdom, opportunity to live their lives in a world where all men and women and children dwell in peace and comradeship."[3]

During the remainder of 1953, the President addressed two additional messages to the Soviets emphasizing the morality of international cooperation for arms control and peace. In April, after Stalin had died, he urged the new Soviet leaders to "help turn the tide of history" by deeds promoting mutual trust and arms reduction. "I know of only one question upon which progress waits," Eisenhower said. ". . . What is the Soviet Union ready to do? . . . If we strive but fail and the world remains armed against itself, it at least need be divided no longer in its clear knowledge of who has condemned humankind to this fate." In a speech before the UN in December, the President further proposed the international stockpiling of fissionable materials for peaceful purposes—an "atoms for peace" program under which the United States and the USSR would make joint efforts to use atomic power for constructive rather than destructive ends. The suggestion, as he later said, once again put the moral burden on the Soviets to join in a worldwide effort for peace. In and of themselves, these proposals had great merit, but the tone of self-righteousness with which they were enunciated tells more about the mood in the United States than about anything Eisenhower expected to happen in international affairs. Indeed, it is clear from the speeches themselves that the President had little hope of the Soviets accepting his proposals, and that the principal benefit he saw in making them was the moral unity they would create in the United States and throughout the "free world."[4]

The Soviets, in fact, were eager to talk. At Stalin's funeral, Georgi Malenkov, Russia's new leader, announced his interest in "peaceful coexistence and competition" with the United States. Shortly after, in a speech to the Supreme Soviet, he spoke of "no disputed or unresolved question that cannot be settled peacefully by mutual agreement of the interested countries. . . . This applies to our relations with all the states, including the United States of America." The Russians followed this with calls for a unified and neutralized Germany, and the announcement that they were ready for "serious businesslike discussions of disputed problems both by means of direct talk and . . . within the framework of the U.N." Churchill, who had returned to power in 1951, declared Britain ready for a summit meeting. "It would be a mistake to assume that nothing could be settled with Soviet Russia unless or until everything is settled," he said.

Churchill's statement was a rebuke to Eisenhower and Dulles, who rejected such talks without prior assurances that positive agreements would result. In his April speech Eisenhower asked for Soviet demonstrations of good intentions as a prelude to any meeting: a peace treaty with Austria; freedom for thousands of prisoners of war held from World War II; a Germany united on the basis of free and secret elections; and full independence for Eastern European nations. Without "definite evidence of good faith" on Russia's part, the President would not enter into talks. As important, Eisenhower and Dulles feared that a positive response to such overtures would weaken Europe's resolve to commit itself to a European Defense Community, a plan for rearming Germany by integrating its armed forces with those of other Western European states. Perhaps even more to the point, the American leaders were asking Soviet conformity to Western standards as a precondition of a dialogue. By positive deeds or "definite evidence of good faith," they meant Soviet acceptance of American values: free and secret elections, full independence, arms reduction, atoms for peace—all symbols and expressions of American life which, from Moscow's perspective, would have played havoc with Russian security. But this hardly registered on the administration or on most Americans, who warmly supported the President's announcements. The objective, at bottom, was less to enter into talks than to insist that the Soviets become more like the United States.[5]

Despite this impulse, by the summer of 1955 Eisenhower felt compelled to meet with the Soviets anyway. Though a fundamental insistence on Soviet conformity to American assumptions continued to govern dealings with the Russians, a number of other considerations propelled the administration into talks. A Western European Union, with a rearmed Germany integrated into NATO, reduced the likelihood that summit discussions would shatter European defense plans. Anthony Eden, who became British prime minister in April 1955, urged the need for a meeting. In the United States, McCarthyism went into eclipse with the Army-McCarthy hearings in 1954, and the right-wing insistence on the dangers of contamination from any contact with the Communists lost some of its hold on the public imagination. The development of the H-bomb by both the United States and the USSR created the feeling, as Eisenhower expressed it, that "there is just no real alternative to peace" and that discussions would have to be tried. Finally, the fact that the Soviets gave concrete evidence of an interest in détente by signing an Austrian peace treaty and offering a substantive proposal for arms control persuaded the President that it was time to meet.[6]

But the goal of converting rather than accommodating the Soviets remained intact. What he wanted to talk about, Eisenhower later recorded, was "the plight of enslaved peoples behind the Iron Curtain, and the aims of international Communism," or "the basic purposes of the international Communist conspiracy." Preliminary discussions offered him "little hope of a truly changed attitude on the part of the Soviets" toward these subjects. Moreover, he prepared himself to counter what his advisers saw as the chief Soviet goal at the conference: "a recognition by the Western powers of the 'moral and social equality' of the Soviet Union." Since this would strengthen the Soviet hold on its satellites and encourage neutralism, American planners urged the President to avoid social gatherings, where he would be photographed with the Russian leaders, and to maintain "an austere countenance" when he was with them before the cameras. As if to emphasize the moral and social differences between the two sides, Eisenhower addressed the nation before he left for Geneva on "the cardinal religious concepts which form the very core of our democratic society." He asked all Americans, on the next Sabbath, to "crowd their places of worship" to ask for help in achieving peace. "This would demonstrate to all mankind that we maintained great armaments only because we must. Our armaments did not reflect the way we wanted to live; they merely reflected the way we had to live." The message was clear: America, the morally superior nation, would go to Geneva hoping, with God's help, to convert the Russians to American ways of peace.

Nothing less would suffice. The three major goals the administration set for itself at Geneva were simply beyond reach. As described by Peter Lyon, an Eisenhower biographer, they were:

> a unified Germany, militarized and safely within NATO; European security, by which was meant fewer Soviet troops stationed in central Europe and a relaxed Soviet grip on the countries of eastern Europe; and a leveling and control of armaments, with the United States retaining an unchallenged superiority of and supervision over nuclear weapons. The likelihood of Soviet concurrence in any of these was nil.[7]

The principal Eisenhower proposal on disarmament— "open skies"—underscores the point. In a dramatic gesture calculated to demonstrate American devotion to arms reduction and peace, the President suggested an exchange of military blueprints of armed forces followed by regular and frequent aerial inspections to verify their accuracy. "I only wish that

God would give me some means of convincing you of our sincerity and loyalty in making this proposal," he declared. It might indeed have required an act of Providence: Since the Russians already knew "the location of most of our installations," Eisenhower told his advisers, "mutual agreements for such overflights would undoubtedly benefit us more than the Russians, because we know very little about their installations." A "gimmick," a ploy by Cold Warriors practicing psychological warfare, in the view of critics, "open skies" evoked Premier Nikita Khrushchev's wrath: "A very transparent espionage device . . . ," he told Eisenhower. "You could hardly expect us to take this seriously."

But the President had little difficulty rationalizing his maneuver. In his view and that of most Americans—who gave him a 79 percent approval rating on his return from Geneva—he was dealing with either "communist zealots or power-mad dictators." In either case, they were unbending in their ambition for world power and their hostility to the United States. At Geneva the Russians "drank little and smiled much. . . . Obviously planned and rehearsed," Eisenhower later observed, "their efforts to ingratiate were carried out with precision and mechanical perfection." Failing to induce the five Soviet leaders at the conference "to reveal their true purposes and ideas" during a gathering at his villa, the President nevertheless found it "a useful evening in that I saw that the implacability of this quintet in a social situation would certainly be encountered in ensuing conferences and we would have to shape our own tactics accordingly." General Georgi Zhukov, his old comrade-in-arms from World War II, was no longer the man he had been in 1945. Subdued, worried-looking, unsmiling, Zhukov impressed the President as well trained for a performance. "He spoke as if he was repeating a lesson that had been drilled into him. . . . My old friend was carrying out orders of his superiors." As for Khrushchev, he was a "ruthless and highly ambitious politician," who cared "nothing for the future happiness of the peoples of the world—only for their regimented employment to fulfill the Communist concept of world destiny."

Eisenhower's observations were more revealing of U.S. attitudes than of Russian realities. From the American perspective, the Soviets were not to be bargained with but converted, won over to the virtues of free elections, independence, disarmament, and peace. Since Soviet intransigence seemed to make this impossible, the next best thing was to demonstrate to peoples everywhere American moral superiority—the principal function, for example, of "open skies." In some abstract way, Eisenhower at Geneva played out the dominant mood in the United States. Intolerant of dissent or anything that could be described as "un-American," the country wanted conformity at home and abroad. "We are all items in a national supermarket," declared one commentator on the American scene, "—categorized, processed, labeled, priced, and readied for merchandising." As a result of fundamental economic and social changes, which made social popularity and acceptance more desirable traits than individualism, Americans took comfort in self-evident truths to which moral people everywhere would subscribe. Just as the nation had no patience with domestic divisions or factional strife, so it saw no room for negotiation with opponents of the U.S. credo overseas. If the Soviets would not abide by American standards of proper behavior in international affairs, they, like nonconformists in the United States, were to be morally ostracized. Eisenhower's moral indignation toward the Soviets at Geneva for refusing to accede to American ideas echoed the moral recriminations felt toward dissenting opinion in the United States. Conformity and orthodoxy at home set the standard for U.S. policy overseas.[8]

American policy in the Middle East further demonstrated how this worked. A central concern of the Eisenhower administration in the first months of its term was to ensure against the spread of Communist power in the area, especially in Iran. In 1951 Dr. Muhammad Mossadegh, Iran's prime minister, nationalized the country's British-controlled oil industry, touching off a boycott of Iranian oil by the largest marketers of world oil supplies and a serious economic crisis in Iran. Though Mossadegh was an anticommunist and a nationalist intent on serving the interests of his people, Eisenhower and Dulles saw him as only opening the way to a Communist Iran. When British Foreign Secretary Anthony Eden visited Washington in March 1953, the President speculated on "the consequences of an extension of Russian control of Iran, which he regarded as a distinct possibility. . . ." To Eden, Eisenhower "seemed obsessed by the fear of a Communist Iran." Consequently, when Mossadegh appealed to Eisenhower for financial aid to stabilize his country, the President rejected his request and approved, instead, a CIA plan to replace the prime minister with a more "reliable" ruler. In a cloak-and-dagger operation Eisenhower later described as "more like a dime novel than an historical fact," the U.S. government secretly helped the shift of power from Mossadegh to Shah Muhammad Reza Pahlevi.

Why did the administration act as it did? Since Mossadegh was not a Communist, or under Communist influence in the spring of 1953, and since American aid to Mossadegh's government might have restored order and stability and headed off possible Communist control, why did Eisenhower reject his request for help? One possible answer is: the influence on the government of U.S. oil interests which wanted to replace the British in Iran. But this conclusion stumbles over the fact that American oil companies, which in 1953 were making great profits from increased production in Kuwait and Saudi Arabia, were content to see a continuation of Mossadegh's government and a boycott of Iranian oil. Moreover, when offered the chance to share control of Iran's oil fields after the shah's successful ouster of Mossadegh, the American companies, fearing a glut, agreed only reluctantly, and on condition that the administration exempt them from U.S. antitrust laws.

The true basis for Eisenhower's action in Iran was the automatic assumption that any government, like Mossadegh's, which was not pro-American was already, or eventually would end up, in the Communist camp. The President's belief "that he had saved Iran from Communism, and even that Mossadegh's government had been a 'Communist-dominated regime' . . . ," historian Barry Rubin writes, "encouraged a tragic confusion between militant nationalism and Marxism-Leninism that plagued United States policy elsewhere in the Third World." Failing to look carefully at Iranian affairs or, perhaps more to the point, bound by the conformist, unthinking mood in the United States which encouraged a Manichean picture of a worldwide Communist-capitalist struggle, Eisenhower committed the United States to act against communism in Iran.[9]

The Baghdad Pact of 1955 grew out of similar concerns. Eager to surround and contain the Soviet Union with alliance systems, the Eisenhower administration added a Southeast Asia Treaty Organization (SEATO) to NATO in 1954. With NATO checking the Soviets from the Baltic to the eastern Mediterranean and with SEATO designed to hold the line from the Philippines to Pakistan, Eisenhower and Dulles wished to close a 3,000-mile gap in the Middle East from Pakistan to Turkey by forming yet another alliance. Spurred by the British, who wished to shore up their influence in the area, Iraq, Pakistan, and Turkey signed a mutual defense treaty, the Baghdad Pact, in early 1955. Though delighted with this anticommunist barrier thrown up by "northern tier" countries and Britain, the administration decided against full American membership in the alliance for fear of antagonizing anti-British Arab states led by Egypt.

But even tacit U.S. support for the pact angered Arab nationalists and helped promote, rather than forestall, Soviet influence in the Middle East. When President Gamal Abdel Nasser asked Moscow to sell Egypt arms in 1955, the Russians readily complied. Had there been no Baghdad Pact supported by the United States, they might have been more cautious, fearing that an arms deal would become an excuse for more vigorous Western action in the area. But with an anticommunist alliance already in place, Moscow apparently saw little to lose and, indeed, something to gain from stronger Soviet-Egyptian ties.[10]

To neutralize the arms sale, Washington agreed to help Nasser finance the building of the Aswan Dam, Egypt's highest economic priority. But the administration soon had second thoughts. Congressional resistance, generated by Israel's supporters, hard-line anticommunists, and southern representatives fearful of expanded Egyptian cotton production and competition, created political problems. More important, Dulles and Eisenhower, who was largely immobilized during this time by serious illness, had substantial reservations about catering to Nasser's neutralism or use of Soviet ties to extract favors from the United States. Consequently, in May 1956, when Egypt recognized Communist China as a way to assure continued arms supplies should Russia agree to an arms embargo in the Middle East, the Eisenhower administration found a good reason to cancel its offer on the Aswan Dam. The issue before us, Dulles later said, "was, do nations which play both sides get better treatment than nations which are stalwart and work with us?" Determined not to give in to "immoral blackmail," the secretary of state believed that canceling the deal would put the Soviets in an impossible position: since Moscow would be unable to fulfill a promise to help build the dam, backing away from the offer would serve to humiliate the Russians and destroy Nasser, "thus demonstrating the perils of neutralism."[11]

But the American leaders badly miscalculated the consequences of their action. Rather than go to the Russians, to whom he did not wish to be bound, Nasser nationalized the Suez Canal, announcing that he would use the tolls to finance the Aswan Dam. Because Dulles was "bent upon pursuing his own highly abstract brand of global anti-Communism," his biographer Townsend Hoopes writes, his "principal aim was to expose what he regarded as the pretensions of Soviet economic aid programs" and, thereby, "break the momentum of the Soviet drive for 'competitive coexistence'. . . ." In his preoccupation with the Soviets, Dulles lost sight of Egyptian realities. "It was precisely Dulles's ignorance of Arabs, his tendency to treat Nasser as an undifferentiated pawn in a larger game," Hoopes points out, "that produced the specifically Arablike and rashly human nationalization of the Suez Canal." Indeed, as in their dealings with Iran, Eisenhower and Dulles practiced a kind of tunnel vision. Because they could see only the Soviet and Communist menace to American values, the Middle East in general and Egypt in particular were lost to view. Policy toward Cairo was predicated not on knowledge and understanding of Egyptian attitudes and affairs but only on what would serve the worldwide anticommunist drive, a policy of orthodoxy that remained highly popular in the United States but undermined American effectiveness in the Middle East and with European allies.[12]

The extent of the problem showed up in the closing months of 1956. Incensed at Nasser's nationalization of the Canal, which made them dependent on Egypt for the continued flow of oil supplies, Britain and France conspired with Israel to break Nasser's power and retake the Suez. On October 31, after Israel had attacked Egypt in the Sinai and London and Paris had issued an ultimatum demanding Egyptian-Israeli withdrawal from the area of the Canal, British and French forces attacked Egypt. The attack enraged Eisenhower. Fearful that such action would drive the Arabs into the Soviet camp and shut off Arab oil to Western Europe, he declared his intention to do everything possible to "stop this thing." Going to the UN "before the U.S.S.R. gets there," the United States supported a cease-fire resolution in the Security Council, which Britain and France vetoed. Eisenhower now personally condemned the attack, refusing to "condone armed aggression—no matter who the attacker, and no matter who the victim. We cannot—" he publicly announced, "in the world, any more than in our own nation—subscribe to one law for the weak, another law for the strong. . . . There can be only one law—or there will be no peace. . . . This we know above all: There are some firm principles that cannot bend—they can only break. And we shall not break ours." In the climate of the fifties this was soothing music to American ears.[13]

It was to take another week before the President was to have his way. But it took extraordinary pressure; a General Assembly resolution calling for a cease-fire, a loss of oil supplies and dollar reserves, plus a threatened Soviet attack on Britain and France, finally brought their invasion to a stop. With the cease-fire in place, Eisenhower looked forward to "action that will minimize the effects of the recent difficulties and will exclude from the area Soviet influence." He shortly wrote Churchill: ". . . The Soviets are the real enemy and all else must be viewed against the background of that truth." This meant filling "the existing vacuum in the Middle East . . . before it is filled by Russia."

To this end, in January 1957, he enunciated the "Eisenhower Doctrine." Russia's rulers, czars and Bolsheviks alike, "have long sought to dominate the Middle East," he told Congress. To prevent this, he requested money for economic and military assistance to Middle Eastern nations trying to preserve their independence, and he asked permission to use American might to defend those countries "requesting such aid" against "overt armed aggression from any nation controlled by International Communism." But as critics at the time pointed out, the principal threat to pro-Western Arab countries came not from "International Communism" but from Arab nationalists who insisted on independence from Western "imperialists." The accuracy of this complaint registered forcefully in the following year, when in response to a successful coup against the pro-Western government in Iraq and threats to the government in Beirut, Eisenhower sent American forces into Lebanon. Though he likened the danger to that experienced by Greece, Czechoslovakia, China, and South Korea, all supposedly victims of indirect Soviet aggression, the threat in Lebanon was Arab nationalism, not Soviet communism. But none of this legitimate criticism of Eisenhower's doctrine could deter the Democratic Congress from following his lead. "America has either one voice or none," Speaker of the House Sam Rayburn answered critics of the doctrine, "and that voice is the voice of the President—whether everybody agrees with him or not."[14]

From 1956 to 1958 the mood of domestic conformity dominated foreign affairs. In the 1956 election campaign, for example, although Democratic candidate Adlai Stevenson took his distance from the Eisenhower foreign policies, astutely pointing to events in the Middle East as "symptoms of a vast new upheaval in the balance of world power," he also felt compelled to espouse Cold War clichés which emphasized his determination to stand up to the Communists. In this, like Eisenhower, he was reflecting the national mood; on matters of foreign policy, Walter LaFeber points out, the election marked "a consensus of ideology," an agreement among the great majority of voters with the central tenets of Eisenhower-Dulles diplomacy. "Brinksmanship," unflinching opposition to communism in the cause of peace, was the conventional wisdom of the day. Yet at times it was so at odds with foreign realities that one suspects it served another purpose—as a device for not only expressing but also reaffirming the virtue of single-mindedness in the United States, where even dissenters shared in the national style of conformity. "We love everything," the Beat writer Jack Kerouac affirmed, "Bill Graham, the Big Ten, Rock and Roll, Zen, apple pie, Eisenhower—we dig it all."[15]

Even more than in the Middle East, the domestic mood of the fifties shaped American thinking and policies toward Asia. As in earlier days, that continent remained an area of the world where Americans most readily thought in parochial terms and paid small attention to local conditions. Policy toward Korea, China, Japan, Indochina, and Southeast Asia generally continued to be more an expression of internal U.S. preoccupations than a response to a recognizable part of the globe where specific realities had to be taken closely into account.

The conclusion of the Korean War is illustrative. When Eisenhower entered the presidency, the Korean War was more than two and a half years old, with no clear end in sight. The heavy cost in human life, money, and domestic tension made continuation of the status quo "intolerable." The alternatives, as the President assessed them, were to negotiate an honorable peace or to launch a major offensive to win the war. He clearly preferred a negotiated settlement. Fighting a wider war would have meant using atomic weapons and might have touched off a worldwide conflict. Under compelling circumstances, Eisenhower could have imagined using such weapons. "My feeling was then, and still remains," he wrote in his memoirs, "that it would be impossible for the United States to maintain the military commitments which it now sustains around the world . . . did we not possess atomic weapons and the will to use them when necessary." The fact, however, that such tactical bombs might prove ineffective against extensive underground fortifications constructed by the Communists made him resistant to the idea. More important, he worried that a decision to use atomic weapons "would have created strong disruptive feelings between ourselves and our allies." A highly successful all-out offensive would "in time" have healed such "rifts," but he worried that such action would have isolated the United States. "If you go it alone in one place," he remarked at the time, "you have to go it alone everywhere. No single nation can live alone in the world." Though fear of a wider and terribly destructive conflict deterred Eisenhower from more aggressive action in Korea and against China, he also preferred a negotiated end to the Korean fighting because it promised unity, or, in the parlance of the day, togetherness, at home and abroad.

To this end, Eisenhower let it be known to the Chinese, Russians, and North Koreans that without satisfactory progress in the peace talks, the United States would "move decisively without inhibition in our use of weapons" and would feel free to carry its military actions beyond the Korean peninsula. By then announcing the withdrawal of the American Seventh Fleet as a buffer between Chiang Kai-shek and mainland China, the expansion of American air power in Korea, and the enlargement of the South Korean Army, the administration apparently pushed the Communists into renewed negotiations. When they reached an impasse in May 1953, however, Dulles sent word through Prime Minister Nehru of India that the United States might "use atomic weapons" and strike at China's Manchurian sanctuaries. This apparently achieved the desired effect, for the Chinese and North Koreans agreed to an armistice on July 27. To ensure that America and its allies would not now relax their vigil, Eisenhower declared that "we have won an armistice on a single battleground, but not peace in the world." Dulles more ominously announced that the consequence of renewed aggression on the peninsula "would be so grave that in all probability it would not be possible to confine hostilities to Korea."[16]

The Korean experience moved the administration to commit itself to a defense strategy popularly described as massive retaliation. Convinced that limited wars like the one in Korea were both an unacceptable drain on the national economy and destructive to unity among Americans and their allies,

Eisenhower, Dulles, and Secretary of the Treasury George Humphrey proposed to halt aggression by "a great capacity to retaliate, instantly, by means and at places of our own choosing." While a genuine concern with defense costs was central to this thinking, the strategy also expressed the administration's conviction that local wars were simply part of an overall Communist drive for global domination. Massive retaliation, in other words, expressed the belief that Americans could think of Asia and all other parts of the non-Western world in the same way—not as separate entities with individual problems but as objects of a worldwide struggle between freedom and Communist control. The strategy of deterrence by massive force rested partly on a psychology of orthodoxy or conformity which observed the world in undifferentiated terms.[17]

This impulse also played a large role in the administration's thinking about Indochina. At the start of Eisenhower's term in 1953 the French and the Communist-dominated Vietminh were beginning the seventh year of a war for control of Vietnam, Laos, and Cambodia. The President believed that French defeat would mean not only the loss of millions of people and strategic supplies to Communist control but also the eventual victory of communism throughout all Southeast Asia, with "incalculable" consequences "to the free world." To prevent this outcome, he urged the French to accord the three Indochinese states the right of self-determination. The effect, Eisenhower believed, "would soon have been . . . to make the war the concern of all nations outside the Iron Curtain, and could have assured France of material help, as well as the support of world opinion." In the spring of 1954, after the French had refused to follow this suggestion and then made the error of challenging the Vietminh to attack them at Dienbienphu, "an exposed position with poor means of supply and reinforcements," they had to ask the United States to save them from defeat.

But Eisenhower would not intervene unless he was assured of "united action" at home and abroad. First, he wished any commitment of American forces in the conflict to rest on prior congressional approval. Secondly, he would not act without a formal request from France and the Associated States of Indochina for American participation. And thirdly, he insisted on joint action by Britain, Australia, New Zealand, Thailand, and the Philippines in conjunction with the United States. Though he now told Churchill that the triumph of Communist arms in Indochina could be "disastrous" for "our and your global strategic position," he refused to budge without full cooperation from the Congress and the allies. "Unilateral action by the United States in cases of this kind," he privately remarked, "would destroy us. If we intervened alone in this case we would be expected to intervene alone in other parts of the world."

As soon as the Geneva Conference in July acknowledged French defeat by declaring an end to the fighting, dividing Vietnam into southern and northern portions at the seventeenth parallel, and scheduling elections for 1956 to determine the fate of all Vietnam, the Eisenhower administration launched a new effort to assure collective action against "further Communist aggression" in Southeast Asia. In South Vietnam it committed itself to provide direct aid to the anticommunist government of Ngo Dinh Diem and simultaneously created a Southeast Asia Treaty Organization (SEATO) to hold the line in the area. Consisting of the United States, Britain, France, Australia, New Zealand, Thailand, the Philippines, and Pakistan, the treaty states acknowledged a need to meet a "common danger." But the pact was more shadow than substance. Lacking automatic provisions for collective action against aggression, the treaty also excluded Cambodia, Laos, and South Vietnam, which the Geneva agreement forbade to join any military alliance. SEATO was, in fact, largely a symbolic coalition, but it satisfied the American desire for demonstrations of "free world" cooperation against a universal Communist foe.[18]

Chinese Communist action against the offshore islands of

Quemoy and Matsu demonstrated how policies like massive re-taliation and SEATO spoke more to American preoccupation with unity and conformity than to the realities of Asian affairs. In the fall of 1954, for example, after the Communists had begun intermittent shelling of the islands, the Eisenhower ad-ministration refused to commit itself to their defense. Though the United States had signed a treaty with the Chinese Nation-alists promising to defend Formosa, where they were now en-sconced, the treaty omitted mention of the offshore islands and was accompanied by an exchange of letters stipulating that Nationalist military action would "be a matter of joint agree-ment" or subject to an American veto. Furthermore, in Jan-uary and February 1955, when the Communists attacked the Tachen Islands, some 200 miles northwest of Formosa, Eisen-hower decided to help the Nationalists evacuate them, while also drawing a "line." Asking Congress for a joint resolution authorizing the defense of Formosa and the Pescadores, the ad-ministration promised not to commit American forces to the defense of Quemoy and Matsu unless it believed that an assault on them was a prelude to an attack on Formosa.

When predictions of an imminent attack on the offshore is-lands filled the press in March, Eisenhower had to decide on a response. To persuade the Communists "of the strength of our determination," he and Dulles announced their readiness to use tactical atomic weapons against "strictly military targets and for strictly military purposes." But knowing that the use of such weapons against "military targets" would have caused as many as 14,000,000 civilian casualties and might have brought on World War III, the President publicly and privately backed away from such a commitment. Asked again by reporters whether or not he intended to use nuclear weapons to defend Quemoy and Matsu, he refused to give a direct response and then told the press that he "did not believe that war was upon us." At the same time he recorded in a diary that "hostilities are not so imminent as is indicated by the forebodings of a number of my associates. . . . Most of the calamities that we anticipate really never occur." Even if this was only wishful thinking on Eisenhower's part, it was a token of how resistant he was to following through on a policy of massive retaliation. Happily he read the situation correctly, and the crisis passed. But three and a half years later, when it flared again and renewed talk of using atomic weapons reactivated earlier fears, Eisenhower assured Britain's foreign secretary that he was "against the use of even tactical atomic weapons in a limited operation." Massive retaliation in Asia was more a figure of speech or an expression of the belief that the Communist threat was global than a policy to which the President was willing to give specific form. As with other Eisenhower foreign policies, it may have told less about what Americans intended to do abroad than what they were thinking and needed at home. Massive retaliation reflected not only the impulse to see most matters in undifferentiated terms but also the desire to rationalize domestic unity or mass conformity as a necessary response to a worldwide Communist threat.[19]

When he entered the presidency, Eisenhower later recorded in his memoirs, he recognized that Latin America had been taken for granted. Because they lay "in our own backyard" and shared a common religious heritage and "ideals of freedom," Americans expected "our sister republics to stand by us automatically on critical world issues." Moreover, preoccupied with European and Asian problems, U.S. officials could not imagine that a "global war would break out as the result of problems in Latin America." His objective on coming to the White House, Eisenhower tells us, was to remedy this neglect.[20]

If so, he failed badly. Capable of freely exercising American power in the region, particularly in Central America, without regard for local realities, Eisenhower abandoned his rational intentions to pay more mind to the area and allowed his administration to think of it in strictly pro- and anticommunist terms.

Guatemala is a principal case in point. In the 1940s this country of extreme poverty, populated chiefly by illiterate Indians, cried out for economic and social reform. Consequently, in 1944, a revolutionary junta overturned the reactionary rule of General Jorge Ubico, who had proudly compared himself to Hitler, banned labor unions, and declared the word "worker" subversive. In the following nine years, the junta instituted a series of constitutional, economic, and social reforms which improved the country's standard of living and eventually brought a democratically elected government under Jacobo Arbenz, an army officer, to power. By accepting some Communists in his government and expropriating idle lands owned by the American-controlled United Fruit Company—the most powerful economic force in Guatemala—Arbenz opened himself to attack from the Eisenhower administration as an agent, whether wittingly or unwittingly, of the worldwide Soviet Communist conspiracy. ". . . The man thought like a Communist and talked like a Communist, and if not actually one," American Ambassador John E. Peurifoy told Dulles, "would do until one came along." Peurifoy warned that "unless Communist influence in Guatemala were counteracted, Guatemala would within six months fall completely under Communist control." Arbenz, Eisenhower concluded, "was merely a puppet manipulated by Communists."

Though it was in fact local conditions rather than Soviet-inspired communism that had produced Guatemala's reform movement, the Eisenhower administration could see it only as a threat to American security. As the president of the United Fruit Company predicted at the start of troubles with the Arbenz regime, "the question is going to be Communism against the right of property, the life and security of the Western Hemisphere." Dulles led sixteen of the twenty other American republics into echoing this point at the Tenth Inter-American

Conference in Caracas, Venezuela, in March 1954. Because "international communism . . . is incompatible with the concept of American freedom" and because its extension to this hemisphere "would constitute a threat to the sovereignty and political independence of the American states," a conference resolution declared, they would take "appropriate action" against "subversive activities."

To this end, Eisenhower authorized the Central Intelligence Agency to arrange the overthrow of Arbenz's government. Seizing upon the fact that Guatemala had received 1,900 tons of arms from Czechoslovakia and that its government, in an attempt to prevent the CIA-planned coup, had arrested several right-wing leaders and suspended civil liberties, the administration aided Colonel Carlos Castillo Armas, an exiled Guatemalan army officer, to cross the border from Honduras with a small army. With U.S. help and the refusal of the Guatemalan Army to support Arbenz, Castillo Armas took control of the country in June 1954. Refusing to acknowledge the decisive role of the United States in the coup, the State Department described the event as "a revolt of Guatemalans against the government," while Dulles announced that the "evil purpose of the Kremlin [was] being cured by the Guatemalans themselves." "Now the future of Guatemala," he added, "lies at the disposal of the Guatemalan people. . . ." Although the Eisenhower administration was also influenced by a desire to serve the interests of the United Fruit Company, the fear of communism seems to have been its central concern. "Thanks to all of you. You've averted a Soviet beachhead in our hemisphere," Eisenhower told the CIA planners after the change of regimes.

The obvious public deception practiced by the administration is less troubling than its unwitting self-deception, the conviction that the Arbenz government was essentially a tool of the Soviets rather than, as it was, a home-grown movement intent on easing Guatemala's plight. The coup, *New York Times* columnist Harrison E. Salisbury has recently written, "was conceived by men who did not understand what was happening in Guatemala, who did not understand the nature of Latin America and its problems and who had no understanding of the consequences of the events they set in motion." Even someone as close to the situation as the American ambassador could not distinguish between Guatemalan motives and concerns and a distant Russian threat. But Peurifoy, like other government officials and Americans generally in the fifties, saw any challenge to the United States as part of a monolithic Soviet attack.

Such an assumption both reflected and reinforced the pressure for domestic conformity. Since so many people in the United States insisted on 100 percent Americanism, defining people and actions as "American" and "un-American," demanding patriotic avowals through loyalty oaths, it was easy for the administration to see the world as sharply divided into pro- and anti-American camps. This projection of domestic assumptions onto the world also reinforced them; if the nation faced so hostile a division abroad, it became all the more essential for Americans to pull together at home.[21]

During the rest of Eisenhower's presidency, Latin America remained a continuing goad to patriotism and unity in the United States. In the spring of 1958, when Vice President Richard Nixon visited eight Latin American countries, he met spontaneous outbursts of anti-Americanism, including a confrontation in Venezuela which jeopardized his life. Outraged that the Eisenhower administration had given a medal and asylum to the recently ousted dictator Marco Pérez Jiménez, who had contributed to a Venezuelan financial crisis by enriching himself, a mob in Caracas attacked Nixon's car with rocks and brickbats. Though Communists unquestionably participated in the riots in Venezuela and elsewhere, it was irrational to blame the hostility exclusively on international communism working to embarrass the United States. But that is what Nixon and Eisenhower did. "This is Communism as it is," Nixon declared. The whole affair fitted into a pattern, the President said, "a sort of pattern around the world—in Burma, in Jakarta, in South America, other places—that looks like there is some kind of concerted idea and plan. . . ." The Vice President's trip, Eisenhower concluded, brought home "the clear truth" that "the threat of Communism in Latin America is greater than ever before." Though some in the United States would declare it "foolish for us to attribute anti-Americanism just to Communist agitation" in the Latin countries, Nixon came home to a hero's welcome. Fifteen thousand, including the entire Cabinet and congressional leaders from both parties, cheered him at Washington's National Airport.[22]

Cuba also served to draw people together in the United States against the Communist threat. At the beginning of 1959 Fidel Castro overturned the government of Fulgencio Batista and started a thoroughgoing revolution aimed at building a balanced economy and ending Cuban dependence on the United States. For all practical purposes, the island was an extension of the U.S. economy: American business interests owned 80 percent of its utilities, 40 percent of its sugar, 90 percent of its mineral resources and held a general control over its economy by determining how much sugar it could send to the American market. ". . . The United States . . . was so overwhelmingly influential in Cuba," the U.S. representative to that country said in 1960, "that . . . the American Ambassador was the second most important man in Cuba; sometimes even more important than the President. . . ."

Although Castro visited the United States in the opening months of his presidency, he had no intention of maintaining Cuba's traditional dependence on Washington. Since he spoke openly of his intention to nationalize American-owned landholdings, it was not surprising that the Eisenhower administration viewed him with suspicion. Nor was it surprising, in light of earlier reactions to other instances of Latin assertiveness, that American officials branded Castro a Communist or, at the very least, a radical under Communist control. While the extent of his initial Communist ties was open to debate, it was predictable that his tensions with the United States should have pushed him firmly into the Soviet camp. By February 1960, the Cuban government had signed a trade agreement with Moscow which expanded commerce with the Soviet bloc in two years from 2 percent to 80 percent of Cuba's entire trade. In the following month Eisenhower ordered the CIA to prepare Cuban exiles for a possible assault on the island.[23]

The administration's insensitivity to Latin problems in the 1950s was troubling. In the midst of the Cold War it was understandable that American officials wanted cordial relations with Latin neighbors that would back the United States against the USSR. But why this alliance could not have included a variety of Latin governments that partly built their affinity for the United States on American willingness to help them fashion their own internal fates is unclear. Of course, U.S. economic interests did help discourage such a hands-off approach. Still, the core of the problem was more a reflexive anti-communism than a fixed determination to hold Latin economies hostage to the United States. Indeed, on considering the pattern of American response to Latin attacks on the status quo, one gets the impression that the Eisenhower administration, reflecting the national mood, almost wanted confrontations with Communist adversaries that would confirm the need for unity, patriotism, and conformity at home. If, to come back again to Riesman, the rise of an other-directed America meant the waning of individualism or inner-directedness in the nation, it was not an easy change. Eisenhower, for example, who preached the rollback of federal influence on domestic life, nonetheless greatly expanded social security and unemployment compensation coverage, established a new Department of Health, Education and Welfare, and increased the federal budget to $76.5 billion in 1960, as against $39.5 billion in 1950. Acceptance of an organization ethic required repeated rationalization for so fundamental a shift in perspective to take hold. It may well be, then, that the need to see significant Communist dangers, where they were either nonexistent or of small consequence, was a way to blame anxiety generated by this fundamental change on forces outside the United States. Further, such fears may also have served to reinforce the feeling that traditional individualism was out of vogue or that only an organization ethic could now assure national survival.

By the latter half of 1957, Townsend Hoopes has written, the Eisenhower "administration had settled into a rather fixed perception of the outer world and an established way of responding to the problems it presented." Its foreign policies, Washington *Post* cartoonist Herblock asserted in 1958, consisted of "frozen attitudes" and "frozen platitudes." This described dealings with the Soviet Union in the last three and a half years of the Eisenhower term.

In the fall of 1957, after the Soviets had fired the world's first intercontinental ballistic missile (ICBM) and launched the first man-made satellites into space, the sputniks, acute anxiety and self-doubt gripped the United States. Talk of a "missile gap" and of a shift in the military balance of power to Moscow became commonplace. A distinguished study panel headed by H. Rowan Gaither, president of the Ford Foundation, advised the Defense Department and the American public that Russia was superior to the United States in weapons technology. By 1959 or 1960, the Gaither report warned, the Soviets could possibly destroy the bomber force of America's Strategic Air Command and inflict huge civilian casualties on the country. Though American intelligence agencies had information indicating that the Soviets were nowhere near achieving such mastery over U.S. arms and though Eisenhower cautioned against crediting the Russians with more power than they had, govern-

ment officials found this picture of a growing Soviet threat irresistible. Democratic senators described Russian ICBM strength
as almost twice what it actually was, while Eisenhower himself
felt compelled to confer with British Prime Minister Harold
Macmillan about ways to counter the Soviet challenge.
"America cannot stand alone, still less 'go it alone,' " he told
Macmillan. Because "self-sufficiency is now out of date," the
leaders announced in a communiqué, they would urge NATO
to adopt "an enlarged Atlantic effort in scientific research and
development." Exaggerated fears of Soviet missile strength and
capacity to injure the United States were additional compelling reasons for uniformity of thought and shared purpose, a
further goad to national "other-direction" for middle-class
Americans still justifying a group ethic to themselves.[24]

This compulsive need to see the Soviets strictly as aggressors
dominated administration thinking in its second term. In the
fall of 1957, in hopes of freeing East Germany and Eastern Europe generally from permanent Soviet domination, George
Kennan proposed the unification of a neutralized Germany
and the withdrawal of all foreign forces from Central Europe, a
policy of disengagement. The response in the United States,
both within and outside the administration, was a sharp de-
nunciation of Kennan's "naïveté." A neutral Germany, critics
argued, would be inevitably forced into the Soviet orbit, with
the ultimate elimination of "independent national life in Western Europe." Better to have a divided Germany with the Federal Republic integrated into NATO and Western Europe reasonably safe, they said, than to risk the loss of all Europe
through German unity and neutrality. Only through free elections, Dulles declared in November 1958, should Germany be
reunified. "We hold to that."

Profoundly fearful of a rearmed West Germany with influence over United States policy, Khrushchev demanded that a
"solution" to the German question be reached in six months—
before the end of May 1959. Although he focused his demand

on settling the "abnormal situation" in Berlin, he apparently wanted a German peace treaty that would prevent West Germany from producing or possessing nuclear weapons. Taking a "granite-like" stance against the Soviets, including readiness to go to the brink of nuclear war and beyond, if necessary, the Eisenhower administration forced Khrushchev to back away from his threat, a demonstration, in Prime Minister Macmillan's judgment, of the fact that Soviet motivations were defensive.[25]

The administration's principal concession to this fact was a willingness to have Eisenhower meet Khrushchev face-to-face. In September 1959 the premier traveled to the United States, where he urged the necessity of a détente between the two nations. "Many Americans nursed serious misgivings" about Khrushchev's visit, Eisenhower recorded in his memoirs. "Some of the more vociferous were those who opposed any kind of contact with the Soviets, but others were persons of standing, not only in political life, but also in business, labor, and the clergy." The exchange of visits, the President assured one of the critics, "implied no hint of a surrender." He was true to his word. When Khrushchev privately declared that the Soviet Union "did not want war" and his conviction that "we realized this fact," Eisenhower "agreed that there was no future in mutual suicide, but remarked that the attitudes shown at the latest meeting of the foreign ministers gave a contrary impression." The "big obstacle on the American side," in the way of better relations, he perceptively told the premier, "was a matter of national psychology," the need for Americans to believe that Soviet communism did not stand for the destruction of the United States. Eisenhower himself bore out this remark. Though Khrushchev agreed "to remove any suggestion of a time limit within which he would sign a Soviet-East German peace treaty" and though "a crisis over Berlin had been averted without the surrender of any Western rights," the President refused to acknowledge that a new positive mood had taken hold of Soviet-American relations. Khrushchev later "talked much about 'the spirit of Camp David,'" but Eisenhower "never used" the term or thought it "valid."[26]

At the same time the President agreed to a summit conference of Britain, France, Russia, and the United States and a subsequent personal visit to the Soviet Union. The distant possibility of a nuclear test ban treaty and the remote chance of a German settlement encouraged him to take these steps. But a combination of bad luck and resistance to an accommodation with the Russians destroyed these plans. On May 1, 1960, two weeks before the summit meeting in Paris, the Soviets shot down an American U-2 spy plane 1,200 miles inside Russia. When Khrushchev announced this fact on May 5, the State Department described the aircraft as a weather research plane which may have "accidentally violated Soviet airspace." When the Soviet premier then introduced the captured pilot and evidence of his mission, the department had to acknowledge that such a flight had been "probably undertaken" as a way to counter Russia's "secret preparation of armed might." In an apparent attempt to save the summit, Khrushchev declared his "willingness to grant that the President knew nothing" or "had no knowledge of a plane being dispatched to the Soviet Union." Eisenhower faced a difficult choice: pretend he knew nothing of the flight and jeopardize Republican chances in the 1960 elections by vulnerability to Democratic complaints of incompetence, or take the unprecedented step of acknowledging responsibility for an act of espionage and destroy the summit talks.

The President saw the second alternative as the only acceptable choice. It promised domestic political gain and allowed him to counter "Khrushchev's outbursts [which] were hypnotizing the world." By publicly accepting responsibility for the U-2 flight, he hoped to make it clear that the Soviets were driving the Americans into distasteful but necessary acts of international espionage. Russian spying, especially in the

United States, Eisenhower said, dwarfed our activities. The issue, then, was not that "both sides conducted intelligence activities, but rather that the conduct and announced intentions of the Communists created the necessity for such clandestine maneuvers." The United States had constantly to guard against "any possible prelude to an infinitely more destructive Pearl Harbor." While such openness seemed certain to destroy even surface signs of geniality with the Soviets, Eisenhower thought it "advantageous" to drop the "false cloak of camaraderie" and honestly confront "the sharply conflicting views both sides held about the major problems of the cold war."[27]

There is no question but that Soviet Russia posed a threat to the United States in the fifties and that the Eisenhower administration needed to defend American and allied interests against excessive Soviet gains. But the more important question about the period is why the United States so consistently overreacted to that threat, why the administration repeatedly saw Russian defensiveness as aggressive and uniformly turned Asian, Latin, and Middle Eastern nationalism into Communist attacks on American security. The answer may be found in the possibility that foreign affairs both reflected and encouraged the national mood or climate of conformity dominating the decade. Foreign policy was as much a way to express and rationalize an other-directed society at home as a means to defend the national interest abroad. It was, in part, a kind of symbolic politics in which the world outside facilitated cultural change within.

8

Cold War Unity:
Kennedy and Johnson

It seemed to me, as I watched the faces of the [inaugural] crowd, that they had forgotten the cold, forgotten party lines and forgotten all the old divisions of race, religion and nation.

Theodore C. Sorensen, *Kennedy* (1965)

We cannot keep what we have and we cannot preserve the brightening flame of hope for others unless we are all—repeat *all* committed. . . .

Lyndon B. Johnson, 1964

In 1960, when the Democrats nominated John F. Kennedy for the presidency, some Americans took hope that the conformity and orthodoxy of the fifties would now give way to a new autonomy in American life. Arthur Schlesinger, Jr., recalled that Kennedy "had wrought an individuality which carried him beyond the definitions of class and race, region and religion. He was a free man . . . in the sense that he was, as much as man can be, self-determined and not the servant of forces outside him." A Kennedy presidency seemed to promise younger Americans "that they could become more than satisfied stockholders in a satisfied nation. It offered hope for spontaneity in a country drowning in its own passivity. . . ." The writer Norman Mailer shared this hope, believing that with Kennedy, "we as a nation would finally be loose again in the historic seas of a national psyche which was willynilly and at last, again, adventurous."

Kennedy's "magic," Schlesinger said, was "the hope that he could redeem American politics by releasing American life from its various bondages to orthodoxy."

At the same time, others observed a conformist quality in Kennedy which promised a continuation of 1950s orthodoxy. "The 'managerial revolution' has come to politics," the commentator Eric Sevareid complained during the campaign, "and Nixon and Kennedy are its first completely packaged products." Personal advancement was the only strong commitment held by these "tidy, buttoned-down men." They were junior executives on the make, representing "the apotheosis of the Organization Man." It was also clear to Kennedy that this conformist side of his personality and career was an asset in a nation drawn to conventional wisdoms and easy answers to difficult problems. In the closing days of the campaign, for example, after a surge of enthusiasm generated by demonstrations of Kennedy's boldness and idealism, he began to lose ground. ". . . It was almost as if," Schlesinger, Jr., believed, "the electorate were having sudden doubts whether it really wanted so intense a leader, so disturbing a challenge to the certitudes of their existence; it was as if the American people commenced to think that the adventure of Kennedy might be too much and that they had better fall back to the safe and familiar Nixon." Sensing this undercurrent in American life, Kennedy recognized that the nation would not be, as Mailer hoped it would be, "brave enough to enlist the romantic dream of itself . . . [and] vote for the image of the mirror of its unconscious."[1]

In sum, the country preferred old clichés to a New Frontier. This was especially true in foreign affairs, where the U-2 episode had strengthened conformist tendencies and weakened impulses toward finding political alternatives to the Cold War. Indeed, as in the fifties, grave threats from Russia and China in the sixties were to remain a useful means of reassuring Americans that shared purposes, togetherness, or "other-direction" were essential in the United States. In short, world affairs partly remained a device for easing internal concerns.

Among other things, Kennedy's presidency served this end. His campaign, for instance, was a celebration of Cold War beliefs. He reproached the Republicans for allowing the Communists to get "eight jet minutes from Florida" and Russia to seize an advantage in missiles over the United States. He urged an "attempt to strengthen the non-Batista democratic anti-Castro forces in exile, and in Cuba itself, who offer eventual hope of overthrowing Castro. Thus far," he complained, "these fighters for freedom have had virtually no support from our Government." At the same time, he emphasized the so-called missile gap between the United States and the Soviet Union, and the need to strengthen America's military tools. If some of this was simply campaign rhetoric, it did not deter Kennedy from further militancy after the election. Though Adlai Stevenson had strong claims on the top Cabinet position, the former presidential nominee was too "controversial" to become secretary of state. He "had taken too many public positions on prickly issues," and he would offend the Congress. Most of all, Kennedy wanted "a Secretary of State who could get along on Capitol Hill." This led him to appoint Dean Rusk, a former assistant secretary for Far Eastern Affairs, the head of the Rockefeller Foundation, and a staunch supporter of the anti-communist policies shaping American actions around the globe.[2]

The tone and direction of Kennedy's foreign policy found expression in his Inaugural Address. It contained no discussion of domestic goals, which had, when included in a preliminary draft of the speech, impressed Kennedy as "partisan" and "divisive." Instead, he focused exclusively on world affairs or matters that could draw the country together. Though in many ways a brilliant and inspiring talk, with accents and rhythms that represented in some ways a fresh departure from those heard in the Eisenhower years, "the fervent anti-communist absolutes of John Foster Dulles were embedded [in its] very bone structure." This new administration, Kennedy said, was ready to "pay any price, bear any burden, meet any hardship, support any friend, oppose any foe to assure the survival and the success of liberty." There was to be "a new alliance for progress" with our sister republics to the south. "But this peaceful revolution of hope" was not to "become the prey of hostile powers. Let all our neighbors know that we shall join with them to oppose aggression or subversion anywhere in the Americas. . . . In the long history of the world," the new President announced, "only a few generations have been granted the role of defending freedom in its hour of maximum danger. I do not shrink from this responsibility; I welcome it. . . . The energy, the faith, the devotion which we bring to this endeavor will light our country and all who serve it, and the glow from that fire can truly light the world." It seemed to Theodore Sorensen, a principal Kennedy adviser, that, under the influence of the President's speech, the inaugural crowd forgot "all the old divisions of race, religion and nation."[3]

During his presidency the tone of Kennedy's foreign policy was strikingly different from Eisenhower's. If the Eisenhower approach to world affairs was "stodgy, unimaginative, and illiberal," Kennedy's seemed fresh and thoughtful. As in earlier years, America was once more to stand for freedom and the inalienable right to rebel against tyranny. Revolution was no longer a dirty word if it meant advancing the interests of the masses against "the poverty and discontent and hopelessness" on which communism and other totalitarian systems fed. Under Kennedy, America's aim was not "to make the world safe for capitalism" but to help genuine democracy wherever it might take hold. A man of great intelligence who clearly recognized the complexities of world affairs, Kennedy understood that none of this would be easy. Nonetheless, he intended to break with Eisenhower's affinity for the status quo or resistance to every revolution as Communist-inspired, and to adopt a more flexible approach to world events. In domestic affairs as well, Kennedy emphasized the need for a more adventurous approach by "a new generation of Americans" abandoning "the middle-aged complacency of the 1950s." And yet it was not long before his presidency came to be dubbed "the third Eisenhower administration." The New Frontier, one critic complained, was no more than "a limited exercise in civilizing the status quo." While the Kennedy presidency was more progressive and innovative on domestic issues than these comments suggest, it did far less to challenge conventional truths than its rhetoric implied.

Similarly, for all his good intentions in international affairs, for all his determination to be more "realistic" and less doctrinaire, Kennedy's foreign policy proved to be more the reflection of Cold War orthodoxies than of the liberal pronouncements so eloquently enunciated by the President and the exceptionally intelligent men surrounding him. In part, this resulted from the fact that by 1961 the Cold War had a life of its own: Soviet-American suspicions and tensions had a self-perpetuating momentum which could be neither turned off nor easily shifted into a lower gear. Whatever its sources on the Soviet side, in the United States, political, economic, and moral influences joined with an organization ethic to fuel this Cold War orthodoxy. Still attached to the country's traditional individualism and uncomfortable with the shift to a society dominated by large bureaucracies, Americans partly reaffirmed the need for this change by exaggerating overseas threats. "For many people," David Riesman observed, "the program of their lives is determined by fear of a fifth column, and what the Russians or their allies do is an urgent and an all-embracing preoccupation. To such persons there is little identification with America in terms of positive aims, but rather a neurotic clinging to a shadow-war in which our national Superman is engaged." What the Kennedy administration "came to fear most," the historian John L. Gaddis writes, ". . . was not communism, which was too fragmented, or the Soviet Union, which was too committed to détente, or even China, which was too impotent, but rather the threat of embarrassment, of humiliation, of appearing to be weak." The administration, Gaddis adds, "could not even appear to withdraw from what were admittedly overextended positions without setting off a crisis of confidence that would undermine American interests everywhere."[4]

It is in this context that the puzzling Bay of Pigs episode becomes more understandable. When Kennedy came to the White House in January 1961, plans for an exiles' invasion of Cuba were already well developed. The new President, however, was free to drop the idea, and in the five months between his first hearing of the plan and its execution, he had ample opportunity to do so. But he found a compelling logic in the arguments advanced in its behalf: An invasion would topple Castro by igniting substantial discontent on the island, and even if this did not occur, the 1,500 invaders could escape into the Escambray Mountains, where they could maintain guerrilla operations. More compellingly, proponents of the plan emphasized that a failure to follow through on the invasion would discredit the United States: Cuban exiles would tell how the American government had lost its nerve, and this would encourage Fidelistas to attack other "democratic regimes," producing pro-Castro revolutions all over the Caribbean. Thus, a failure to attack Castro's rule would jeopardize the security of the United States.

A few dissenting voices argued against this idea. Senator J. William Fulbright, chairman of the Foreign Relations Committee, opposed the operation as "wildly out of proportion to the threat." He told Kennedy: "The Castro regime is a thorn in the flesh; but it is not a dagger in the heart." Likewise, Arthur Schlesinger, Jr., advised the President that Cuba was not "so grave and compelling a threat to our national security as to justify a course of action which much of the world will interpret as calculated aggression against a small nation in defiance both of treaty obligations and of the international standards as we have repeatedly asserted against the Communist world."

These arguments left Kennedy unmoved. Nor did he and his principal advisers give sufficient weight to the possibility that as a successor to Batista's brutal regime, Castro's government, whatever its failings, might enjoy popular support. Moreover, though the failure of the invasion moved Kennedy to wonder how a rational and responsible government could have become involved in so irrational a project, he held to the idea that he had been striking a blow for freedom and security against worldwide Communist totalitarianism. ". . . You should recognize," the President answered a note of complaint from Premier Nikita Khrushchev, "that free peoples in all parts of the world do not accept the claim of historical inevitability for communist revolution. . . . The great revolution in the history of man, past, present and future, is the revolution of those determined to be free." Further, he publicly announced that "if the nations of this Hemisphere should fail to meet their commitments against outside Communist penetration . . . this Government will not hesitate in meeting its primary obligations which are to the security of our Nation!" The lesson of Cuba, he asserted, was that the Communists intended to "pick off vulnerable areas one by one in situations which do not permit our own armed intervention." This was a "new and deeper struggle" occurring all over the globe. It required new concepts and tools and a new sense of urgency if America was not to lose its security through subversion and infiltration.[5]

The primary lesson Kennedy took from the Bay of Pigs failure was not to rely on experts. But he overlooked a more important lesson—namely, that national security is not easily defined and that appeals to the idea can mask a variety of motives. The more than twenty years of Castro's rule in Cuba largely refutes the argument that America's safety requires an end to his regime, and suggests that the unrealism of both the Eisenhower and Kennedy administrations about the dangers posed by his continuing power rested on something more central to national than to international affairs. A determining influence was the ongoing need to rationalize the virtues of the cooperative or organization ethic in American life. A nation threatened by powerful foreign forces, military and otherwise, was more at peace with the idea of surrendering traditional habits of individualism than one relatively free from serious external threats.

This perception of a Communist threat, it should be emphasized, was not simply the result of displaced feelings about internal concerns. Khrushchev gave Kennedy and his countrymen reason to fear Soviet intentions. In a speech on January 6, 1961, two weeks before Kennedy entered the White House, the Soviet premier had predicted the triumph of socialism through wars of national liberation. What made Khrushchev's assertion so troubling was not the rhetoric but the fact that democracy seemed everywhere in retreat and communism everywhere on the march: The Soviets had developed the hydrogen bomb, surpassed the United States in long-range missiles, exceeded America's rate of industrial growth, and supported successful revolutions in Algeria, Cuba, and North Vietnam.[6]

Moreover, in a meeting between Kennedy and Khrushchev in Vienna in June, the Soviet leader aggressively bullied the President, asserting that communism would inevitably triumph over capitalism, that a nuclear test ban treaty would have to be based on Soviet terms, and that the West would have to sign a German peace treaty within six months, turning West Berlin into a "free city." If the West refused, Russia would sign a treaty on its own and fight any effort to maintain Western occupation rights. The treaty decision was irrevocable, Khrushchev said, and if the United States insisted on war, the Soviet Union was ready to accept the challenge. "It was a very somber 2 days" in Vienna, the President told a national audience on his return. It demonstrated "how long and hard a struggle must be our fate as Americans in this generation as the chief defenders of the cause of liberty." Privately, Kennedy described Soviet policy as "designed to neutralize West Germany as a first step in the neutralization of Western Europe." West Germany was "the key as to whether Western Europe will be free." Furthermore, he saw the Berlin "outpost" as "not an isolated problem" but as part of a threat endangering Europe, Southeast Asia, and the Western Hemisphere. To counter it, Kennedy asked for a 25 percent increase in American military power, called up national reserve forces, and proposed an accelerated fallout shelter program.[7]

However provocative Khrushchev had been, the administration overreacted. It was as reasonable to assume that Soviet truculence rested less on a determination to snuff out freedom all over the globe than on a fear of the West: Announcements in March and May of plans to expand American missile strength, a tougher stance on Berlin than Eisenhower's, a West Germany which might acquire nuclear weapons, and a prosperous West Berlin drawing thousands of East Germans to migrate each week, all frightened the Russians. Kennedy himself later wondered whether it was not these conditions that had chiefly worked to strain Soviet-American relations in the spring of 1961. It is understandable that he saw an immediate threat to West Berlin in Khrushchev's pronouncements. But his impulse to translate Soviet aggressiveness toward Germany into a general European and worldwide threat may be partly explained as a spontaneous reinforcement of the need for "a shadow war" compelling "togetherness" in the United States.[8]

Soviet-American difficulties as a goad to conformity were in ample supply during the remainder of 1961 and most of 1962. In August 1961, the Soviets built the Berlin Wall to prevent further migration of skilled East German workers to the West. Two weeks later, the Russians broke a three-year moratorium on nuclear weapons tests, and the United States, after unsuccessfully trying to revive arms limitation talks, resumed atmospheric testing in April 1962. At the same time, Khrushchev tried to resolve the Berlin stalemate and simultaneously check Chinese power, with which the Soviet Union was in growing conflict. Although Khrushchev announced in the fall of 1961 that the Berlin Wall had made an immediate peace treaty with Germany unnecessary, he also emphasized the continuing need for a final settlement. To this end, and in the hope of deterring China from gaining a nuclear capability, he arranged to emplace in Cuba nuclear missiles which could reach a large part of the United States. Khrushchev's plan, according to historian Adam Ulam, was to appear in November 1962 before the United Nations, where he would announce the existence of these missiles and a proposal to remove them in return for American agreement to a peace treaty with Germany and atom-free zones in Central Europe and the Pacific. The consequence of the latter would dissuade the Chinese from building a nuclear arsenal, which would appeal not only to the Soviets but also to the Americans, still locked in deep conflict with Communist China.[9]

The Kennedy administration's realistic and successful action to compel Soviet dismantling of the missiles without these concessions produced a significant improvement in Soviet-American relations. Although Kennedy recognized that Soviet missiles in Cuba would not have significantly tipped the strategic military balance toward Russia, he felt that it "would have politically changed the balance of power. It would have appeared to, and appearances contributed to reality," he later said. Consequently, he announced a naval blockade of military shipments to Cuba to prevent the Soviets from completing the installation of their missiles. When Khrushchev offered to remove the missiles in return for American promises not to invade Cuba and to withdraw Jupiter missiles from Turkey, Kennedy agreed only to the first condition. Khrushchev then defused the worst Soviet-American crisis in the postwar period by announcing that Russia would dismantle its Cuban missile sites. Although the peaceful conclusion of the confrontation hardly signaled the end of the Cold War, it greatly eased tensions. Soviet efforts to force the United States into drawing up a German peace treaty making West Berlin a "free city" ended, while Kennedy no longer saw "a likely Soviet military threat against Europe. . . . Relations with the Soviet Union," he now concluded, "could be contained within the framework of mutual awareness of the impossibility of achieving any gains through war." In line with this conviction, he publicly urged a "world safe for diversity" and successfully negotiated a nuclear test ban treaty with Moscow. Over the objections of a minority predicting the loss of America's future safety, the Senate approved the treaty, which was supported by 80 percent of the country. The fears of Russia, which had partly served to abet the change in national values from individualism to other direction, now shifted to China and Southeast Asia.[10]

In 1961, deteriorating Sino-Soviet relations suggested to Kennedy that a détente with the Soviet Union would not assure improved relations with China. The day before Kennedy took office, Eisenhower emphasized the problems the new administration would face in Asia. Eisenhower said Laos was the key to all Southeast Asia, and urged unilateral intervention, if necessary, to keep it out of Communist hands. Following that advice, in his State of the Union message Kennedy declared:

> In Asia, the relentless pressures of the Chinese Communists menace the security of the entire area—from the borders of India and South Vietnam to the jungles of Laos, struggling to protect its newly-won independence. We seek in Laos what we seek in all Asia, and, indeed, in

all of the world—freedom for the people and independence for the government. And this Nation shall persevere in our pursuit of these objectives.[11]

Though Laos initially commanded Kennedy's attention, South Vietnam soon became the focus of his concern in Asia. While negotiations with the Soviets led to the neutralization of Laos, no such solution was possible for a more independent Vietnam. By the time Kennedy came to office in 1961, the American-backed Diem government in South Vietnam was under siege from guerrilla forces supported by the North Vietnamese and the Chinese. Kennedy had some doubts about the validity of Eisenhower's domino theory, according to which the "loss" of any country in Southeast Asia would inevitably lead to Communist control of the entire area. Nonetheless, confronted by commitments made under his predecessor, and reluctant to disavow a theory that, whatever its flaws, impressed him as containing a large measure of truth, he expanded American involvement in Vietnam. Instead of concluding that the Vietnamese struggle was essentially an indigenous contest for power, he viewed it as part of a worldwide Communist drive that the United States would have to answer with "counter-insurgency warfare." The battle of "freedom versus tyranny" was being fought in Vietnam, he told the Congress in May 1961.[12]

Kennedy had substantial support among high American officials for his view of Vietnam. In the spring of 1961, after visiting South Vietnam, Vice President Lyndon Johnson urged Kennedy to understand that the time for "the basic decision in Southeast Asia is here. We must decide whether to help these countries to the best of our ability or throw in the towel in the area and pull back our defenses to San Francisco and a 'Fortress America' concept." If we did not make "a major effort to help these countries defend themselves," the Vice President advised, it would signal to the world that we "don't live up to our treaties and don't stand by our friends." In October, after the Viet-cong had demonstrated their growing power in South Vietnam by seizing a provincial capital, Kennedy sent General Maxwell Taylor and Walt W. Rostow, a member of the White House national security staff, to evaluate the situation. Like Johnson, they strongly recommended a major American effort, including a military task force of possibly 10,000 men. ". . . As I knew from experience with my French friends," George Ball, Kennedy's Under Secretary of State, later recalled, "there was something about Vietnam that seduced the toughest military minds into fantasy."

Because, Schlesinger recalls, he was skeptical about con-verting the conflict "into a white man's war," which he feared "we would lose as the French had lost a decade earlier," Ken-nedy asked for another evaluation of the Vietnam situation from John Kenneth Galbraith, then ambassador to India. Gal-braith described the problem there as political and not mili-tary. A change of rule from the totally ineffectual Diem regime to a more popular and effective government would probably allow the Vietnamese Army to defeat the guerrillas. "While no one can promise a safe transition," Galbraith wrote, "we are now married to failure." He urged the rule "that nothing suc-ceeds like successors."

In the end, deciding that the military knew best and that the whole world balance might hinge on what the United States now did in Vietnam, Kennedy adopted the Taylor-Ros-tow plan. The commitment had "the sound and solemnity of a religious oath," George Ball observes, citing a government memorandum: "We now take the decision to commit ourselves to the objective of preventing the fall of South Vietnam to Communism. . . ." To Kennedy's satisfaction, moreover, the policy seemed to work. In 1962, Secretary of Defense Robert McNamara reported that "every quantitative measurement we have shows we're winning this war." General Taylor echoed this conclusion, and by the start of 1963 Kennedy was telling the nation that "the spearpoint of aggression has been blunted in South Vietnam."[13]

He felt this was particularly important because of China. In the aftermath of the Cuban missile crisis, he saw Chinese power as "the great menace in the future to humanity, the free world, and freedom on earth. . . . The Chinese," he said privately, "would be perfectly prepared, because of the lower value they attach to human life, to sacrifice hundreds of millions of their own lives, if this were necessary in order to carry out their militant and aggressive policies." This distorted portrait of Chinese intentions found confirmation in the Sino-Indian War of November 1962. Although it was in fact the Indians who had provoked the conflict, and the Chinese voluntarily limited the border areas they occupied after defeating Indian forces, Americans within and outside the government could only view China's action as evidence of the reckless ambition of Peking. Indeed, by the beginning of 1963, China had replaced Russia as the principal menace to America and all the "free world."[14]

It is difficult to understand, even in the context of 1963, how rational men could hold this belief. Measured against the actualities of Chinese power and intentions, images of a Communist China sweeping across Southeast Asia and out into the Pacific, where it would compel a U.S. retreat to Hawaii and San Francisco, seem ludicrous. Even many intelligent Americans who did not take such assertions at face value still persuaded themselves that an aggressive, dangerous China was a piece of international "reality" upon which the nation needed to act, especially in Vietnam. To be sure, Chinese and Vietnamese Communist hostility to America, coupled with memories of Chinese intervention in Korea, encouraged combativeness in the United States. But the need for an ongoing menace that diverted middle America from unhappy feelings over diminished autonomy and reaffirmed the need for unity at home was part of the backdrop from which fear of China and Communist expansion in Vietnam emerged.

It is this peculiar tension over the character of American life that at least partly explains U.S. unrealism toward Vietnam. Despite the rosy pictures painted by high American officials in 1962, the Diem government made little progress toward winning the war. But U.S. military and Foreign Service officers in Vietnam refused to accept this fact. When American journalists in Saigon conscientiously reported Diem's failings, a U.S. admiral asked: "Why don't you get on the team?" Although the reporters assumed that these American officials were deliberately lying to them and their people, the truth is that they "believed their own reports. They were deceiving not only the American government and people," concluded Arthur Schlesinger, Jr., "but themselves."

The administration in Washington was as gullible. In spite of evidence to the contrary in the first half of 1963, the State Department continued to see progress in Vietnam. Dean Rusk saw a "steady movement toward a constitutional system resting upon popular consent." Even when widespread protests against the Diem government in the summer of 1963 demonstrated the unpersuasiveness of this idea, the American government refused to give up its support of Diem or to consider withdrawing from the country. In a press conference Kennedy counseled against rendering "too harsh a judgment." The United States wanted "a stable government there, carrying on a struggle to maintain its national independence. . . . For us to withdraw from that effort would mean a collapse not only of South Vietnam but Southeast Asia. So we are going to stay there."

The central objective of American policy remained the victory of an anticommunist regime that would presumably stem the general expansion of communism in Asia and improve the security of the United States. In September and October of 1963, therefore, when continuing domestic upheaval in South Vietnam finally made Diem seem incapable of providing this, the U.S. government acquiesced in a military coup against his regime. By publicly urging "changes in policy and perhaps . . . personnel" on the Saigon government and by cutting off some aid to Diem, the Kennedy administration gave tacit backing to a change of rule. Though the execution of Diem disgusted American officials, they greeted his fall from power with undisguised relief and high hopes that their aims in Vietnam might now be achieved.[15]

While Kennedy kept saying that the war was for the Vietnamese to win or lose, he saw a substantial American stake in the conflict. By the time of his assassination in November 1963, he had put 16,000 troops in South Vietnam. In his judgment and that of most officials, this was not only a contest for all Southeast Asia but also a test of American ability to combat Communist-inspired wars of "national liberation." Yet it was neither. Communist control of all Vietnam did not mean the advance of monolithic communism through all Southeast Asia. Nor did it presage the triumph of "national liberation" wars anywhere else.

The unrealism of Kennedy and many of his contemporaries about Vietnam partly arose from their preoccupation with internal concerns. Kennedy's rhetoric and personal style paid homage to the individualism of an earlier day. But his actions largely encouraged existing trends toward organizational conformity. Like Eisenhower, he exaggerated and misread external dangers, first from Russia and then from China and Vietnam, allowing foreign affairs in part to reflect and rationalize needs for personal "belongingness" or dependency within the United States. Judged from his private comments, he was uncomfortable with these influences on world affairs. But like most other Americans, he was moved by tensions in the changing national character he himself did not fully understand.

Lyndon Johnson was a striking example of the new character type predominant in the United States. ". . . Johnson's story provides a panoramic view of the changing nature of American life in the twentieth century," Doris Kearns has written.

The world in which Johnson grew up was a different world from the one he came to lead. He grew up in an America where almost every household contained the text and the message of Horatio Alger—the triumph of character, determination, and will over all adversity. Success or failure was determined by the individual himself; structural barriers simply did not exist.

By the time Johnson came to the White House, the country had become congealed into large units in which accommodation and conformity were more likely to make a man's career than individual initiative. This change in the culture did not, however, throw Johnson into sharp conflict with national trends. Having grown up in a household where he had learned to avoid passionate and emotional divisions over issues, he was also a superb consensus politician skilled at pasting over differences and knitting together opposing forces. Thus, powerful impulses toward individualism and conformity resided in him side by side. But, facing a world in which the latter was now more valued than the former, he found ways to rationalize his own and the country's accommodation to this change.[16]

One means was through international relations. Of all the presidents in the post-1945 era, none believed more strongly in foreign affairs as a unifying force in American life than Lyndon Johnson. Long before he entered the White House, Johnson had concluded that presidential direction of foreign policy was not a fit subject for domestic debate. "I am the only President you have," he was fond of saying. And when the safety of the nation was at stake, he considered it unpatriotic for Americans to question the government's policy. On matters of foreign affairs, he often referred to the Alamo: It was a case of us against them, and any act of dissent was bound to weaken the fortress and give aid to hostile forces. "When they lead your boy down to that railroad station to send him into boot camp and put a khaki uniform on him to send him some place where he may never return, he doesn't debate foreign policy," Johnson said. "They send you to defend the flag, and you go."[17]

Like his immediate predecessors, he also saw the United States locked in conflict with Communist aggression around the globe. Since any show of weakness in world affairs impressed him as likely to undermine American security abroad and his political standing at home, Johnson made clear that he would vigorously meet every challenge to U.S. power. In January 1964, therefore, when rioting in the Canal Zone led Panama's President Roberto Chiari to break relations with the United States and demand renegotiation of the 1903 Panama Canal Treaty, the U.S. President took a hard line. He refused to knuckle under to a "banana republic" no larger than the city of St. Louis. Though he sent Thomas C. Mann, his staunchly anticommunist assistant secretary for Latin American affairs, to Panama City for talks, he would not hold formal "discussions and negotiations," publicly proposed by representatives of the Organization of American States. The OAS "couldn't pour piss out of a boot if the instructions were written on the heel," Johnson said. Determined to do nothing which would allow the Republicans to describe him as "weak" in the upcoming presidential campaign, he agreed to no more than a "review" of outstanding issues between Panama and the United States.[18]

But it was less Johnson's assertiveness than his restraint in foreign affairs which helped make him more appealing than Barry Goldwater in the 1964 presidential campaign. By contrast with Johnson, who believed that a hard-line approach to the Cold War could be coupled with peaceful coexistence, Goldwater had a record of opposing any negotiation or compromise with the Communists. He wanted withdrawal from the United Nations, an end to diplomatic relations with Russia, and a repudiation of disarmament agreements. Goldwater insisted on seeing the Communist world as a uniform bloc with no internal differences, and in his book *Why Not Victory?* he posited a life-or-death struggle with this monolithic communism which must end in either victory or defeat. Only a final triumph over communism could save American freedom. His Democratic opponents, referring to his apparent readiness to risk nuclear war in this cause, effectively paraphrased Goldwater's campaign slogan, "In your hearts you know he's right," to read: "In your hearts you know he might."

Goldwater's ideas had considerable appeal for some Americans. Accepting his assertion that nuclear weapons were simply a more effective means of destruction, and remembering the tradition of free security in which the United States paid little for national defense, his supporters believed that his program would return the country to an earlier, less difficult time. ". . . What seems most remarkable," Richard Hofstadter wrote in 1965, "is not that many should respond wholeheartedly to the pseudo-conservative interpretation of events, but that our statesmanship has been as restrained as it has usually been and that this restraint has won preponderant public support."[19] The reason lay primarily in the desire to avoid a nuclear holocaust. But it may also be explained by the fact that a continuing Cold War served the shift in national character from individualism to other-directed habits. In calling for a victory over the Communists, Goldwater was indirectly urging the elimination of the external threat that helped make "togetherness" or the organizational ethic an imperative of American life. Just as in domestic affairs, where he wished to throw off the "bureaucratic shackles" eroding "individual worth," so he wished to abolish the external conditions compelling an enlarged role for government and conformity in the United States. In an America no longer beset by foreign dangers, the individual would find greater freedom to go his own way. But a majority of Americans, fearing nuclear war, largely resisted Goldwater's ideas. In addition, more attached to the organized, industrial life than to the individualism Goldwater preached, Americans did not want to repeal the New Deal or end the Cold War. Whereas the former insulated them from the economic and social insecurities of an earlier time, the latter allowed them to resist emotional ties to a reputedly more heroic nineteenth-century life.

Johnson's use of foreign affairs to confirm the need for conformity is neatly demonstrated in his dealings with the Dominican Republic in the spring of 1965. On April 24, rebel forces committed to overturning an unpopular government headed by Donald Reid Cabral, and replacing it with a more liberal regime under Juan Bosch, launched a revolt. Informed by the U.S. Embassy in Santo Domingo that American lives and property were in jeopardy and that the rebel forces included some Communists or Communist sympathizers, Johnson at once decided to send in the Marines. ". . . Where American citizens go, that flag goes with them to protect them," he said. In subsequent public remarks, he explained that he had had to land troops or American blood would have run in the streets. At a news conference in June, Johnson told reporters that

> Some fifteen hundred innocent people were murdered and shot, and their heads cut off, and six Latin American embassies were violated and fired upon over a period of four days before we went in. As we talked to our Ambassador to confirm the horror and tragedy and the unbelievable fact that they were firing on Americans and the American Embassy, he was talking to us from under a desk while bullets were going through his windows and he had a thousand American men, women, and children assembled in the hotel who were pleading with their President for help to preserve their lives.

The President also emphasized the Communist threat. "People trained outside the Dominican Republic are seeking to

gain control," he declared. He spoke of an "international conspiracy" working toward "a Communist seizure of the island,"
and added: "We don't propose to sit here in our rocking chair
with our hands folded and let the Communists set up any government in the Western Hemisphere." He pledged not to allow
another Cuba and promised to defend "every free country" in
the Americas. To demonstrate the point, the American Embassy issued a list of fifty-eight "identified and prominent Communist Castroite leaders" in the rebel camp.

Much of this was fabrication or at the very least exaggera-
tion on Johnson's part. There was little reason to believe that
without a U.S. landing American blood would have run in the
streets of Santo Domingo. There was no considerable loss of life
visible to reporters in the Dominican capital, no 1,500 (if any)
people had been beheaded, only one embassy had been violated, the American ambassador had not shielded himself from
bullets while talking to the President, and no American civilian
had been hurt. Moreover, the list of fifty-eight prominent Communist leaders advancing an "international conspiracy" to
seize the island impressed American newspapermen on the
scene as "propaganda, not fact." Three of the names on the list
turned out to be a diehard conservative, a right-wing naval officer, and a fifteen-year-old boy. With considerable justice,
Juan Bosch complained that "this was a democratic revolution
smashed by the leading democracy of the world."[20]

But Johnson could not see it that way. Convinced that
there was a genuine Communist threat and pleased by the fact
that a relatively free election held in the following year produced a stable anticommunist government, he felt justified in
what he had done and said. In his memoirs he asserted that
during the upheaval, power, for the most part, "rested with the
Communists and their armed followers and with the dissident
military officers and enlisted men." Though there were not
great numbers of Communists, they "were well armed, tightly
organized, and highly disciplined. Perhaps more important,
they included dedicated professional revolutionaries trained to

exploit the kind of situation in which they then found themselves." Adding this danger to the possible "slaughter of American citizens" in the Dominican Republic, Johnson found ample reason for military action.[21]

The fact that he misrepresented conditions on the island suggests that something other than Dominican realities moved him to act as he did. Undoubtedly, he was influenced by unspoken fears of infectious instability in the Caribbean and as well by domestic political considerations—the need to avoid giving the Republicans any grounds for charges of hesitant leadership. But a chance to reaffirm the need for shared purposes and other-directed habits probably also played a part. Drawn to the simpler, more autonomous world Goldwater described, but unwilling to relinquish the material gains of the corporate world in which they lived, Johnson and numerous Americans wished to reaffirm that they could not turn back the clock. An America in jeopardy from foreign forces was one means to this end. Exaggerated dangers in the Dominican Republic made the unorganized individualism of an earlier day a luxury the country could not afford.

Vietnam echoed the point. Like Eisenhower and Kennedy, Johnson could not think of Vietnam as a local struggle between Vietnamese; rather, it was a contest for all of Southeast Asia and a major test of American staying power in the Cold War. It was also a potentially sensitive domestic issue. "... If we walked away from Vietnam and let Southeast Asia fall," Johnson later wrote, "there would follow a divisive and destructive debate in our country.... A divisive debate about 'who lost Vietnam' would be, in my judgment, even more destructive to our national life than the argument over China had been." Worse yet, he believed that withdrawal from Vietnam would tempt Moscow and Peking into bolder actions which would lead to a nuclear war with the United States. As in Korea, a strong stand in Vietnam would prevent a wider war. At the start of his presidency, these assumptions moved Johnson to declare privately and publicly that he was "not going to lose South Vietnam."

In 1952, the English historian Denis Brogan described the central problem of American foreign relations as "The Illusion of American Omnipotence." Johnson's ideas about Vietnam in the mid-sixties suggests that someone would have done well to restate the problem as "The Omnipotence of American Illusion." From the perspective of the eighties, one can see clearly that Johnson was wrong on every count about Vietnam: it was not a contest for all of Southeast Asia, its "loss" to communism did not spark "a divisive and destructive debate" in the United States, and American withdrawal did not lead to a nuclear war.

Why did Johnson so badly miscalculate the consequences of a U.S. withdrawal from Vietnam? False assumptions about Communist intentions, excessive moralism, and memories of McCarthyism provide part of the answer. Another piece of the puzzle may be found in Johnson's compelling concern that a pullback from the Cold War might open the way to a destabilizing shift from large-scale organization and uniformity to romantic individualism or renewed inner direction in the United States. "We would like to live as we once lived," Johnson quoted Kennedy in explanation of American policy in Vietnam. "But history will not permit it." In 1966, Johnson affirmed what he saw as an "overriding rule": "that our foreign policy must always be an extension of our domestic policy. Our safest guide to what we do abroad is always what we do at home. . . ." Explicitly, he meant leaving the "footprints of America" on Vietnam—"schools and hospitals and dams," turning the Mekong river area into a Tennessee Valley. Implicitly, he meant that foreign policy must expand unity abroad and reinforce it at home: The Vietnamese would become more like Americans, and Americans would mute differences in the name of national security. "We cannot keep what we have and we cannot preserve the brightening flame of hope for others unless we are all—repeat *all* committed; all—repeat *all* willing to sacrifice and to serve wherever we can, whether it be in Vietnam, whether it be at home," Johnson said in 1964.[22]

Vietnam as a unifying force was a constant Johnson theme. In his first briefings on the subject, he complained to his advisers that there had been too much bickering among Americans in Vietnam, and he asked that "all senior officers of the government will move energetically to insure the full unity of support for established U.S. policy in South Vietnam." Johnson also felt that American actions which had helped topple Diem were a serious blunder. It opened a period of deep political confusion in Saigon, during which seven different governments held power. It would have been far better to leave Diem in place and for critics in both Vietnam and the United States to have shown greater understanding and patience.

The President wished to ensure that divisive steps of this sort would not again undermine the defense of Vietnam. Consequently, in August 1964, after he had ordered American air strikes against North Vietnamese ports in retaliation for attacks on American destroyers by North Vietnamese torpedo boats, he asked Congress for a resolution supporting his policy, and more: "the advance support of Congress for anything that might prove to be necessary." Should Hanoi "overreact and launch an all-out invasion of South Vietnam" or "ask the Chinese Communists to join them in battle . . . , I wanted us to be ready for the worst." Concealing the fact that the American destroyers had been supporting South Vietnamese raids on North Vietnam and insisting that the attacks on the U.S. ships "were unprovoked" acts of "open aggression on the high seas," Johnson persuaded the Congress to let him "prevent further aggression" and take "all necessary steps" to defend any Southeast

Asian nation asking help "in defense of its freedom." The Tonkin Gulf Resolution, he remarked, was "like grandma's nightshirt—it covered everything." As important in his judgment, a unanimous vote in the House and a vote of 88 to 2 in the Senate gave "indisputable" evidence of united American action in Vietnam.[23]

A united America was again a central consideration in Johnson's next major action on Vietnam in February 1965. When Vietcong attacks on U.S. installations in November and December 1964 took American lives, the President concluded that "public opinion" was ready for stronger action. By February, in fact, his principal advisers as well as an influential part of the press and the Congress were pushing him to do more in Vietnam. Hence, a Vietcong attack in February on an American base at Pleiku, 240 miles northeast of Saigon, became the catalyst for air strikes against the North. Three weeks later the President ordered continuous bombing of North Vietnam as a means of forcing Hanoi to negotiate an end to the war. This, he thought, would take between twelve and eighteen months, a period of time not likely to arouse much frustration in the United States or to undercut the unity Johnson assumed would be a part of the expanded fighting. He believed that the great bulk of the country would accept the proposition "that in our nation's relations with the outside world partisanship should be left behind."[24]

But to his great dismay the war produced not a year of general unity but almost immediate dissent. The President's bombing program at once created "a tremendous outcry" in the United States. It sparked a series of university teach-ins, the first widespread organized opposition to the war. It also touched off protests from allies and adversaries abroad, culminating in an appeal from seventeen nonaligned nations in April for "termination of the conflict ... through negotiations." In response, Johnson declared his willingness "to go anywhere at any time, and meet with anyone whenever there is promise of progress toward an honorable peace." In a speech at Johns Hopkins University on April 7, he announced his readiness for "unconditional discussions" with the "governments concerned" and a messianic appeal for an Asian development plan, a cooperative effort of industrialized and underdeveloped countries to improve living standards throughout Southeast Asia. But by limiting any talks to the "governments concerned," Johnson was excluding the Vietcong, Saigon's principal adversary in Vietnam, and the possibility of serious negotiations. Convinced that the Communists would not negotiate as long as they were winning, Johnson largely made the speech to blunt domestic criticism.[25]

Though the President now recognized that a continuing war would split the country and jeopardize his Great Society programs, he believed that ending the conflict in an unsatisfactory way would cause even greater division in the United States. If he agreed to a settlement in Vietnam which allowed the Communists to gain eventual control, Johnson expected political opponents to accuse his administration of "softness" toward communism and to provoke a new round of McCarthyism that would tear the country apart. He "preached rationality and compromise," Doris Kearns writes, "but continually feared and imagined the emergence of unreasoning passions and unyielding ideologies. His conduct and words expressed a will to believe, a fear of his own doubts. Johnson was always afraid that he himself might give way to irrational emotions; control came to appear a requirement of survival of the self." In terms of the conflict over national character, this meant that Johnson dreaded the loss of consensus and unity as leading to a kind of political and social diffusion more appropriate to nineteenth-century American life. In personal terms, he seemed constantly on guard against the inner-directed impulses which, however attractive, impressed him as no longer viable in a mid-twentieth-century world.[26]

Because he was apprehensive, above all of losing the war,

while being worried at the same time that continuing and expanding it would also undermine the domestic unity and progress he wished to maintain, Johnson did all in his power to disguise and play down the extent of American involvement in Vietnam. At the same time that he unleashed an air campaign against the North, he agreed to expand the number and role of U.S. troops in the South. By the end of April 1965 some 50,000 American soldiers were in Vietnam to defend air bases and support Vietnamese units in serious trouble. By June U.S. troops were free to undertake combat missions on their own. In July, on the recommendation of six of his leading advisers, Johnson agreed to send 150,000 more troops as a way to "stave off defeat in the short run" and produce "a favorable settlement in the longer run." Urged by his advisers to declare a "state of emergency" and alert the country and the Congress to the fact that they were involved in a major war, Johnson refused. Fearing that such action would touch off "a right-wing stampede" and shatter the Great Society, he decided to fight "a covert full-scale war" instead. "By pretending there was no major conflict, by minimizing the level of spending, and by refusing to call up the reserves or ask Congress for an acknowledgment or acceptance of the war," Johnson hoped to preserve domestic unity, fulfill reform goals, and save Vietnam. "I was determined to be a leader of war *and* a leader of peace," he later said. "I refused to let my critics push me into choosing one or the other."[27]

Though the war was supposed to draw the nation more tightly together, mounting American casualties in the fighting after 1964 dissolved Johnson's domestic consensus. Critics on the left denounced the war outright, while opponents on the right complained about the restraint with which it was being fought. Johnson, however, rejected both arguments as likely to lead to World War III: If the United States withdrew from Vietnam, it would embolden the Communists and force a larger, far more destructive war later on; if America struck harder at Hanoi, it would draw in the Russians and the Chinese and cause the nuclear exchange a limited war in Vietnam was supposed to prevent. Such a conflict, Johnson said, "would have meant the end of everything we know." Though he surely believed this, it is difficult to see him responding rationally to world affairs. Assumptions that the Soviets and the Chinese were ready to risk nuclear war in response to events in Vietnam tell more about the proponents of such a view than about Moscow and Peking. Indeed, when the President saw a radical change in policy toward Vietnam as leading to "the end of everything we know," he may be understood as partly saying that an end to the Cold War would have encouraged a shift from an organized, other-directed America to an outdated individualism that would tear the country apart.

There is evidence for this in the way Johnson reacted to the critics of the war. In his view, he was dealing with the "crazies" of the left and the right. He saw himself pursuing a moderate middle course aimed at saving Vietnam, ensuring American security, and advancing prosperity in the United States. He described his critics as motivated by self-interest and jealousy, or even as disloyal to their country. They were "nervous Nellies" ready to "turn on their own leaders, and on their country, and on our own fighting men." His liberal critics were under the influence of the Russians, who told them what to say. ". . . Isn't it funny that you could always find [Soviet Ambassador] Dobrynin's car in front of [*New York Times* columnist James] Reston's house the night before Reston delivered a blast on Vietnam?" Johnson said. Convincing himself that his opponents did not represent majority sentiment in the United States, the President felt justified in pursuing a steady course in Vietnam. When critics, for example, argued that he no longer commanded a consensus on the war, he declared himself confident that the people "loved" him "a great deal. . . . Deep down," he told Doris Kearns, "I knew—I simply knew—that the American people loved me." Whatever the opposition to the war, he could not let go of the idea that it promoted domestic unity or was a bar to internal divisions destructive to recent gains in American life.[28]

The tension between Johnson and young war critics further illustrates the point. Many young opponents of the war berated the President and his generation as automatons, mindless patriots stamped out by an impersonal machine society. By contrast, these young people celebrated the virtues of the "old West, the simple life, the life of adventure." The West was "an escape from the sober responsibilities and acquiescence to impersonal authority that characterized the civilized East." Yet the two generations were never as far apart as young people liked to think. "The values of any new generation," psychoanalyst Erik Erikson has explained, "do not spring full blown from their heads; they are already there, inherent if not clearly articulated in the older generation.... The younger generation makes overt what is covert in the older generation; the child expresses openly what the parent represses." Johnson himself demonstrated this when he wondered, why didn't young people "realize I'm really one of them? I always hated cops when I was a kid, and just like them I dropped out of school and took off for California. I'm not some conformist middle class personality. I could never be bureaucratized." But of course, he had been. And in fighting the war in Vietnam, rejecting the arguments of his critics, questioning their motives, and denying their influence, Johnson was partly fighting for the organizational ethic in American life. Like his young opponents, he was also drawn to the romantic individualism of his youth. But unlike Goldwater, Johnson and most Americans feared this impulse as destructive to the economic and political stability developed over the past seventy-five years. Indeed, the President's emotional commitment to the war in Vietnam may be seen as less the product of a realistic concern with preventing World War III than of a deep-felt need to check powerful longings for an earlier, more autonomous style of life.[29]

Why, then, in 1968, did Johnson decide to deescalate the war and withdraw from public life? It was not, as Kearns points out, because the public had lost faith in his policies; a majority of Americans in 1968 continued to support the war in Vietnam and the Great Society. But it had lost confidence in Johnson's ability to lead. His presidency had brought not unity and advance but a "credibility gap" and riots in the streets. In the first 1968 presidential primary in conservative New Hampshire, for example, Senator Eugene McCarthy of Minnesota, an all but unknown liberal member of the upper house, came within less than 1 percent of beating Johnson. An analysis of the vote showed McCarthy with more support from hawks than doves, suggesting that people were more interested in voting against Johnson than for his opponent.

In the face of this reality, on March 31 the President announced his withdrawal from the presidential race in order to devote himself to making peace in Vietnam and at home:

> This country's ultimate strength lies in the unity of our people. There is division in the American house now. There is divisiveness among us all tonight. And holding the trust that is mine, as President of all the people, I cannot disregard the peril to progress of the American people and the hope and prospect of peace for all people.... With America's future under challenge right here at home ... I do not believe that I should devote an hour or a day of my time to any personal partisan causes. Accordingly, I shall not seek, and will not accept, the nomination of my party for another term as your President.[30]

Although the means now changed, Johnson's goal remained the same: Unable to achieve a cohesive society through an expanded war in Vietnam, he sought the same end through de-escalation and retirement from political life. As with his immediate predecessors, the principal aim of foreign policy was more a sense of shared purpose at home than the containment of exaggerated dangers abroad.

9

Cold War "Liberalism": Nixon and Kissinger

Nixon is at one with Woodrow Wilson and Herbert Hoover in all things that united those earlier Presidents. He believes in, he summarizes, he is the apt spokesman for (and the final product of) classical liberalism ... the ideal of self-government, of the self-disciplined self-made man.

Garry Wills, *Nixon Agonistes: The Crisis of the Self-Made Man* (1969)

In 1968, under the weight of political, economic, and social disarray, the American system seemed ripe for collapse. Opposition to a "pointless" war, political assassinations, riots in the streets, and mounting inflation threatened to end the "American way of life." In these circumstances, it was not surprising that the country (though narrowly) chose Richard Nixon over Hubert Humphrey for the presidency. As Johnson's vice-president, Humphrey was identified with all the failings of the Johnson administration. But Nixon's victory, wrote Garry Wills in 1969, was also "the nation's concession of defeat, an admission that we have no politics left but the old individualism, a web of myths that have lost their magic." However strong the wish to return to that "Golden Age," however great the need to continue believing in "what Wilson called 'the man on the make,' the self-making man," this ideal had become, Wills argued, "a cruel hoax. The middle-class earner, given initial advantages, uses them to build walls of security, pensions, free schools, government unemployment checks, union guarantees of a job or a wage." Those who preach the gospel of individualism "find themselves guilty of the thing they curse in others—*dependence,* reliance on other men, the lack of self-made autonomy. Self-made men are not the bold swashbucklers imagined once, laughing, spontaneous, free. They are cramped, full of pretense, diminished things—Dick Nixons."[1]

As a character type, Nixon, like so many of his followers, is two men in one, a deeply divided personality. Having risen to the White House from modest beginnings in Southern California, an American frontier in the first fifty years of this century, Nixon is a latter-day Horatio Alger, a rugged opportunist fighting his way to the top. At the same time, he is the quintessential organization man, the "team player" unswervingly loyal to the Republican party, the consummate patriot best remembered for his conventionality.

Nixon's presidency was largely a playing out of these character traits. In domestic affairs, rhetoric and action ran along separate parallel lines that rarely converged. His initial words and deeds on civil rights, Supreme Court appointments, and national economic policy encouraged conservatives hoping for a return of states' rights and traditional individualism. But he ultimately disappointed them by embracing the political and economic assumptions of a post-New Deal America. "I am now a Keynesian," Nixon declared in January 1971, and seven months later he attacked economic "stagflation," recession combined with persistent inflation, with wage and price controls, a tax cut, and devaluation of the dollar. He even took up social reform, declaring under the influence of Daniel P. Moynihan, his chief urban affairs adviser, that "Tory men with liberal principles are what has enlarged democracy in this world."[2]

Nowhere in his presidency did Nixon vent this duality in his own and the national character more fully than in international affairs. Foreign policy was his special domain, the field of presidential action he felt best prepared to manage. Whereas he believed himself limited in both expertise and opportunity for change in domestic affairs, he saw the opposite in international relations. Through extensive reading and travel he had readied himself for major undertakings abroad, and more than any predecessor in the White House he devoted himself to solving world problems. Yet the same tension in domestic affairs between old-style liberalism and modern bureaucratic trends also helped shape Nixon's foreign policies. For all of Nixon's genuine realism about the outside world, internal conditions remained of central importance in determining how his administration acted overseas.[3]

In shaping international affairs, Nixon found a congenial partner in Henry Kissinger. Though the two men came from vastly different backgrounds, they thought along similar lines. Kissinger was a Jewish migrant from Hitler Germany who grew up in New York City and became a successful academic at Harvard with close ties to the foreign policy establishment, and his experiences seemed strikingly removed from Nixon's. Yet, like the President, Kissinger was very much a self-made man, who praised the openness of a society that allowed someone of his background to rise so high. But again, like Nixon, he was also the product of an institutional world—Harvard, the Council on Foreign Relations, the Rockefeller family entourage, the staff of White House consultants—through which he moved comfortably. Bureaucratic management, consensus, fundamental agreement along national lines were central considerations of his years in office. Nixon and Kissinger, then, embodied similar national characteristics, which, for all their sophistication and determination to be coldly realistic about foreign affairs, played a significant part in guiding what they tried to accomplish abroad.[4]

In designing a foreign policy, Nixon and Kissinger began with the assumption that they were facing a new era in international relations, one in which the power configurations emerging from the Second World War had largely disappeared. "... The rigid bipolar world of the 1940s and 1950s," Nixon declared in 1971, had given way "to the fluidity of a new era of multilateral diplomacy." In the twenty-five years since its establishment, membership in the United Nations had grown from 51 to 127 countries. Further, many of these nations, having "found identity and self-confidence," were "acting autonomously on the world scene." Moreover, even among the Communists, the Stalinist bloc had "fragmented into competing centers of doctrine and power." The President concluded: "It is an increasingly heterogeneous and complex world. ..."

In response to these developments, Nixon and Kissinger wished to encourage local and regional initiatives and foster national independence and self-sufficiency. Other nations were now to "define the nature of their own security and determine the path of their own progress," Nixon stated in 1971. "... Without the foundations of self-help and regional help, American help [to other peoples] will not succeed. ... We in this generation," he also said, "have before us an historic opportunity to turn the transformations of the last twenty-five years into new avenues for peace, and to realize the creative possibilities of a pluralistic world."

At the same time that these initiatives were promoting autonomy and self-sufficiency, they were also meant to create "an enduring structure of peace" through widespread international cooperation. "In coming years," Nixon predicted,

> we will therefore be engaged in a broad and deep discussion with others concerning foreign policy and the nature of our respective roles. ... To promote this dialogue is to improve the prospects that America, together with others, will play its vital part in fashioning a global structure of peace. A peace that will come when all have

a share in its shaping. A peace that will last when all have a stake in its lasting.

The rhetoric and vision were pure Wilson; self-determination and universal cooperation for peace were echoes from World War I.[5]

Kissinger was the administration's most effective spokesman for this grand design. Systematically cultivating an image of himself as an Old World politician who understood the nature of power and how to defend American interests, he captured the imagination of the press and the public. Emphasizing the European idea of geopolitics, offering brilliant monologues on world affairs in his German accent, encouraging the impression of a bon vivant—"Power is an aphrodisiac," he declared—Kissinger created a widespread view of himself as America's first true *Real*politician, capable of meeting every challenge abroad. Watergate, moreover, actually enhanced his hold on the public imagination. "As an individual I led a charmed life," Kissinger writes. "I became the focal point of a degree of support unprecedented for a nonelected official. It was as if the public and Congress felt the national peril instinctively and created a surrogate center around which the national purpose could rally." The objective was to create unified support at home for unprecedented cooperation overseas. And where this could not be done by traditional political means, Nixon and Kissinger relied on covert intimidation or the arbitrary use of executive power.[6]

Although the Nixon-Kissinger "structure of peace" had the virtue of encouraging détente with Russia and China, it was also vague and unrealistic. The proposed "structure of peace," asserts the foreign policy scholar Seyom Brown, "was particularly mystifying, for there was no accompanying design, or even outline, of the characteristics of the international order that was supposed to be produced by these policies."[7] Kis-

singer's call for a grand design, political scientist Stanley Hoffmann points out, was "nowhere accompanied by a description
of the kind of world [he] was trying to bring about." If there
was such a vision, "we are left free to guess what it might have
been." Moreover, in Hoffmann's estimate, a fundamental unrealism marred the Nixon-Kissinger policies: They "assumed
a far greater ability to force the Soviets to play 'our' game than it
was wise to expect," and they focused excessive attention on
Moscow and too little on local conditions elsewhere—"a recipe
for disaster." They failed to see how dividing "the world into
friends and foes resembles the crusaders' itch to divide it into
good and evil," and how teaching " 'our people to face their
permanent responsibility' " would inevitably produce a new
swing toward the sentimentalism in foreign affairs they wished
to end. Ultimately, Hoffmann says, "it is not surprising if
no substantial conception of world order emerges. Religions
are poor at describing paradise: it is with this world that they
deal. And geopolitics is Kissinger's religion—its god is the
balance of power, its dogma is linkage, faith is credibility, the
high priest is a United States acting on Henry Kissinger's
maxims."

Moreover, Hoffmann argues, the Nixon-Kissinger grand
design was little more than an old-style commitment to holding
Russia in check. It "is not at all adequately described by the
word détente," Hoffmann states.

> It was a scheme for universal, permanent, and successful
> containment, marshaling all our instruments of power
> more effectively than before, and aiming at "an end to
> the constant probing for openings and the testing of
> every equilibrium." Kissinger, indeed, appears as the
> Compleat Cold Warrior. To be sure, he would allow for
> some cooperation with Moscow, but as a reward for
> good behavior, as an incentive to moderation, and be-
> cause of the risks in the nuclear age.[8]

If this grand design was more a religion than a scheme for world order, and if it rested more on the old containment idea than on recognition of the new state of international affairs, it was also an outlook spawned by enduring domestic tensions over national character. In describing a new era in which nations would act autonomously along individual national lines, Nixon and Kissinger were projecting old-style American liberalism or Wilsonianism onto the world. It was not only their rhetoric about self-help, self-sufficiency, autonomy, and heterogeneity which suggests that this colored their thinking, but also the fact that their grand design implied an end to the Cold War era and the emergence of a peaceful world in which Americans could return to individual pursuits. At the same time, however, their foreign policy also reflected the attachments both men had to the organizational discipline that had partly shaped their lives. Their inclination, for example, to see the Soviet-American struggle as a permanent fixture on the world scene, and their intolerance of any dissent from White House thinking about foreign questions, suggest the need, as in the immediate past, to make international affairs a vehicle for rationalizing large-scale military-industrial power and domestic conformity. The Nixon-Kissinger foreign policy was the product not only of old and new ideas about world politics but also of clashing views on the character of American life.

To create a "structure of peace" and open the way to greater autonomy for peoples everywhere, Nixon and Kissinger saw the need first to end the war in Vietnam. But a preoccupation with issues external to Vietnam or with making it a test case for American and international principles caused this to be a singularly difficult task. "Psychologists or sociologists may explain some day," Kissinger notes in his memoirs, "what it is about that distant monochromatic land [Vietnam], of green mountains and fields merging with an azure sea, that for millennia has acted as a magnet for foreigners who sought glory there and found frustration, who believed that in its rice fields and jungles some principle was to be established and entered them only to recede in disillusion." While Nixon and Kissinger did not view it this way, they too dealt with Vietnam more as a proving ground for wider goals than as a local state of affairs beyond their control.

Their objective was to make an honorable settlement which would "preserve the independence of South Vietnam," prevent a "terrible" domestic upheaval over the loss of another Asian ally, and prevent miscalculations about American resoluteness that could encourage new aggression and a wider war. In aiming at self-determination for South Vietnam, the administration had little chance of success. From its inception in 1954, South Vietnam had been a client state ruled by unstable governments lacking significant popular support. Since American leaders could neither "preserve" what did not exist—South Vietnamese independence—nor create from the outside what had to develop from within, their policy was fundamentally flawed. Furthermore, their assumption that a Communist victory in South Vietnam would tear apart the United States suggests that they were better at reading the past than at foreseeing the future: American distress over "losing" China did not automatically translate into outrage over Communist power in South Vietnam. Finally, the assumption that abandoning Vietnam to the Communists would endanger international stability and peace was not borne out by subsequent events. All in all, the uniform unrealism of the Nixon-Kissinger policy toward Vietnam suggests that it was other concerns, both at home and overseas, that principally shaped their views.[9]

To achieve an honorable peace in Vietnam, Nixon and Kissinger began by urging Hanoi to negotiate. If the North Vietnamese would agree to withdraw their forces from South Vietnam and restore the demilitarized zone at the seventeenth parallel as a boundary between North and South, the United

States would simultaneously remove its troops. When the North Vietnamese rejected this proposal and launched attacks across the demilitarized zone, the administration retaliated by secretly bombing Communist forces and supply lines in Cambodia. Aware that an avowal of such a campaign would provoke a fresh burst of antiwar activism in the United States and abroad, Nixon decided to hide it from public view. "The reason for secrecy," Kissinger writes, "was to prevent the issue from becoming an international crisis, which would almost certainly have complicated our diplomacy or war effort." And Nixon explains: "My administration was only two months old, and I wanted to provoke as little public outcry as possible at the outset."[10]

In the fall of 1969, after the attempts at negotiation and the Cambodian attacks had brought no significant move toward peace, Nixon announced a program of Vietnamization. In a nationwide speech on November 3, he declared that the United States would go on fighting until the Communists had negotiated a "fair and honorable peace or until the South Vietnamese were able to defend themselves on their own—whichever came first." The pace of American withdrawal was to be linked to the progress of Vietnamization unless Hanoi made such a defense program unnecessary by first agreeing to a settlement. Further, Nixon emphasized that U.S. policy "would not be affected by demonstrations in the streets," and he called upon "the great silent majority of my fellow Americans" to support him in this peace plan. "Let us be united for peace," he concluded. "Let us also be united against defeat. Because let us understand: North Vietnam cannot defeat or humiliate the United States. Only Americans can do that."

Vietnamization was an unrealizable goal. But it served other ends. In pursuing it, Nixon and Kissinger were not only struggling to find a way out of Vietnam, but also playing out inner tensions over domestic affairs: Vietnamization was partly an assertion of the earlier autonomy or self-determination

Nixon wished to regain for Americans. Self-determination for Vietnam echoed Woodrow Wilson's international view as well as the hope for greater self-expression or individual freedom from organized control in the United States. To judge from the public reaction to Nixon's speech, a majority of Americans shared their President's feelings: Of those listening, 77 percent approved of the speech, while the number of telegrams and letters arriving at the White House surpassed that previously received in response to any presidential address. Although much of this reaction was undoubtedly an expression of grass-roots patriotism, the implicit vision of greater freedom for the individual may also have contributed to the positive response.[11]

Continuing unrealism in 1970 reaffirmed the idea that domestic crosscurrents significantly influenced administration policy in Southeast Asia. Though American advisers helped expand and modernize South Vietnam's armed forces and encouraged the restoration of village autonomy through local elections and control of civic and military affairs, Saigon's ability to defend itself or to command the loyalty of South Vietnam's peasants remained well below what was needed to assure survival as an independent state. Despite this and the fact that negotiations with Hanoi remained at a standstill, Nixon announced an additional phased withdrawal of 150,000 U.S. troops beginning in the spring of 1970, an assertion that Vietnamization was working. The announcement was more an expression of his determination to reduce American involvement in the fighting and attraction to self-determination than a realistic assessment of conditions in Vietnam.[12]

Nevertheless, Nixon clung doggedly to Vietnamization. In April 1970, in spite of the likelihood of sharp opposition, he attacked North Vietnamese forces in Cambodia with combined U.S.-South Vietnamese ground units. Though justified as "limited, temporary," and "indispensable for Vietnamization," the assault touched off protests in the United States, which the President tried to counter with a speech. On April 30 he told the country that if "the world's most powerful nation acts like a pitiful helpless giant, the forces of totalitarianism and anarchy will threaten free nations and free institutions throughout the world." He said he would not allow America to prove itself "unworthy to lead the forces of freedom in this critical period in world history. I would rather be a one-term President and do what I believe is right than to be a two-term President at the cost of seeing America become a second-rate power and to see this Nation accept the first defeat in its proud 190-year history."[13]

While polls showed that Nixon's action commanded considerable public support, his speech did not blunt the sense of outrage felt by opponents of the war. A "tidal wave of media and student criticism powerfully affected the Congress" and caused "the very fabric of government" to begin falling apart. In his memoirs, Kissinger explains that he had a special feeling for student protesters, whom "my generation had failed . . . by encouraging self-indulgence and neglecting to provide roots." In a sense, the Nixon-Kissinger policy toward Southeast Asia was an attempt to provide those roots by celebrating the virtues of self-determination and autonomy. But the unrealism of self-determination as a goal for South Vietnam made it impossible for many young people to follow the President's lead.[14]

In the year after the Cambodian "incursion," the administration's policy toward Vietnam did not change. Vietnamization, continuing troop withdrawals, expanded American air attacks, fresh offers to negotiate, and repression of domestic opponents occurred through the first half of 1971. By then public sentiment and the approach of the 1972 election had moved the government to adopt a more flexible stance toward negotiating an end to the war. With 71 percent of Americans saying it was a mistake to have sent troops, with only 31 percent supporting Nixon's Vietnam policy, and with a majority favoring removal of U.S. forces by the end of 1971, even if it meant a Communist victory, the administration offered to pull out all forces within six months after signing a peace agreement which would say nothing about a North Vietnamese withdrawal from the South. Hanoi agreed to renewed peace talks, but they broke down in the fall of 1971 over an American refusal to abandon Nguyen Van Thieu's government in Saigon or to abandon the hope that Vietnamization could still guarantee an independent South Vietnam.[15]

This goal was put in immediate jeopardy in March 1972, when North Vietnam launched a major invasion across the demilitarized zone. Convinced that Hanoi would have to come to terms if Saigon survived this assault and that America's ability to deal with Moscow would be appreciably weakened by a South Vietnamese collapse, Nixon and Kissinger decided to "blunt the offensive." Authorizing massive B-52 attacks on North Vietnam, the President privately declared that "the bastards have never been bombed like they're going to be bombed this time." In June he ordered the mining of Haiphong Harbor and a naval blockade of North Vietnam. With American planes also flying round-the-clock missions against North Vietnamese forces in the South, the campaign simply raised the stalemate to a new level of violence. Consequently, in the summer of 1972 both sides agreed to return to the negotiating table. The administration perceived at least two compelling reasons for such action. First, although domestic opposition to this latest round of bombing had been restrained, it seemed certain that congressional and public action against the war would shortly erupt into new domestic explosions. Secondly, a continuation of the fighting promised further delays in negotiations with Russia and China for the international "structure of peace." Finally, since Nixon and Kissinger continued to hope for a settlement that would support South Vietnam's survival, they saw persuasive reasons to return to the peace talks.[16]

The negotiations moved forward rapidly. Convinced that a settlement now would not jeopardize its long-term goal of

Communist control in the South, that it needed a respite from the fighting, and that it would do better to make peace before Nixon won a mandate to another presidential term, Hanoi agreed to a cease-fire. Under its terms, North Vietnamese troops were to remain in the South, all American forces were to withdraw, and a tripartite electoral commission including the Vietcong was to take responsibility for a future political settlement. When Kissinger presented this agreement to Thieu in October, however, the latter rejected it as inimical to South Vietnam's interests. He refused to sign a cease-fire allowing North Vietnamese forces to stay in the South and recognizing the legitimacy of the Vietcong. Although Nixon advised Thieu that he thought the agreement "the best we will be able to get and that it meets my *absolute* condition—that the GVN must survive as a free country," he refused to override Thieu's objections. He saw a preelection settlement as likely to undermine his margin of victory. A peace agreement in late October would have seemed opportunistic and indifferent to South Vietnamese concerns, should Thieu openly oppose it. While Kissinger declared on October 26 "that peace is at hand," he could not make good on his forecast.[17]

The introduction of Thieu's demands when talks with the North Vietnamese resumed in November produced a new deadlock and an American decision to force both North and South Vietnam into an agreement. In the twelve days between December 17 and 29, 1972, the United States dropped more tons of bombs on North Vietnam than in the entire period from 1969 to 1971. "I don't want any more of this crap about the fact that we couldn't hit this target or that one," Nixon told the Chairman of the Joint Chiefs of Staff. "This is your chance to use military power to win this war, and if you don't, I'll consider you responsible." As for Thieu, he presented him with an additional billion dollars in military equipment, together with "absolute assurances" that if Hanoi broke the peace agreement, he would order "swift and severe retaliatory action." He also gave Thieu an ultimatum: either accept America's lead in the negotiations or "go our separate ways."[18]

Neither of the Vietnams could resist Nixon's pressure. Suffering extensive destruction in Hanoi and Haiphong and numerous civilian casualties, the North Vietnamese agreed to return to the peace table. Unable to survive without continued American support, Thieu also acquiesced to American demands. Consequently, after only six days of negotiation in January, all sides agreed to the terms of the cease-fire as essentially laid down in October. "Peace with honor," a supposedly independent South Vietnam, an America allegedly unashamed of the outcome in Vietnam, and a world presumably convinced that the United States honored its commitments came at a high price. In the four additional years of fighting under Nixon, more than 500,000 Vietnamese and over 20,000 Americans had lost their lives.[19]

On the American side at least, it was all for naught. Twenty-seven months after "peace with honor" came to Vietnam, Saigon fell to Communist arms. Though Nixon promised to "respond with full force" if Hanoi broke the agreements, telling Thieu in March 1973, "You can count on us," he did not reckon with the inhibitions on his power imposed by the Watergate scandal. Indeed, by the end of 1973, Nixon "was virtually powerless" to do anything more in Southeast Asia. With the Congress determined to halt America's "endless support for an endless war," neither Nixon nor Gerald Ford after him could provide significant additional military or financial aid to Saigon. This weakened South Vietnam's capacity and will to resist, and Thieu's government collapsed less than two months after North Vietnam had begun a major offensive in March 1975.

The collapse demonstrated the bankruptcy of Vietnamization. After ten years of massive American aid, the Saigon government lacked the military and political wherewithal to stand on its own. The two other assumptions of the Nixon-Kissinger policy—that losing Vietnam would provoke domestic strife and further Communist aggression—proved to be equally unrealistic. Instead of a bitter debate over who "lost" Vietnam, the end of the struggle produced a collective show of indifference in the United States. "Today it is almost as though the war had never happened," a columnist wrote in October 1975. "Americans have somehow blocked it out of their consciousness. They don't talk about it. They don't talk about its consequences." Likewise, though Cambodia and Laos fell under Communist control, the rest of Southeast Asia remained intact. Moreover, Communist domination of Indochina, far from igniting Soviet and Chinese aggression around the globe, led rather to Sino-Soviet tensions over a Chinese attack in 1979 on Vietnam.

The Nixon-Kissinger failure in Southeast Asia demonstrated that something other than a realistic perspective on Vietnam shaped their policy. Certainly, domestic opposition to the war was a contributing influence. Believing that their political survival depended on an end to the fighting, both men rationalized American withdrawal with unrealistic assertions about Vietnamization or the ability of South Vietnam to defend itself. The portrayal of a stable Vietnam was also aimed at discouraging the belief that the United States had run out on an ally. But in pursuing Vietnamization, it should be pointed out, Nixon and Kissinger did not willfully deceive the public. "We were . . . not just getting out under the cynical cover of a 'decent interval' before the final collapse," Kissinger says. "We hoped for a decent settlement. . . . With the proper mixture of rewards and punishments for Hanoi, we thought we had a reasonable chance to maintain the uneasy equilibrium in Indochina. . . ." The policy was a form of self-deception, of persuading themselves that they had found a satisfactory means of simultaneously ending the war, serving their political interests, and defending national security. But it was also a form of displacement, of making Vietnam the focus of internal tensions over national character which continued to agitate many Americans. Vietnamization was partly a reaffirmation of individual self-determination, a vicarious expression of faith in nineteenth-century American values. But like "the self-making man" of the seventies, Vietnamization was "a cruel hoax," a "cramped," "diminished" version of the individualism that Nixon no longer felt free to pursue in a meaningful way in the United States.[20]

By ending the war in Vietnam, Nixon and Kissinger freed themselves to meet what they described as "a new era of international relations" with "a new approach to foreign policy." The postwar period, they said, was now over. The years of American military predominance, anticommunist nations' dependence on the United States, and a unified Communist bloc had passed. Instead, the world now faced a Soviet-American military balance of power and insistence by Western, Communist, and newly emerging states on independence from superpower control. Similarly, the mood in the United States had changed. Changing conditions abroad coupled with disillusionment over Vietnam had shattered postwar American convictions about containment. In light of all this, Nixon and Kissinger urged the need for a new international order or structure of peace that would reduce Cold War tensions and create a fresh foreign policy consensus in the United States.

As it emerged during Nixon's first term, this was the policy of détente—the opening to China and the attempt to reach a stable accommodation with the USSR. Though both initiatives grew out of a realistic perception of a need to deal with the two Communist superpowers in more conciliatory ways, they also rested on traditional American assumptions about individualism, independence, and self-determination. Indeed, a close reading of the Nixon-Kissinger policies toward China and Russia suggests that they were as much a reaffirmation of old American habits as a sincere attempt to create a new structure of peace.

In February 1972, in an effort to achieve a rapprochement,

Nixon traveled to Peking. Ostensibly, his objective was to end twenty-two years of mutual hostility and join the United States and China in curbing Moscow's "geopolitical ambitions." But the trip was also a celebration of old American values. "What brings us together," Nixon told Chairman Mao, "is a recognition of a new situation in the world and a recognition on our part that what is important is not a nation's internal political philosophy. What is important is its policy toward the rest of the world and toward us." He told Chou En-lai: "We know you believe deeply in your principles, and we believe deeply in our principles. We do not ask you to compromise your principles, just as you would not ask us to compromise ours." In short, independence and self-determination for individual nations were the time-honored American way of life. "So, let us . . . ," Nixon declared in a banquet toast, "start a long march together, not in lockstep, but on different roads leading to the same goal, the goal of building a world structure of peace and justice. . . ." He proposed in another toast: ". . . We join the Chinese people, we the American people, in our dedication to this principle: That never again shall foreign domination, foreign occupation, be visited upon . . . any part of China or any independent country in this world."

The Shanghai communiqué issued at the close of the talks echoed the theme of self-determination. Acknowledging that they could not then settle existing differences, they agreed to disagree. ". . . The communiqué," Nixon recalls in his memoirs, "broke diplomatic ground by stating frankly the significant differences between the two sides on major issues rather than smoothing them over." On the question of Taiwan, for example, the Chinese described it as their province and its liberation as China's internal affair. While the United States would not agree to abandon Taiwan, it acknowledged that the island was a part of China and urged a peaceful settlement of the issue "by the Chinese themselves." On the larger matter of Asian and Pacific security, however, both sides agreed to oppose "efforts by any other country or group of countries to establish . . .

hegemony." This, Nixon says, was a clear statement of American and Chinese opposition to the denial of self-determination or great power domination of Asia. The communiqué, Kissinger later said, was "a symbol to the world and our two peoples." As such, it had to squelch criticism from the conservative right in America—not only by avoiding suggestions that the United States would abandon Taiwan but also by trumpeting classical liberalism, the principles of individualism and national self-determination.

Kissinger, for all his determination to eliminate sentimental considerations from his dealings with China, could not resist the impulse to apply traditional American standards. Mao Tse-tung was a study in "concentrated willpower. . . . He dominated the room . . . by exuding in almost tangible form the overwhelming drive to prevail." He was the consummate self-made man. "[His] very presence testified to an act of will. His was the extraordinary saga of a peasant's son from southern China who conceived the goal of taking over the Kingdom of Heaven, attracted followers, led them on the long march of six thousand miles, which less than a third survived, and from a totally unfamiliar territory fought first the Japanese and then the Nationalist government, until finally he was ensconced in the Imperial City. . . . There were no trappings that could account for the sense of power Mao conveyed. . . . [He] emanated vibrations of strength and power and will." When Kissinger told a Chinese official that "The relations of our two countries were on a sound basis because neither asked anything of the other," Mao rebutted this "banality," as Kissinger himself subsequently called it. "If neither side had anything to ask from the other, why would you be coming to Peking? If neither side had anything to ask, then why . . . would we want to receive you and the President?" Mao would not let this exercise in wishful thinking pass. Nixon's presence in Peking was an ironic demonstration of the fact that the era of American self-sufficiency was over.[21]

Yet the implicit promise of rapprochement with China was

a new world order which would ultimately free Americans from the constraints of the Cold War—the external inhibitions on renewed autonomy in the United States. Indeed, the insistent description of the new Sino-American relationship as an exercise in self-determination demonstrated that the Nixon-Kissinger policy aimed not only at a new equilibrium abroad but also at resurgent autonomy at home. Détente with the Soviets rested on the same hopes.

The basis of the Nixon administration's policy toward the Soviet Union, Kissinger explains in his memoirs, was the belief that the Soviets have a distinctive system with which we could negotiate meaningful agreements. Past administrations had assumed either that Moscow was reforming itself to become more like the West or that basic changes in Russian behavior could be forced by a "liturgical belligerence, as if the emphatic trumpeting of anti-Communism would suffice to make the walls come tumbling down." Both the advocates and the opponents of negotiation "agreed in their fundamental assumptions," Kissinger pointed out:

> They were in accord that an effective settlement presupposed a change in the Soviet system. They were at one in thinking that Western diplomacy should seek to influence Soviet internal developments. . . . They differed primarily about the issue of timing. The opponents of negotiation maintained that the Soviet change of heart was still in the future, while the advocates claimed that it had already taken place. . . .

By contrast, Nixon and Kissinger assumed that the Soviet Union, like the United States, was a unique state that would maintain its separate identity but would also support a new world order compatible with Soviet interests. The principle of autonomy, as with China, was to be a hallmark of fresh dealings with the USSR.[22]

Nixon and Kissinger echoed this theme at the summit talks in Moscow in May 1972. "I know that my reputation is one of being a very hard-line, cold-war oriented, anticommunist," Nixon told the Soviet leaders. "It is true that I have a strong belief in our system . . . but at the same time I respect those who believe just as strongly in their own systems. There must be room in this world for two great nations with different systems to live together and work together. We cannot do this, however, by mushy sentimentality or by glossing over differences which exist." In discussing Vietnam, the unsentimental, realistic Nixon declared that ". . . Our goal is the same as yours. We are not trying to impose a settlement or a government on anybody." After a three-hour discussion on Vietnam, in which the Russians made it clear that they would not sacrifice the gains they hoped to achieve at the summit for the sake of North Vietnam, Nixon and Soviet Premier Alexei Kosygin agreed that it was a good omen for future relations that after so much "hard-hitting" talk, "we could still have a relaxed and personally friendly conversation over dinner. . . . We must recognize our differences and discuss them honestly," Nixon declared. During the summit, Kissinger echoed the President's feeling that the starting point for better relations was a recognition of enduring Russian distinctiveness. "A glimpse of that ocean of land that is Russia" reminded Kissinger that invading hordes had streamed across this expanse over the centuries. "In the end, each was overcome by the enduring patience of a people stubbornly clinging to its native soil and preserving its own identity amidst all violence and cruelty—even that inflicted by its own leaders."[23]

Yet for all this talk of differences, Nixon could not resist the belief that the Russian leaders were just like him and other self-made Americans. "Brezhnev's office was the same room in which I had first met Khrushchev, thirteen years before," Nixon recalls in his memoirs. ". . . I was sure that neither of us, standing shoulder to shoulder in the kitchen at the American

Exhibition thirteen years before, had imagined that we would one day be meeting at the summit as leaders of our countries." And Nixon told Kissinger:

> We constantly misjudge the Russians because we judge them by their manners, etc., and we do not look beyond to see what kind of character and strength they really have. Anybody who gets to the top of the Communist hierarchy and stays at the top has to have a great deal of political ability and a great deal of toughness. All three of the Soviet leaders have this in spades, and Brezhnev in particular. . . . Like an American labor leader, he has what it takes. . . .

He also reminded Nixon of "a big Irish labor boss, or perhaps an analogy to Mayor [Richard] Daley [of Chicago] would be more in order. . . ." But whomever he called to mind, he was the consummate self-made man with "a great deal of animal magnetism and drive which comes through whenever you meet him."

What also appealed to the two Americans about the Russians was their freedom to act without substantial bureaucratic and public constraints. During World War II, Nixon told Brezhnev, differences between American and Soviet subordinates "were usually overcome at the top level" by Stalin and FDR. "That is the kind of relationship that I should like to establish with the General Secretary. . . . If we leave all the decisions to the bureaucrats, we will never achieve any progress. . . . They would simply bury us in paper!" Brezhnev "laughed heartily and slapped his palm on the table." Kissinger notes condescendingly: "Neither of the leaders having achieved high office through their mastery of detail, the only agreement they could reach at this point was on the untrustworthiness and inadequacy of their bureaucracies."[24]

Kissinger, however, was a staunch advocate of this view. Determined to run foreign policy from the White House, Nixon and Kissinger consistently bypassed the bureaucracy—the many officials in the State, Defense, and Treasury departments and the CIA responsible for the technical details of foreign affairs. For Kissinger, Stanley Hoffmann writes, "the job of the U.S. bureaucracies was to give him the data for the decisions he and Nixon would make, and to carry out these decisions." The summit meetings in Peking and Moscow, for example, were arranged without the State Department's participation, and although Secretary of State William Rogers attended both conferences, he and his advisers played distinctly limited parts. Further, at the Moscow summit, Nixon and Kissinger made no direct use of the U.S. experts in Helsinki who had negotiated the Strategic Arms Limitation Treaty (SALT). Because they failed to bring these authorities to Moscow until it was time to sign the treaty, some critics have complained that the Russians gained strategic advantages over the United States. More a matter of personal style than a rational device for making an effective foreign policy, the Nixon-Kissinger disdain for the bureaucracy was a case study in how self-made men can use power. "Kissinger's emphasis in *White House Years*," the historian Alan Henrikson writes,

> is much more on motives, intentions, and purposes—at the level of the individual—than on effects, results, and outcomes—at the larger historical level. . . . Kissinger appears to believe, perhaps without fully realizing the selfish and undemocratic implications of doing so, that the significance of a political act lies in its meaning for the actor himself, and *only* for that person.[25]

However much their impulse to see the Russians as an autonomous people was the product of a personal perspective, it was also a more realistic means of dealing with them. By assuming that they were a separate nation with special interests which could be accommodated for the sake of peace, Nixon and Kissinger achieved success at the summit. To assure that the U.S. rapprochement with China did not turn into a full-scale alliance, that the West would accept the postwar boundaries in Eastern Europe, and that they would improve their economic well-being through reduced military spending and greater trade with the United States, the Soviets agreed to an arms limitation treaty, wider commercial exchange, and an avoidance of international tensions which could play havoc with Soviet-American détente and the new structure of peace. Kissinger accurately describes the summit as "a major success for American policy. . . . The fundamental achievement was to sketch the outline on which coexistence between the democracies and the Soviet system must be based . . . : a willingness to confront Soviet expansionism and a simultaneous readiness to mark out a cooperative future."

Still, as he freely acknowledges, the Nixon administration never fully implemented this vision or strategy. Watergate or "the erosion of Nixon's domestic base," Kissinger argues, "prevented the full fruition of the prospects then before us, not only in nurturing U.S.-Soviet relations but more generally in developing a new structure of international relations." He exaggerates the influence of Watergate and underestimates other difficulties in the way of détente, such as Nixon-Kissinger policies which intensified Soviet suspicions of the United States. Indeed, at the same time that they moved toward accommodation with the Russians, Nixon and Kissinger demonstrated an affinity for a reflexive anticommunism in Asia, Latin America, and the Middle East which undermined détente. Even the most rational approach to the Russians did not ensure a softening of their deeply embedded fears. But the continuation of a Cold War orthodoxy based more on unresolved internal tensions over national self-image than on genuine foreign threats was bound to drive the two sides farther apart.[26]

While Nixon and Kissinger pressed for détente, a peaceful world of autonomous peoples, they also practiced a familiar globalism, the containment of Soviet power and the insistence on a worldwide Communist threat requiring a unified response in the United States. The reaction to the Indian-Pakistani conflict over Bangladesh in 1971 is an example of this enduring perspective.

For Nixon and Kissinger, the Indian-Pakistani War was less a local struggle than a challenge to détente and the emerging structure of peace. It was a conflict between client states that could unsettle administration plans to play China off against the USSR and create a new world order. "India's opportunity to humiliate Pakistan," Kissinger writes,

> was also the Soviet Union's opportunity to humiliate China. . . . The Soviets encouraged India to exploit Pakistan's travail in part to deliver a blow to our system of alliances, in even greater measure to demonstrate Chinese impotence. Since it was a common concern about Soviet power that had driven Peking and Washington together, a demonstration of American irrelevance would severely strain our precarious new relationship with China.

Further, the Soviet-Indian action threatened stability in the Middle East and American credibility with other allies. A successful Soviet-backed war in South Asia also would have encouraged Egypt to settle its grievances by war and "would have disheartened allies like Iran and Turkey, which sympathized with Pakistan, had the same commitment from us [as Pakistan had to its security], and looked to our reaction as a token of American steadiness in potential crises affecting them." This was the rationale for the administration's tilt toward Pakistan.[27]

It produced a sharp outcry at home. Convinced that Pakistan was responsible for the crisis, in which it was brutally repressing Bengali rebels, and that the struggle was essentially a local or regional affair, in which the United States should not interfere, State Department officials, congressional leaders, and liberal journalists vigorously opposed administration policy. Critics objected that the Nixon-Kissinger approach to the conflict was essentially a throwback to a Cold War orthodoxy that had involved the nation in Vietnam. The point was well taken. Both men saw Pakistan as an ally the United States needed to support if other key countries were to continue relying on its word. "The dismemberment of Pakistan by military force and its eventual destruction without any American reaction," Kissinger believes, "thus would have profound international repercussions." But his and Nixon's linkage of Pakistan's fate to so much else in world affairs was unpersuasive. That other nations in the Middle East and elsewhere would use events in South Asia as a basis for their own actions was a highly questionable proposition which took insufficient account of national and regional influences.

Yet even if this assumption was flawed, it appealed to Nixon and Kissinger as a means of rebuilding a foreign policy consensus and reaffirming an organization ethic in the United States. Kissinger's discussion of the "India-Pakistan crisis of 1971," for example, is as much a consideration of these concerns as of events abroad. "It was nearly impossible to implement" their Pakistan policy, he complains, "because our departments operated on different premises. . . . The result was a bureaucratic stalemate in which White House and State Department representatives dealt with each other as competing sovereign entities, not members of the same team. . . ." Kissinger adds: "The history of the 'tilt' is less a tale of Presidential self-will than of the complexity of managing a modern government. . . . Who was right in this dispute is irrelevant; Presidents must be able to count on having their views accepted even if these run counter to bureaucratic preconceptions." When the administration could not bend its opponents to its will, it resorted to intimidation or police-state tactics—spying on its own officials, for example. One would think, the journalist Tad

Szulc points out, that such action "would be ordered only under the most critical conditions affecting national security in its most serious sense. But the chronology of events . . . does not suggest that such critical conditions ever existed. What *did* exist was a police-state mentality in the White House."[28]

If dangers abroad cannot fully account for these actions, one may view them as partly an expression of internal fears— the need of men torn between inner- and other-directed impulses to see threats requiring conformity to an organizational standard. Indeed, it is striking that for all its contempt for unimaginative bureaucrats, the Nixon administration insisted on a greater measure of institutional conformity than ever before asked in American history. Simultaneously drawn to and fearful of an outdated autonomy with which they and the country could no longer live, Nixon and Kissinger rationalized the need for organized discipline by pointing to exaggerated foreign threats. In this, they continued a pattern set by their predecessors in the previous twenty years.

Their fear of communism in Chile, for example, was much out of proportion to the threat. In 1962 and 1964 Presidents Kennedy and Johnson had authorized nearly $4,000,000 in expenditures by the CIA to prevent Salvador Allende, leader of a left-wing coalition, from gaining power in Chile. Beginning in 1970, the Nixon administration extended and intensified this effort to control Chilean politics. Convinced that an Allende victory would mean a Marxist government, which would align itself with the Soviet Union and Cuba and threaten U.S. interests throughout Latin America, Nixon and Kissinger felt justified in doing all in their power to keep Chile in the anticommunist camp. "If Allende should win, and with Castro in Cuba," Nixon quoted an Italian businessman approvingly, "you will have in Latin America a red sandwich. And, eventually, it will all be red."

The State Department and some members of the CIA were skeptical of this conclusion. A CIA report in the fall of 1970, for example, "concluded that the United States had no vital interests within Chile, the world military balance of power would not be significantly altered by an Allende regime, and an Allende victory in Chile would not pose any likely threat to the peace of the region." At worst, "an Allende victory would threaten hemispheric cohesion and would represent a psychological setback to the U.S. as well as a definite advance for the Marxist idea." In August 1971, nine months after Allende had come to power, America's military intelligence agencies described Allende as charting an independent, nationalistic course committed to a policy of nonalignment. They did not think that he or the Chilean armed forces would tolerate a permanent Soviet military force in Chile. In September 1973, almost three years after Allende had gained power, and only a week before a military coup overturned his rule, these same agencies saw him as presenting no "Marxist danger," and predicted "a political standoff" in the country. After the coup, in which Allende died, a Senate Select Committee on Intelligence Activities concluded that "the more extreme fears about the effects of Allende's election were ill-founded; there never was a significant threat of a Soviet military presence; the 'export' of Allende's revolution was limited, and its value as a model more restricted still. . . ."

"Nevertheless," the report also noted, "those fears, often exaggerated, appear to have activated officials in Washington." This was shorthand for the fact that the Nixon administration did all it could to topple Allende. Supplying money to political opponents, suspending economic assistance, discouraging international financial institutions from offering fresh credits, and encouraging the Chilean military to act against Allende's regime, the administration helped make a coup possible. Publicly, Nixon would not let on that the United States was working to overthrow a legitimately constituted government. On the contrary, in a 1972 foreign policy report to the Congress, he declared that "the hemisphere community is big enough, mature enough and tolerant enough to accept a diversity of national approaches to human goals. We therefore deal realistically with governments as they are—right and left. . . . We respect the hemispheric principle of non-intervention."

This was not simply hypocrisy on Nixon's part. He believed sincerely in this principle of autonomy or self-determination for nations. But it also frightened him; the risks of true diversity were too great. Just as the progressives, for all their talk of individualism, were not ready to abandon the benefits flowing to them from the new large-scale organizations of their day, so Nixon could not let go of concentrated power and organized togetherness in his time. Indeed, the pattern was to preach autonomy and then find reasons why it could not work. In terms of this world view, Chile was a dangerous regime in America's backyard and this was reason enough to impose firm organizational discipline, with no disagreement or dissent allowed. In 1970, for example, when State Department officials expressed doubts about administration policy in Latin America, Kissinger declared their statement "an act of treason."[29]

A similar pattern operated in policy toward the Middle East. As with South Asia and Latin America, Nixon and Kissinger thought of the area principally in terms of Soviet-American tensions. "The difference between our goal and the Soviet goal in the Middle East," the President told Secretary of State Rogers in 1969, "is very simple but fundamental. *We* want peace. *They* want the Middle East." Nixon declared in 1970: "We are *for* Israel because Israel in our view is the only state in the Mideast which is *pro*-freedom and an effective opponent to Soviet expansion." And he told the Israeli ambassador in August 1970: ". . . The Soviets are the main cause of Middle East tensions, and . . . if they were removed from the situation Israel would be able to handle matters without difficulty." Explosive tensions over the Palestinians and boundaries made this unlikely. To be sure, Arab threats to Israel without Soviet support would have been less dangerous to world peace, but the "main cause of . . . tensions" sprang more from local conditions than from Soviet involvement in the region.

Though Kissinger had a more sophisticated understanding of the complexities of the region than Nixon did, he nevertheless shared the President's belief that it was "essential to reduce the scope of Soviet adventurist policies in the Middle East." To this end, he initially tried to negotiate a Middle East settlement with the Russians, aiming at the same time to tie these discussions to broader concerns, especially Vietnam. While this first effort came to nothing, Nixon and Kissinger continued through Nixon's term to see the Middle East largely as a problem in Soviet-American relations.

This perspective was to mislead the administration on more than one occasion. The conflict between Syria and Jordan in September 1970, for example, proved to be more a local struggle than an extension of Soviet designs. The lesson of that bloodshed, some American officials concluded, was that Middle East "solutions were possible only if they were based on the 'dynamics of the area.' " But Nixon and Kissinger, who continued to focus on Soviet influence, refused to concede this point—believing, for example, that an Arab-Israeli peace settlement depended more on Russia than on Egypt, the most important Arab military power. Consequently, in 1972, after President Anwar Sadat had expelled Russian advisers from Egypt and made overtures to the United States to take a new initiative for peace, Nixon and Kissinger turned them aside. ". . . Opportunities were missed (and the October [1973] war made more likely)," Stanley Hoffmann points out, "partly by Kissinger's fixation on the Soviet angle of the Middle Eastern problem, partly by the simple fact that the summits and Vietnam left him little time, partly by the fact that 1972 was an election year. . . ." Moreover, despite strong indications that Egypt and Syria would attack Israel sometime in the second half of 1973, the American leaders refused to draw that conclusion. Distracted by Watergate and convinced that Soviet commitments to détente would prevent such an attack, they underestimated Egyptian and Syrian freedom to follow their own lead.[30]

A central element of Middle East policy making, as with most of Nixon's diplomacy, was tension between the White House and the State Department. Joseph Sisco, assistant secretary of state for Near Eastern and South Asian affairs, Kissinger writes, "spent as much time mediating between Rogers and me as between the Arabs and Israelis." Both the White House and the State Department agreed that the nub of the issue in the Middle East was to blunt Soviet influence. The disagreement was over how to do it, with each side implying that failure to follow its approach would strengthen Russian power in a vital region and undermine the security of the United States. The battle was over which side could appropriate the Soviet threat to compel conformity to its design. Although Russian ambitions in the Middle East were a reality that sensible leaders could not ignore, preoccupation with a new world order and a need to rationalize an undifferentiated approach to internal affairs or to legitimize adherence to a common standard moved the Nixon administration to exaggerate the threat.[31]

If Nixon and Kissinger shared a greater cosmopolitanism of outlook than most of their immediate predecessors and possibly all of their more remote ones, they nevertheless partly shaped foreign policy in the same way other U.S. leaders had since the end of the nineteenth century. As was true of these earlier Americans, tensions over national character or self-image, the clash between individualism and organized conformity, autonomy and centralized control, remained important influences on actions overseas. Displacing internal concerns onto the world outside, before 1945 the country turned relations with other nations partly into a quest for democracy, freedom, personal fulfillment, social harmony, and universal justice. The war with Spain, dealings with other American republics, involvements in East Asia, World Wars I and II—all became symbolic extensions of domestic hopes and fears. After World War II, however, when a more crowded, organized, and constricted society seemed fixed on the national scene, the country quieted its longings for a simpler, freer time by using foreign affairs to persuade itself that a nineteenth-century style of life had permanently passed. Torn between the advantages of the modern and the allure of the old, Americans exaggerated dangers abroad to ease their acceptance of new habits at home.

Yet, as the record makes clear, such displacement, whether in the Spanish-American War or in the building of a structure of peace, is an unconstructive way to deal with international relations. No one sensitive to the difficulties involved in the national shift to modern currents of behavior would deny the usefulness of illusions in easing America's way into the twentieth century. Nevertheless, it seems essential to recognize that the American style of unrealism in foreign policy is not a sound way to assure the national well-being. Using outside events in even limited ways for internal purposes will neither solve domestic difficulties nor serve our external aims. Indeed, until we detach problems abroad from our social dilemmas at home, we will continue to jeopardize the security and peace we yearn for in world affairs.

Notes

Introduction

1. George Kennan, "On Nuclear War," *The New York Review of Books,* vol. XXVIII (January 21, 1982), p. 12.

2. Bailyn is quoted in Michael P. Kammen, ed. *The Past Before Us: Contemporary Historical Writing in the United States* (Ithaca, N.Y., 1980), p. 38.

3. Fritz Stern, *The Politics of Cultural Despair: A Study in the Rise of Germanic Ideology* (New York, 1956 ed.), p. 12.

4. Richard Hofstadter, *The Paranoid Style in American Politics and Other Essays* (New York, 1967), p. ix.

5. David Riesman, *Individualism Reconsidered* (Glencoe, Ill., 1954), pp. 112–13.

Chapter 1

1. For the Populist platform see Samuel Eliot Morison, Henry Steele Commager, and William E. Leuchtenburg, *A Concise History of the American Republic* (New York, 1979), p. 439. The Cleveland quote is in Ernest R. May, *Imperial Democracy: The Emergence of America as a Great Power* (New York, 1961), p. 91; May's conclusion is on p. 268.

2. See Walter LaFeber, *The New Empire: An Interpretation of American Expansion, 1865–1898* (Ithaca, N.Y., 1963), especially pp. 40, 46, 106, 181.

3. Lee Benson, "The Historical Background of Turner's Frontier Essay," *Agricultural History,* vol. 25 (April 1951), pp. 59–82, especially p. 67 ff. LaFeber, *The New Empire,* pp. 60–80.

4. Ruth Miller Elson, *Guardians of Tradition: American Schoolbooks of the Nineteenth Century* (Lincoln, Neb., 1964), pp. 298–99, 160–61. For foreign influences encouraging American expansion in the 1870s, 1880s, and 1890s, see Ernest R. May, *American Imperialism: A Speculative Essay* (New York, 1968), chaps. VI and VII.

5. James D. Hart, *The Popular Book: A History of America's Literary Taste* (New York, 1950), pp. 169–71, 174–77. James A. Field, Jr., "American Imperialism: The Worst Chapter in Almost Any Book," *The American Historical Review,* vol. 83 (June 1978), emphasizes Strong's concern with domestic matters, p. 647; Elson, *Guardians of Tradition,* chap. 8.

6. Field, Jr., "American Imperialism," pp. 644–68; the quote is from p. 654. Thomas A. Bailey, *A Diplomatic History of the American People,* 9th ed. (New York, 1974), p. 391.

7. LaFeber, *The New Empire,* chap. VI, emphasizes the economic considerations. May, *Imperial Democracy,* p. 33 ff., sees the Venezuela crisis as the result of political and moral forces. Richard Hofstadter, "Cuba, the Philippines, and Manifest Destiny," in *The Paranoid Style in American Politics and Other Essays,* stresses the emotional pressures; the quotes are on pp. 150 and 154.

8. See Bailey, *A Diplomatic History of the American People,* p. 440, for the Lodge quote. For the rest, see Charles S. Campbell, *The Transformation of American Foreign Relations, 1865–1900* (New York, 1976), chap. 11, especially pp. 206, 211–13.

9. May, *Imperial Democracy,* chap. XV. Margaret Leech, *In the Days of McKinley* (New York, 1959), chap. 7, especially pp. 151–53.

10. May, *Imperial Democracy,* chaps. VII, VIII, and X; see pp. 77, 81 for the quotes.

11. *Ibid.,* pp. 133–43.

12. Gerald F. Linderman, *The Mirror of War: American Society and the Spanish-American War* (Ann Arbor, Mich., 1974), chap. II. May, *Imperial Democracy,* pp. 144–45.

13. Linderman, *Mirror of War,* pp. 24–34. May, *Imperial Democracy,* pp. 146–47, 151–59. Hofstadter, "Cuba, the Philippines, and Manifest Destiny," pp. 156–58.

14. For a discussion of newspaper reaction, see Joseph E. Wisan, *The Cuban Crisis as Reflected in the New York Press* (New York, 1934). See Elinor Fuchs and Joyce Antler, *Year One of the Empire* (Boston, 1973), p. 6, for the headlines.

15. For the argument that the war grew out of American domestic tensions, see Hofstadter, "Cuba, the Philippines, and Manifest Destiny," pp. 158–61. Also see Linderman, *Mirror of War,* pp. 4–8, who agrees that the war was a way to strike out at America's business interests.

16. John Higham, "The Reorientation of American Culture in the 1890's," in *The Origins of Modern Consciousness,* ed. John Weiss (Detroit, Mich., 1965), pp. 25–33.

17. Linderman, *Mirror of War*, pp. 91–98. Higham, "Reorientation of American Culture in the 1890's," pp. 37–40. Morton Keller, *Affairs of State: Public Life in Late Nineteenth Century America* (Cambridge, Mass., 1977), pp. 593–94. William E. Leuchtenburg, "Progressivism and Imperialism: The Progressive Movement and American Foreign Policy, 1898–1916," in *Essays in American Diplomacy,* ed. Armin Rappaport (New York, 1967), p. 181. Hofstadter, "Cuba, the Philippines, and Manifest Destiny," pp. 160, 163–64.

18. Linderman, *Mirror of War*, pp. 115, 120–27. Elson, *Guardians of Tradition*, pp. 150–56. Leuchtenburg, "Progressivism and Imperialism," p. 174.

19. Walter Millis, *The Martial Spirit* (Cambridge, Mass., 1931), pp. 154–59. Linderman, *Mirror of War,* chaps. III–IV, especially pp. 62–64, 82–84, 105–07.

20. Theodore Roosevelt, *The Rough Riders* (New York, 1961 ed.), pp. 27–28, 37–38, 43–45, 62–63, 86–92, 110. Linderman, *Mirror of War,* pp. 70, 94–95, 106, 110–13.

21. Frank Freidel, *The Splendid Little War* (New York, 1962 ed.), chaps. 3 and 5. Millis, *Martial Spirit,* pp. 150–52, 159–60, 211–15, 241–49, 255–58.

22. Freidel, *Splendid Little War,* chaps. 7–9, especially pp. 118–19, also pp. 23–30 and 164–65. Millis, *Martial Spirit,* chap. X.

23. For the Dunne quote, see Thomas C. Leonard, *Above the Battle: War-making in America from Appomattox to Versailles* (New York, 1978), pp. 61–62.

24. For the Hay quote, see Freidel, *Splendid Little War,* p. 9.

25. Hofstadter, "Cuba, the Philippines, and Manifest Destiny," pp. 169–74. Julius W. Pratt, *Expansionists of 1898: The Acquisition of Hawaii and the Spanish Islands* (Chicago, 1964 ed.), p. 319. May, *Imperial Democracy,* pp. 244, 248–49, 255–59. H. Wayne Morgan, *William McKinley and His America* (Syracuse, N.Y., 1963), pp. 403–04, 407–08.

26. For the influence of the imperial elite, see Hofstadter, "Cuba, the Philippines, and Manifest Destiny," pp. 162–68. For the shift in the business community and the economic influences, see Pratt, *Expansionists of 1898,* chap. 7; and LaFeber, *The New Empire,* especially pp. 407–17.

27. Frederick Merk, *Manifest Destiny and Mission in American History: A Reinterpretation* (New York, 1963), pp. 228–66. Pratt, *Expansionists of 1898,* chap. I. Julius W. Pratt, "The Large Policy of 1898," *Mississippi Valley Historical Review,* vol. XIX (September 1932), pp. 219–42. Julius W. Pratt, "The Ideology of American Expansion," in *Essays in Honor of William E. Dodd by His Former Students at the University of Chicago,* ed. Avery Craven (Chicago, 1935), pp. 335–53.

28. Hofstadter, "Cuba, the Philippines, and Manifest Destiny," emphasizes the "psychic" influences. The foreign influences are described by May in *American Imperialism*.

29. For the James and Watterson quotes, see Hofstadter, "Cuba, the Philippines, and Manifest Destiny," pp. 161–62, 180–81.

30. For these quotes, see May, *Imperial Democracy*, pp. 248, 257; Pratt, *Expansionists of 1898*, pp. 355–56; May, *American Imperialism*, pp. 186, 196, 227.

31. For attitudes in the United States toward imperialism after the annexation of the Philippines, I have leaned on May, *American Imperialism*, pp. 206–23; also see his chap. V. The explanation, however, of why the Filipino uprising had the impact it did on imperialist thought is my own. For anti-imperialism, see Robert L. Beisner, *Twelve Against Empire: The Anti-Imperialists, 1898–1900* (New York, 1968), and E. Berkeley Tompkins, *Anti-Imperialism in the United States: The Great Debate, 1890–1920* (Philadelphia, 1970).

32. On the search for solutions to American domestic problems, 1877–1920, see Robert H. Wiebe, *The Search for Order, 1877–1920* (New York, 1967). On Herbert Croly, see Leuchtenburg, "Progressivism and Imperialism," pp. 184–85.

Chapter 2

1. Quoted in David McCullough, *The Path Between the Seas: The Creation of the Panama Canal, 1870–1914* (New York, 1977), p. 490.

2. On progressivism, see Morison, Commager, and Leuchtenburg, *Concise History of the American Republic*, pp. 499–501. On TR, see John Morton Blum, *The Republican Roosevelt*, 2nd ed. (Cambridge, Mass., 1977), pp. 56, 140; also see pp. x, 63. Richard Hofstadter, *The American Political Tradition* (New York, 1948), pp. 230–31.

3. Blum, *The Republican Roosevelt*, pp. 125–27, 137. Robert E. Osgood, *Ideals and Self-Interest in America's Foreign Relations* (Chicago, 1953), pp. 66–70, 75–78, 88–91. Bailey, *Diplomatic History of the American People*, p. 515.

4. Leuchtenburg, "Progressivism and Imperialism," describes progressive militancy in foreign policy; on the distinction between populist and progressive imperialism, see Richard Hofstadter, *The Age of Reform* (New York, 1955), pp. 270–73. For the argument that progressivism was fundamentally concerned with establishing social and economic order, see Wiebe, *The Search for Order*, especially chaps. 6–7. Also see Blum's comment that, whatever the disagreements among historians about progressivism, they all agree that TR and progressives like him aimed "to discipline the

uncertainties of American life by imposing upon it . . . consolidation, stability, and control," *The Republican Roosevelt,* p. xi.

5. On the moral impulse behind progressivism, see Hofstadter, *Age of Reform,* especially pp. 5, 9–11.

6. See Howard K. Beale, *Theodore Roosevelt and the Rise of America to World Power* (New York, 1962, Collier Books ed.), pp. 101–08. McCullough, *Path Between the Seas,* pp. 255–59.

7. *Ibid.,* pp. 329–41. On progressive antagonism to big business and TR's appeal to this sentiment, see Hofstadter, *Age of Reform,* pp. 134, 163–72, 213 ff. George Mowry, *The Era of Theodore Roosevelt and the Birth of Modern America, 1900–1912* (New York, 1958), pp. 130–31. Hofstadter, *American Political Tradition,* p. 224.

8. Mowry, *Era of Theodore Roosevelt,* pp. 150–52. McCullough, *Path Between the Seas,* pp. 345, 350–51, chap. 13, and pp. 387–94.

9. Bailey, *Diplomatic History of the American People,* pp. 494–95. Mowry, *Era of Theodore Roosevelt,* pp. 154–55. McCullough, *Path Between the Seas,* pp. 380–86. *The Works of Theodore Roosevelt: National Edition: State Papers as Governor and President, 1899–1909,* vol. 15 (New York, 1926), pp. 202–14. *Addresses and Presidential Messages of Theodore Roosevelt, 1902–1904* (New York, 1904), pp. 427–63.

10. For the contradictions in progressivism, see Hofstadter, *Age of Reform,* pp. 210–12, 134, 214–15.

11. Mowry, *Era of Theodore Roosevelt,* p. 158. Alfred H. Lewis, ed., *A Compilation of the Messages and Speeches of Theodore Roosevelt, 1901–1905* (Washington, D.C., 1906), p. 47. Elting E. Morison and John M. Blum, eds., *The Letters of Theodore Roosevelt,* vol. III (8 vols.; Cambridge, Mass., 1951–54), p. 116. *The Works of Theodore Roosevelt: State Papers,* vol. 15, p. 116.

12. Mowry, *Era of Theodore Roosevelt,* pp. 156–57. Dana G. Munro, *Intervention and Dollar Diplomacy in the Caribbean, 1900–1921* (Princeton, N.J., 1964), pp. 65–76. For the point about the "lesson" of 1898, see May, *Imperial Democracy,* p. 269.

13. Mowry, *Era of Theodore Roosevelt,* pp. 158–59. Munro, *Intervention and Dollar Diplomacy,* pp. 77–94. William H. Harbaugh, *The Life and Times of Theodore Roosevelt* (New York, 1975, new rev. ed.), pp. 187–90. *Letters of Theodore Roosevelt,* vol. IV, pp. 724, 801.

14. Munro, *Intervention and Dollar Diplomacy,* pp. 77, 92–93. *Letters of Theodore Roosevelt,* vol. IV, pp. 821–22. *Works of Theodore Roosevelt: State Papers,* vol. 15, pp. 256–58.

15. Mowry, *Era of Theodore Roosevelt,* pp. 159–61. Harbaugh, *Life and*

Times of Theodore Roosevelt, pp. 190–93. Munro, *Intervention and Dollar Diplomacy,* pp. 94–111. *Works of Theodore Roosevelt: State Papers,* vol. 15, pp. 303–06.

16. Beale, *T.R. and America's Rise to World Power,* pp. 159–65, 175–80, 225–29.

17. Mowry, *Era of Theodore Roosevelt,* pp. 181–84. Beale, *T.R. and America's Rise to World Power,* pp. 231–38.

18. *Ibid.,* pp. 238–39, 242–65, 272–73.

19. *Ibid.,* pp. 264–68. On TR's domestic appeal, see Hofstadter, *American Political Tradition,* pp. 221–31.

20. Bailey, *Diplomatic History of the American People,* pp. 519–20. Beale, *T.R. and America's Rise to World Power,* pp. 268–69, 273–81.

21. Charles E. Neu, *An Uncertain Friendship: Theodore Roosevelt and Japan, 1906–1909* (Cambridge, Mass., 1967), chap. II.

22. Beale, *T.R. and America's Rise to World Power,* pp. 41–47. Mowry, *Era of Theodore Roosevelt,* pp. 92–93. Neu, *Uncertain Friendship,* chaps. III and VII, and pp. 313–14.

23. *Ibid.,* chaps. IV and X. Bailey, *Diplomatic History of the American People,* pp. 524–25.

24. Neu, *Uncertain Friendship,* chap. XI.

25. Blum, *The Republican Roosevelt,* pp. 138, 60–61. Hofstadter, *Age of Reform,* pp. 196–203, describes the progressives' view of society as embodying a clash of immoral, selfish impulses that needed to be restrained by an aroused citizenry.

26. Beale, *T.R. and America's Rise to World Power,* pp. 109–25. Mowry, *Era of Theodore Roosevelt,* pp. 161–63. Bailey, *Diplomatic History of the American People,* pp. 507–10. On the importance of legal rules to the progressives, see Hofstadter, *Age of Reform,* pp. 201–03.

27. Bailey, *Diplomatic History of the American People,* p. 527. Beale, *T.R. and America's Rise to World Power,* pp. 291–93. *Letters of Theodore Roosevelt,* vol. IV, p. 987; vol. V, pp. 25–26, 30–31.

28. *Ibid.,* vol. IV, pp. 1092–93, 1118–19, 1121–22, 1208–09; vol. V, pp. 463, 601, 641. Beale, *T.R. and America's Rise to World Power,* pp. 293–94, 301–02. *Works of Theodore Roosevelt: State Papers,* vol. 15, pp. 295–300.

29. Beale, *T.R. and America's Rise to World Power,* pp. 302–03. Mowry, *Era of Theodore Roosevelt,* pp. 191–92.

30. *Ibid.,* pp. 192–95. Bailey, *Diplomatic History of the American People,* p. 511. Beale, *T.R. and America's Rise to World Power,* pp. 306–34.

31. Osgood, *Ideals and Self-Interest,* p. 75.

Chapter 3

1. On similarities in the Roosevelt and Wilson foreign policies, see Hofstadter, *Age of Reform*, p. 274, n. 3.

2. On this shift in attitude, see *ibid.*, pp. 227, n. 5, 278–79, and John L. Gaddis, *Russia, the Soviet Union and the United States: An Interpretive History* (New York, 1978), pp. 27–32, who sees this shift beginning in the late nineteenth century and attributes it to the rise of "popular nationalism."

3. Arthur S. Link, *Woodrow Wilson: Revolution, War, and Peace* (Arlington Heights, Ill., 1979), pp. 6–7.

4. Arthur S. Link, *Woodrow Wilson and the Progressive Era, 1910–1917* (New York, 1963 ed.), pp. 93–94. Arthur S. Link, *Wilson: The New Freedom* (Princeton, N.J., 1956), pp. 319–20, 327–30. Munro, *Intervention and Dollar Diplomacy*, pp. 269–74, 533–34.

5. Link, *Wilson: The New Freedom*, pp. 330–42. Arthur S. Link, *Wilson: The Struggle for Neutrality, 1914–1915* (Princeton, N.J., 1960), chap. XV. *The Public Papers of Woodrow Wilson*, vol I, *The New Democracy, 1913–1917*, eds. Ray S. Baker and William E. Dodd (New York, 1926), pp. 439–45.

6. Link, *Wilson and the Progressive Era*, pp. 107–15. Link, *Wilson: The New Freedom*, pp. 347–61. *Public Papers of Wilson, 1913–1917*, vol. I, pp. 45–51.

7. Link, *Wilson and the Progressive Era*, pp. 115–18. Link, *Wilson: The New Freedom*, pp. 361–74. *Public Papers of Wilson, 1913–1917*, vol. I, pp. 64–69.

8. Link, *Wilson and the Progressive Era*, pp. 119–26. Link, *Wilson: The New Freedom*, pp. 379–409. *Public Papers of Wilson, 1913–1917*, vol. I, pp. 99–105, 111–22.

9. Link, *Wilson and the Progressive Era*, pp. 127–44. Link, *Wilson: The New Freedom*, pp. 409–16. Link, *Wilson: The Struggle for Neutrality*, chaps. VIII, XIV, XVIII. Arthur S. Link, *Wilson: Confusions and Crises, 1915–1916* (Princeton, N.J., 1964), chaps. VII, X. Arthur S. Link, *Wilson: Campaigns for Progressivism and Peace, 1916–1917* (Princeton, N.J., 1965), pp. 51–55, 120–23, 130–34, 328–39.

10. Link, *Wilson and the Progressive Era*, pp. 82–84. Link, *Wilson: The New Freedom*, pp. 283–88.

11. Link, *Wilson and the Progressive Era*, pp. 84–87. Link, *Wilson: The New Freedom*, pp. 289–304. Michael Schaller, *The United States and China in the Twentieth Century* (New York, 1979), pp. 19–22.

12. Harold M. Vinacke, "Woodrow Wilson's Far Eastern Policy," in

Wilson's Foreign Policy in Perspective, ed. Edward H. Buehrig (Bloomington, Ind., 1957), pp. 81–89. Link, *Wilson: The Struggle for Neutrality,* pp. 192–96, and chap. IX.

13. For a summary of these events, see Bailey, *Diplomatic History of the American People,* pp. 635–36, and Link, *Wilson: Revolution, War, and Peace,* pp. 9, 93, 114. For detailed discussions, see Russell H. Fifield, *Woodrow Wilson and the Far East: The Diplomacy of the Shantung Question* (New York, 1952), pp. 78 ff., and Burton F. Beers, *Vain Endeavor: Robert Lansing's Attempts to End the American-Japanese Rivalry* (Durham, N.C., 1962), chap. 9 and pp. 149–69.

14. For the development of these two attitudes, see Link, *Wilson and the Progressive Era,* chap. 6 (the quote is on p. 165), and Link, *Wilson: Revolution, War and Peace,* chap. 2.

15. Alexander and Juliette George, *Woodrow Wilson and Colonel House: A Personality Study* (New York, 1956), p. 133. Link, *Wilson: The New Freedom,* pp. 469–71.

16. For a discussion of America's unrealistic response to World War I, see Osgood, *Ideals and Self-Interest,* pp. 111–13, chaps. IX–XI. The point about an unrelenting concern with domestic ills is mine. Although German- and Irish-Americans vigorously opposed participation in the fighting against Germany, they were essentially isolated groups which could not significantly influence policy. See Ernest R. May, *The World War and American Isolation, 1914–1917* (Chicago, 1966), pp. 344–45.

17. For Wilson's peace initiative, see Link, *Wilson and the Progressive Era,* pp. 160–62, and Link, *Wilson: The Struggle for Neutrality,* chap. VII. For Wilson's initial reluctance to take up mediation, see George and George, *Wilson and House,* pp. 161–62; also see their comment about Wilson's "insatiable ambition": "No sooner did Wilson put through one reform plan than he would discover another great work calling for his attention. . . . His ambition, in other words, was compulsive," pp. 320–21.

18. Link, *Wilson and the Progressive Era,* pp. 162–69, 174–90, 197–205. Link, *Wilson: The Struggle for Neutrality,* chaps. X–XIII, XVI–XVII, XIX. Link, *Wilson: Confusions and Crises,* chaps. II–IV.

19. Link, *Wilson and the Progressive Era,* pp. 205–17. Link, *Wilson: Confusions and Crises,* chaps. V–VI, VIII–IX.

20. Link, *Wilson and the Progressive Era,* pp. 217–51. Link, *Wilson: Campaigns for Progressivism and Peace,* chaps. I, III–IV.

21. On the threatened railroad strike, see *ibid.,* pp. 83–91, 207, 392–93. Hofstadter's observations are in *Age of Reform,* pp. 213–15.

22. For Wilson's mediation effort, see Link, *Wilson and the Progressive Era,* pp. 252–66. Link, *Wilson: Campaigns for Progressivism and Peace,* chap. V.

23. For movement toward involvement in the war, see Link, *Wilson and the Progressive Era*, pp. 266–82; Link, *Wilson: Campaigns for Progressivism and Peace*, chaps. VII–IX; and Link, *Wilson: Revolution, War, and Peace*, chap. 3. The Hofstadter quote is in *Age of Reform*, p. 279. Wilson's request for war is in *The Public Papers of Woodrow Wilson*, vol. II, *War and Peace, 1917–1924*, eds. Ray S. Baker and William E. Dodd (New York, 1927), pp. 6–16. For the point that progressives saw the war as the way to further reform, see David M. Kennedy, *Over Here: The First World War and American Society* (New York, 1980), pp. 246–47.

24. Osgood, *Ideals and Self-Interest*, pp. 256–61.

25. For Wilson's peace aims, see Link, *Wilson: Revolution, War, and Peace*, chap. 4, especially pp. 82–86; Thomas A. Bailey, *Woodrow Wilson and the Lost Peace* (Chicago, 1963 ed.), chap. 2, and pp. 333–36; the quote is from Hofstadter, *Age of Reform*, pp. 276–77. For a different interpretation of Wilson's peace program, which argues that it was highly sensitive to international issues, see Arno J. Mayer, *Wilson vs. Lenin: Political Origins of the New Diplomacy, 1917–1918* (Cleveland, 1964 ed.), chap. 9 and the Epilogue. Also see N. Gordon Levin, *Woodrow Wilson and World Politics* (New York, 1968), Introduction and Part One.

26. Osgood, *Ideals and Self-Interest*, pp. 273–81. George and George, *Wilson and House*, p. 211. Bailey, *Wilson and the Lost Peace*, pp. 59–65.

27. George and George, *Wilson and House*, pp. 202–04, 237–38. Hofstadter, *Age of Reform*, p. 278.

28. George and George, *Wilson and House*, pp. 223, 225. William E. Leuchtenburg, *The Perils of Prosperity, 1914–1932* (Chicago, 1958), p. 54. Osgood, *Ideals and Self-Interest*, pp. 288–93. Bailey, *Wilson and the Lost Peace*, chap. 13.

29. *Ibid.*, p. 290 ff.; George and George, *Wilson and House*, chap. XIII; Link, *Wilson: Revolution, War, and Peace*, pp. 88–103. For the argument that Wilson's approach to the peace negotiations was much more mindful of international affairs than I suggest, see Levin, *Wilson and World Politics*, Part Two and Epilogue.

30. For Wilson's campaign, see Thomas A. Bailey, *Woodrow Wilson and the Great Betrayal* (Chicago, 1963 ed.), and Link, *Wilson: Revolution, War, and Peace*, chap. 5. For the quotes, see *Public Papers of Wilson, 1917–1924*, vol. II, pp. 523–24, 535, 551–52, 634–45.

31. Osgood, *Ideals and Self-Interest*, pp. 293–94, and Link, *Wilson: Revolution, War, and Peace*, p. 124. On domestic conditions, see Leuchtenburg, *Perils of Prosperity*, chap. IV and pp. 84–89.

32. My point is an expansion of one made by the Georges: that Wilson

"did not *want* to reach a compromise agreement with the Senate. He wanted to defeat the Senate and especially Lodge. If he could not overcome his enemies, it would be less painful to him to sacrifice the Treaty than to make concessions. He could relieve his sense of guilt for having provoked his own defeat by picturing himself martyred in a great cause and by seeking vindication from 'the people'—a vindication for which he strove to his dying day." *Wilson and House,* p. 311. While I agree with the Georges that Wilson sacrificed the treaty, I see another and, to my thinking, equally plausible motive for his action, which I have described in the text. For the argument that Wilson's failure to compromise is better understood as a consequence of his physical illness, see Edwin A. Weinstein, "Woodrow Wilson's Neurological Illness," *Journal of American History,* vol. LVII (September 1970), pp. 324–51. Also see Edwin A. Weinstein, James William Anderson, and Arthur S. Link, "Woodrow Wilson's Political Personality: A Reappraisal," *Political Science Quarterly,* vol. 93 (Winter 1978), pp. 585–98; and a rebuttal by Alexander L. George and Juliette L. George, *"Woodrow Wilson and Colonel House:* A Reply to Weinstein, Anderson, and Link," *Political Science Quarterly,* vol. 96 (Winter 1981–82), pp. 641–65.

Chapter 4

1. For domestic developments in general, see Leuchtenburg, *Perils of Prosperity,* pp. 66 ff. On progressivism, see Hofstadter, *Age of Reform,* pp. 280–300, and Arthur S. Link, "What Happened to the Progressive Movement in the 1920s?," *The American Historical Review,* vol. LXIV (July 1959), pp. 833–51. Also see the comment on Link's article in Richard M. Abrams and Lawrence W. Levine, eds., *The Shaping of Twentieth-Century America* (Boston, 1965), pp. 345–47.

2. The quote is from Osgood, *Ideals and Self-Interest,* p. 327.

3. The Herrick quote is in *ibid.,* p. 311. Hofstadter, *Age of Reform,* p. 280.

4. Examples of the people I am referring to are: Jane Addams, Devere Allen, Florence E. Allen, Newton Baker, Arthur Deerin Call, Carrie Chapman Catt, John Bates Clark, John Hessin Clarke, John Dewey, Manley O. Hudson, Charles H. Levermore, Salmon O. Levinson, Frederick Libby, Reinhold Niebuhr, Kirby Page, Raymond Robins, Norman Thomas. For a detailed description of how this worked, see Robert Dallek, *Democrat and Diplomat: The Life of William E. Dodd* (New York, 1968), chap. 8.

5. See Charles DeBenedetti, *Origins of the Modern American Peace Move-*

ment, 1915–1929 (Millwood, N.Y., 1978), chaps. 1–3; the quotes are on pp. 51, 62–63, 83, 112–13. Also see Charles Chatfield, *For Peace and Justice: Pacifism in America, 1914–1941* (Knoxville, Tenn., 1971), chap. V, especially p. 139.

6. *Ibid.,* chap. IV. Robert H. Ferrell, "The Peace Movement," in *Isolation and Security,* ed. Alexander DeConde (Durham, N.C., 1957), especially pp. 89, 93, 101–02.

7. Roger Dingman, *Power in the Pacific: The Origins of Naval Arms Limitation, 1914–1922* (Chicago, 1976), chap. 9, especially pp. 140 and 150, and C. Leonard Hoag, *Preface to Preparedness* (Washington, D.C., 1941), chaps. V–VI. Also see John Chalmers Vinson, *The Parchment Peace: The United States Senate and the Washington Conference, 1921–1922* (Athens, Ga., 1955), chap. 8; DeBenedetti, *Origins of the American Peace Movement,* pp. 69–70, 85–86; and Osgood, *Ideals and Self-Interest,* p. 338. For a description of the social tensions which raised "febrile anxieties about the very integrity of the social fabric," see Kennedy, *Over Here,* pp. 270–79, 287.

8. Osgood, *Ideals and Self-Interest,* pp. 338–46; Hoag, *Preface to Preparedness,* chap. VIII.

9. The prospect of reduced government spending was a major reason for public support of the treaties, but this does not explain the exaggerated American reaction to the Washington settlement. For evidence of this nostalgia for a nineteenth-century culture during the twenties, see Kennedy, *Over Here,* pp. 224–30, 287. For a somewhat different argument from mine about the importance of domestic politics, see Dingman, *Power in the Pacific,* chap. 12 and Conclusion.

10. Osgood, *Ideals and Self-Interest,* pp. 346–47. DeBenedetti, *Origins of the American Peace Movement,* pp. 60–62, 186–93.

11. Leuchtenburg, *Perils of Prosperity,* pp. 81–83, 208, 132–33, 220–24. DeBenedetti, *Origins of the American Peace Movement,* pp. 190–91, 194.

12. Bailey, *Diplomatic History of the American People,* pp. 649–51. Osgood, *Ideals and Self-Interest,* pp. 347–50. L. Ethan Ellis, "Frank B. Kellogg," in *An Uncertain Tradition: American Secretaries of State in the Twentieth Century,* ed. Norman A. Graebner (New York, 1961), pp. 164–66. Norman A. Graebner, ed., *Ideas and Diplomacy* (New York, 1964), pp. 520–23.

13. On this shift in mood, see Bryce Wood, *The Making of the Good Neighbor Policy* (New York, 1961), Introduction. Also see Richard W. Leopold, *The Growth of American Foreign Policy* (New York, 1964), chap. 36.

14. *Ibid.,* pp. 464–65. Wood, *Making of the Good Neighbor Policy,* pp. 18–21. John D. Hicks, *Republican Ascendancy, 1921–1933* (New York, 1960), pp. 153–57.

15. *Ibid.,* pp. 157–59. Wood, *Making of the Good Neighbor Policy,* chap. 1, see p. 22 for the *New York Times* quote. Elting E. Morison, *Turmoil and Tradition: A Study of the Life and Times of Henry L. Stimson* (Boston, 1960), pp. 222–30.

16. Wood, *Making of the Good Neighbor Policy,* pp. 4–6. Hicks, *Republican Ascendancy,* pp. 159–63. Alexander DeConde, *Herbert Hoover's Latin American Policy* (Stanford, Calif., 1951). Robert Dallek, *Franklin D. Roosevelt and American Foreign Policy, 1932–1945* (New York, 1979), pp. 60–66, 81–84, 122, 132–34.

17. These explanations of American economic nationalism are in: Hicks, *Republican Ascendancy,* pp. 54–59, 135–44, 219–23; Robert Freeman Smith, "American Foreign Relations, 1920–1942," in *Towards a New Past: Dissenting Essays in American History,* ed. Barton J. Bernstein (New York, 1967), pp. 232–62; and Kennedy, *Over Here,* chap. 6, especially pp. 337–47.

18. Bailey, *Diplomatic History of the American People,* pp. 655–70. L. Ethan Ellis, *Republican Foreign Policy, 1921–33* (New Brunswick, N.J., 1968), pp. 191–214. Melvyn Leffler, "The Origins of Republican War Debt Policy, 1921–1923: A Case Study in the Applicability of the Open Door Interpretation," *Journal of American History,* vol. LIX (December 1972), pp. 585–601. Joan Hoff Wilson, *American Business and Foreign Policy, 1920–1933* (Lexington, Ky., 1971), chap. 5, especially pp. 153–56.

19. Link, *Wilson and the Progressive Era,* pp. 36–43. Hicks, *Republican Ascendancy,* pp. 54–59.

20. *Ibid.,* pp. 219–23. Wilson, *American Business and Foreign Policy,* chap. 3.

21. Dallek, *FDR and American Foreign Policy,* chap. 2 and pp. 84–85, 91–93.

22. Leuchtenburg, *Perils of Prosperity,* chap. IV and pp. 204–05.

23. *Ibid.,* pp. 205–13. John Higham, *Strangers in the Land: Patterns of American Nativism, 1860–1925* (New York, 1963 ed.), chaps. 10–11. Christopher Lasch, *The American Liberals and the Russian Revolution* (New York, 1972 ed.), pp. 217–18.

24. Bailey, *Diplomatic History of the American People,* pp. 629–31. Hicks, *Republican Ascendancy,* pp. 145–46. Ellis, *Republican Foreign Policy,* pp. 68–75.

25. Dallek, *FDR and American Foreign Policy,* pp. 70–71, 95–96.

26. Higham, *Strangers in the Land,* pp. 324–30.

27. Bailey, *Diplomatic History of the American People,* pp. 695–99. Ellis, *Republican Foreign Policy,* pp. 328–63. Robert H. Ferrell, *American Diplomacy in the Great Depression: Hoover-Stimson Foreign Policy, 1929–1933* (New York, 1970 ed.), chaps. 8–11.

28. Dallek, *FDR and American Foreign Policy*, chaps. 1–4, *passim*, especially pp. 95–97.

29. Manfred Jonas, *Isolationism in America, 1935–1941* (Ithaca, N.Y., 1966), especially pp. 17, 67, 71.

30. Dallek, *FDR and American Foreign Policy*, pp. 147–52.

31. *Ibid.*, pp. 132–33, 136–37, 530.

Chapter 5

1. For an excellent summary of what the New Deal meant to the country, see chap. 14 of William E. Leuchtenburg, *Franklin D. Roosevelt and the New Deal, 1932–1940* (New York, 1963). On isolationism in the period 1939–1941 and the country's response to it, see Jonas, *Isolationism in America*, especially chaps. VII and VIII.

2. *Ibid.*, pp. 225–32.

3. *Ibid.*, pp. 244–50.

4. *Ibid.*, pp. 222, 266–71.

5. *Ibid.*, pp. 259, 211–15.

6. These events are described in Dallek, *FDR and American Foreign Policy*, chaps. 9–11.

7. *Ibid.*, pp. 201, 289, 530.

8. *Ibid.*, pp. 281–85, 296–98, 247, 310.

9. Jonas, *Isolationism in America*, pp. 234–38.

10. Wendell L. Willkie, *One World* (New York, 1943), pp. 171–72. Sumner Welles, *The Time for Decision* (New York, 1944). Jerome S. Bruner, *Mandate from the People* (New York, 1944), chap. II and pp. 233–42. Robert A. Divine, *Second Chance: The Triumph of Internationalism in America During World War II* (New York, 1967), pp. 39–40, 68–70, 85, 110, 252.

11. *Ibid.*, pp. 178–81. Ronald Steel, *Walter Lippmann and the American Century* (Boston, 1980), pp. 409–11, 414–15.

12. Bruner, *Mandate from the People*, pp. 50, 239–40, 27–28, 31–33. Divine, *Second Chance*, pp. 182–83, 252–53, 304.

13. Dallek, *FDR and American Foreign Policy*, p. 506. Divine, *Second Chance*, pp. 168–71.

14. Bruner, *Mandate from the People*, pp. 5–7, 230. Divine, *Second Chance*, p. 135.

15. Bruner, *Mandate from the People*, pp. 28, 233, 44–48. Divine, *Second Chance*, pp. 252–53.

16. Charles C. Alexander, *Nationalism in American Thought, 1930–1945* (Chicago, 1969), especially pp. viii–ix, 86.

17. Richard Weiss, "Ethnicity and Reform: Minorities and the Ambience of the Depression Years," *Journal of American History,* vol. LXVI (December 1979), pp. 566–85, especially pp. 573 and 577. Willkie, *One World,* pp. 192–94.

18. *Ibid.,* pp. 2, 157.

19. See John L. Gaddis, *The United States and the Origins of the Cold War, 1941–1947* (New York, 1972), chap. 2. Cf. Ralph B. Levering, *American Opinion and the Russian Alliance, 1939–1945* (Chapel Hill, N.C., 1976).

20. Gaddis, *The U.S. and the Origins of the Cold War,* pp. 38–39, 57–58. Levering, *American Opinion and the Russian Alliance,* p. 115.

21. Willkie, *One World,* chaps. 4–5, especially pp. 69–70, 73, 83–84, 92, 97–98. Dallek, *FDR and American Foreign Policy,* p. 439.

22. Gaddis, *U.S. and the Origins of the Cold War,* p. 46. Levering, *American Opinion and the Russian Alliance,* pp. 141–45, 155–56.

23. Dallek, *FDR and American Foreign Policy,* p. 387. Michael Schaller, *The United States and China in the Twentieth Century,* p. 74.

24. Dallek, *FDR and American Foreign Policy,* pp. 329, 391. Willkie, *One World,* pp. 133–35, 145–46.

25. *Ibid.,* pp. 115–22, 108–09.

26. Barbara Tuchman, *Stilwell and the American Experience in China, 1911–1945* (New York, 1971), pp. 349–50. Dallek, *FDR and American Foreign Policy,* p. 391. Henry R. Luce, "The American Century," *Life* (February 17, 1941), pp. 61–65.

27. Gaddis, *The U.S. and the Origins of the Cold War,* chap. 4, especially pp. 95–101, 114–21.

28. Bruner, *Mandate from the People,* pp. 126–35, 138–39, 141–42, 145–46. *Public Opinion Quarterly,* vol. 8 (Summer 1944), pp. 296, 448–49; vol. 9 (Spring 1945), pp. 91, 93. In their patriotic zeal during World War I, Americans renamed sauerkraut "liberty cabbage" and called the dachshund the "liberty pup."

29. Gaddis,*The U.S. and the Origins of the Cold War,* pp. 126–32, 236–38.

30. Bruner, *Mandate from the People,* pp. 127, 129–31, 133–35, 146, 151. *Public Opinion Quarterly,* vol. 8 (Summer 1944), p. 448; vol. 9 (Spring 1945), p. 94; vol. 9 (Fall 1945), p. 386.

31. Herbert Feis, *Contest over Japan* (New York, 1967), pp. 25, 160–61, 167–68, 171–73. Robert E. Ward, "The Legacy of the Occupation," in *The United States and Japan,* ed. Herbert Passin (Englewood Cliffs, N.J., 1966), pp. 48–51. For the argument that during the war many Japanese leaders shared with Americans a Wilsonian vision of postwar international cooperation that helped set the stage for later accommodation, see Akira

Iriye, *Power and Culture: The Japanese-American War, 1941–1945* (Cambridge, Mass., 1981).

32. For the quotes, see Bruner, *Mandate from the People,* pp. 151–52, 127.

33. For examples of these criticisms of FDR's leadership, see William H. Chamberlin, *America's Second Crusade* (Chicago, 1950); Chester Wilmot, *The Struggle for Europe* (New York, 1952); Gaddis Smith, *American Diplomacy During the Second World War, 1941–1945* (New York, 1965); Gaddis, *The U.S. and the Origins of the Cold War;* and James MacGregor Burns, *Roosevelt: The Soldier of Freedom* (New York, 1970).

34. See Dallek, *FDR and American Foreign Policy,* especially "Epilogue: Roosevelt as Foreign Policy Leader," and Robert Dallek, "Franklin Roosevelt as World Leader," *The American Historical Review,* vol. LXXVI (December 1971), pp. 1503–13.

35. Dallek, *FDR and American Foreign Policy,* pp. 470–72, 520–21.

36. *Ibid.,* pp. 429–30, 460–61, 513, 536–37.

Chapter 6

1. Lewis Einstein, *A Diplomat Looks Back,* ed. Lawrence E. Gelfand (New Haven, Conn., 1968), pp. 26–27.

2. William E. Leuchtenburg, *A Troubled Feast: American Society Since 1945,* rev. ed. (Boston, 1979), pp. 23–26.

3. Peter G. Boyle, "The British Foreign Office View of Soviet-American Relations, 1945–46," *Diplomatic History,* vol. 3 (Summer 1979), pp. 307–20, especially p. 311.

4. George F. Kennan, *American Diplomacy, 1900–1950* (Chicago, 1951), pp. 93–101.

5. George F. Kennan, *Realities of American Foreign Policy* (Princeton, N.J., 1954), pp. 109–10.

6. Eric F. Goldman, *The Crucial Decade—and After: America, 1945–1960* (New York, 1960), chap. II, especially pp. 19–28. Robert J. Donovan, *Conflict and Crisis: The Presidency of Harry S. Truman, 1945–1948* (New York, 1977), chaps. 3, 12, 13, 18, 22, 24.

7. *Public Opinion Quarterly,* vol. 9 (Winter 1945–46), p. 512, for the polls on national problems. For indications of conflicting public feelings about domestic and foreign affairs, see the polls on pp. 514–18 and 531; vol. 10 (Spring 1946), pp. 106–08, 112, 116, 120–21; (Summer 1946), pp. 247, 263–64, 280, 282–84; (Fall 1946), pp. 401, 416–17, 423, 432; (Winter 1946–47), pp. 618, 640.

8. Gaddis, *U.S. and Origins of the Cold War,* chap. 7, especially pp. 198–206, 224–30. Leuchtenburg, *A Troubled Feast,* p. 69.

9. *Ibid.,* pp. 230–36. Adam Ulam, *The Rivals: America and Russia Since World War II* (New York, 1971), pp. 67–70. Steel, *Lippmann and the American Century,* pp. 420–21.

10. Donovan, *Conflict and Crisis,* pp. 81–82, 85–86, 89. Gaddis, *U.S. and Origins of the Cold War,* p. 243.

11. *Ibid.,* pp. 263–69. *Public Opinion Quarterly,* vol. 9 (Winter 1945–46), p. 531.

12. Herbert Feis, *The China Tangle: The American Effort in China from Pearl Harbor to the Marshall Mission* (Princeton, N.J., 1953), chaps. 35–37. Tang Tsou, *America's Failure in China, 1941–1950,* 2 vols. (Chicago, 1953). Ulam, *The Rivals,* pp. 87–88, 90–91. Donovan, *Conflict and Crisis,* pp. 149–51.

13. Gaddis, *U.S. and Origins of the Cold War,* pp. 283–84, 289, 299–308, 310–15, 318–21.

14. Goldman, *Crucial Decade—and After,* pp. 46–52. Donovan, *Conflict and Crisis,* pp. 230–31.

15. Gaddis, *U.S. and Origins of the Cold War,* pp. 273–81, 286, 289. Leuchtenburg, *A Troubled Feast,* pp. 106–07.

16. *Ibid.,* p. 309. Donovan, *Conflict and Crisis,* pp. 190–92. Walter La-Feber, *America, Russia and the Cold War, 1945–1980,* 4th ed. (New York, 1980), p. 43.

17. Gaddis, *U.S. and Origins of the Cold War,* pp. 331–35. Donovan, *Conflict and Crisis,* pp. 203–07.

18. Gaddis, *U.S. and Origins of the Cold War,* pp. 261–63, 341–43. Donovan, *Conflict and Crisis,* pp. 127–28, 165–66, 199–200. *Public Opinion Quarterly,* vol. 10 (Winter 1946–47), p. 640.

19. Gaddis, *U.S. and Origins of the Cold War,* p. 322.

20. *Ibid.,* pp. 337–41. Alonzo L. Hamby, *Beyond the New Deal: Harry S. Truman and American Liberalism* (New York, 1973), pp. 127–34. Donovan, *Conflict and Crisis,* chap. 23, and pp. 229, 263. *Public Opinion Quarterly,* vol. 11 (Summer 1947), p. 297.

21. Hamby, *Beyond the New Deal,* pp. 134–38. Donovan, *Conflict and Crisis,* pp. 229–38. Goldman, *Crucial Decade—and After,* pp. 56–57.

22. Donovan, *Conflict and Crisis,* pp. 239–42, 272–74, 246–48. *The China White Paper: August 1949,* 2 vols. (Palo Alto, Calif., 1967 ed.), vol. I, pp. 217–20; vol. II, pp. 686–95.

23. Gaddis, *U.S. and Origins of the Cold War,* pp. 346–52. Donovan, *Conflict and Crisis,* pp. 279–85. Steel, *Lippmann and the American Century,* pp. 437–39.

24. *Public Opinion Quarterly*, vol. 11 (Spring 1947), p. 155.

25. Donovan, *Conflict and Crisis*, chap. 31. Goldman, *Crucial Decade—and After*, pp. 60–61.

26. Donovan, *Conflict and Crisis*, chap. 32. *Public Opinion Quarterly*, vol. 11 (Summer 1947), pp. 285–86; (Fall 1947), p. 497; (Winter 1947–48), pp. 677–78.

27. Robert Dallek, ed., *Dynamics of World Power: A Documentary History of U.S. Foreign Policy, 1945–1973: Western Europe*, gen. ed. Arthur M. Schlesinger, Jr., 5 vols. (New York, 1973), pp. 52–54. LaFeber, *America, Russia and the Cold War*, pp. 58–64. Donovan, *Conflict and Crisis*, pp. 280, 282–83, 287–90. Steel, *Lippmann and the American Century*, pp. 440–43.

28. George F. Kennan, "Sources of Soviet Conduct," *Foreign Affairs*, vol. XXV (July 1947), pp. 566–82. Walter Lippmann, *The Cold War* (New York, 1947). Steel, *Lippmann and the American Century*, pp. 443–49.

29. Donovan, *Conflict and Crisis*, chaps. 35–37.

30. *Ibid.*, chap. 38.

31. *Ibid.*, pp. 358–60. Steel, *Lippmann and the American Century*, pp. 450–53. George F. Kennan, *Memoirs, 1925–1950* (Boston, 1967), pp. 377–79, 397–404. Goldman, *Crucial Decade—and After*, pp. 78–79.

32. Donovan, *Conflict and Crisis*, chaps. 41–43. Kennan, *Memoirs*, pp. 404–14.

33. On why the United States did not intervene more fully in China, see Ernest R. May, *The Truman Administration and China, 1945–1949* (Philadelphia, 1975), pp. 34–49, 97–99.

34. Hamby, *Beyond the New Deal*, pp. 268, 274, 293–94.

35. *Ibid.*, pp. 366–70. *China White Paper*, vol. I, pp. vii, xiv–xvii. Dean Acheson, *Present at the Creation: My Years in the State Department* (New York, 1969), pp. 349–52, 354–56.

36. Goldman, *Crucial Decade—and After*, pp. 100–12, 134–45.

37. On McCarthy's appeal, see Hofstadter, *The Paranoid Style in American Politics*, chaps. 2 and 3. For the poll results, see Glenn D. Paige, *The Korean Decision, June 24–30, 1950* (New York, 1968), pp. 44–46.

38. *Ibid., passim*, and Ernest R. May, *"Lessons" of the Past: The Use and Misuse of History in American Foreign Policy* (New York, 1973), chap. III.

39. John W. Spanier, *The Truman-MacArthur Controversy and the Korean War* (New York, 1965 ed.), chap. V.

40. Goldman, *Crucial Decade—and After*, pp. 158–60, 164–65, 171.

41. Spanier, *Truman-MacArthur Controversy*, pp. 87–88. Walter Millis, *Arms and the State: Civil-Military Elements in National Policy* (New York, 1958), pp. 272–79.

42. Spanier, *Truman-MacArthur Controversy*, Parts II and III.

43. For an analysis of these domestic crosscurrents, see the essays in Daniel Bell, ed., *The Radical Right* (New York, 1964 ed.). The quotes are in Spanier, *Truman-MacArthur Controversy*, pp. 269–70.

Chapter 7

1. David Riesman, *The Lonely Crowd: A Study of the Changing American Character* (New York, 1953 ed.); also his *Individualism Reconsidered*, chap. 6, especially pp. 106, 108, 112–13. William H. Whyte, Jr., *The Organization Man* (New York, 1956). Goldman, *Crucial Decade—and After,* p. 219 ff., especially pp. 219–20, 305–06. Leuchtenburg, *A Troubled Feast,* pp. 53, 69–73, 78–91, 289.

2. Robert A. Divine, *Eisenhower and the Cold War* (New York, 1981), pp. 12–17. Dallek, ed., *Dynamics of World Power: Western Europe,* pp. 213–14. LaFeber, *America, Russia, and the Cold War,* pp. 149–52. For a more positive or "revisionist" picture of Eisenhower's leadership, see Stephen E. Ambrose, "The Ike Age," *The New Republic* (May 9, 1981), pp. 26–34.

3. Dwight D. Eisenhower, *The White House Years: Mandate for Change, 1953–1956* (New York, 1963), pp. 139–40, 143–44.

4. *Ibid.,* pp. 144–47, 251–55. Peter Lyon, *Eisenhower: Portrait of the Hero* (Boston, 1974), pp. 532–33, 584–85.

5. *Ibid.,* pp. 531, 533–34, 536–38. Divine, *Eisenhower and the Cold War,* pp. 108–09.

6. *Ibid.,* pp. 116–18. Goldman, *Crucial Decade—and After,* pp. 262–63. Eisenhower, *Mandate for Change,* pp. 504–06.

7. *Ibid.,* pp. 506–10. Lyon, *Eisenhower,* p. 656.

8. *Ibid.,* pp. 653, 660–65. Eisenhower, *Mandate for Change,* pp. 517–25. Also see Divine, *Eisenhower and the Cold War,* pp. 118–23, who offers a more positive interpretation of Eisenhower's actions at Geneva than I do.

9. Lyon, *Eisenhower,* pp. 543–54. Divine, *Eisenhower and the Cold War,* pp. 71–79. Barry Rubin, *Paved with Good Intentions: The American Experience and Iran* (New York, 1980), pp. 75–90.

10. Townsend Hoopes, *The Devil and John Foster Dulles* (Boston, 1973), pp. 302–28. Lyon, *Eisenhower,* pp. 679–84. Divine, *Eisenhower and the Cold War,* pp. 79–80.

11. Hoopes, *The Devil and John Foster Dulles,* chap. 21. Lyon, *Eisenhower,* pp. 687–92. Divine, *Eisenhower and the Cold War,* pp. 80–81.

12. Hoopes, *The Devil and John Foster Dulles,* pp. 342–46.

13. *Ibid.,* chaps. 22–23. Dwight D. Eisenhower, *The White House Years:*

Waging Peace, 1956–1961 (New York, 1965), p. 83. Divine, *Eisenhower and the Cold War*, pp. 81–86.

14. *Ibid.*, pp. 86–104. Eisenhower, *Waging Peace*, pp. 96, 680–81.

15. LaFeber, *America, Russia, and the Cold War*, pp. 193–94.

16. Eisenhower, *Mandate for Change*, chap. VII. Hoopes, *The Devil and John Foster Dulles*, pp. 185–87. Divine, *Eisenhower and the Cold War*, pp. 27–31.

17. For the interpretation that massive retaliation was a way to deal with domestic economic problems, see Divine, *Eisenhower and the Cold War*, pp. 33–39.

18. Eisenhower, *Mandate for Change*, chap. XIV. Divine, *Eisenhower and the Cold War*, pp. 39–55.

19. The Quemoy-Matsu crises are described in Eisenhower, *Mandate for Change*, chap. XIX, *Waging Peace*, chap. XII; and Divine, *Eisenhower and the Cold War*, pp. 55–70.

20. Eisenhower, *Mandate for Change*, p. 420.

21. LaFeber, *America, Russia, and the Cold War*, pp. 159–61. Lawrence S. Wittner, *Cold War America: From Hiroshima to Watergate* (New York, 1978 ed.), pp. 153–55. Lyon, *Eisenhower*, pp. 588–92, 596–97, 607–14. Eisenhower, *Mandate for Change*, pp. 421–27. See Stephen Schlesinger and Stephen Kinzer, *Bitter Fruit: The Untold Story of the American Coup in Guatemala* (Garden City, N.Y., 1982), pp. xv and 218 for two of the quotes, and the entire book for the fullest account of what happened.

22. Eisenhower, *Waging Peace*, pp. 519–20. Lyon, *Eisenhower*, pp. 768–69. Wittner, *Cold War America*, pp. 166–67.

23. LaFeber, *America, Russia, and the Cold War*, pp. 211–13. Lyon, *Eisenhower*, pp. 789–90, 807–08. Wittner, *Cold War America*, pp. 167–69. Eisenhower, *Waging Peace*, pp. 520–25, 533.

24. Hoopes, *The Devil and John Foster Dulles*, pp. 415, 424–28. Lyon, *Eisenhower*, pp. 753–58. LaFeber, *America, Russia and the Cold War*, pp. 199–200.

25. Hoopes, *The Devil and John Foster Dulles*, chap. 29. LaFeber, *America, Russia, and the Cold War*, pp. 206–10. Ulam, *The Rivals*, pp. 294–95.

26. Hoopes, *The Devil and John Foster Dulles*, pp. 493–96. Eisenhower, *Waging Peace*, pp. 435–36, 446–49.

27. Hoopes, *The Devil and John Foster Dulles*, pp. 499–502. Divine, *Eisenhower and the Cold War*, pp. 140–52. Eisenhower, *Waging Peace*, pp. 543–56.

Chapter 8

1. Arthur M. Schlesinger, Jr., *A Thousand Days: John F. Kennedy in the White House* (Boston, 1965), pp. 64–65, 74–75, 113–17.

2. LaFeber, *America, Russia, and the Cold War*, pp. 213–16. Schlesinger, Jr., *A Thousand Days*, pp. 72–73, 138–41.

3. Theodore C. Sorensen, *Kennedy* (New York, 1966 ed.), pp. 269–78.

4. Ulam, *The Rivals*, pp. 316–17. Schlesinger, Jr., *A Thousand Days*, pp. 225, 245, 291, 298–301, 304. Leuchtenburg, *A Troubled Feast*, pp. 129–35. Riesman, *Individualism Reconsidered*, p. 108. John L. Gaddis, *Strategies of Containment: A Critical Appraisal of Postwar American National Security Policy* (New York, 1982), pp. 212, 235–36.

5. Schlesinger, Jr., *A Thousand Days*, chaps. X–XI.

6. *Ibid.*, pp. 301–03.

7. *Ibid.*, pp. 344–49, 358–74, 379–80. Ulam, *The Rivals*, pp. 320–23. Dallek, ed., *Dynamics of World Power: Western Europe*, pp. 692–93. *Public Papers of the Presidents: John F. Kennedy: 1961* (Washington, D.C., 1962–64), pp. 533–40.

8. Schlesinger, Jr., *A Thousand Days*, pp. 347–48.

9. LaFeber, *America, Russia, and the Cold War*, pp. 220–21. Ulam, *The Rivals*, pp. 323–40.

10. On the missile crisis, see Graham Allison, *Essence of Decision: Explaining the Cuban Missile Crisis* (Boston, 1971). For Kennedy's comments, see Gaddis, *Strategies of Containment*, p. 213, and LaFeber, *America, Russia, and the Cold War*, pp. 232–33. On the test ban treaty, see Wittner, *Cold War America*, pp. 231–32.

11. Chester L. Cooper, *The Lost Crusade: America in Vietnam* (Greenwich, Conn., 1972 ed.), pp. 212–13.

12. Schlesinger, Jr., *A Thousand Days*, pp. 367–68, 321–23, 536–40. Cooper, *The Lost Crusade*, pp. 215–17. LaFeber, *America, Russia, and the Cold War*, pp. 234–35.

13. Schlesinger, Jr., *A Thousand Days*, pp. 540–50. George Ball, *The Past Has Another Pattern: Memoirs* (New York, 1982), pp. 365, 368–69.

14. LaFeber, *America, Russia, and the Cold War*, pp. 232–34.

15. Schlesinger, Jr., *A Thousand Days*, pp. 981–98. Cooper, *The Lost Crusade*, chap. IX. LaFeber, *America, Russia, and the Cold War*, pp. 235–38.

16. Doris Kearns, *Lyndon Johnson and the American Dream* (New York, 1976), pp. ix–x, 369–74.

17. Eric F. Goldman, *The Tragedy of Lyndon Johnson* (New York, 1974 ed.), pp. 488–90.

18. Rowland Evans and Robert Novak, *Lyndon B. Johnson: The Exercise of Power* (New York, 1968 ed.), pp. 420–27. Goldman, *Tragedy of Lyndon Johnson*, pp. 86–91.

19. Barry Goldwater, *Why Not Victory?* (New York, 1963). Richard Hofstadter, "Goldwater, and Pseudo-Conservative Politics," in *The Paranoid Style in American Politics*, pp. 124–37.

20. Goldman, *Tragedy of Lyndon Johnson*, pp. 467–70. LaFeber, *America, Russia, and the Cold War*, pp. 248–50.

21. Lyndon Baines Johnson, *The Vantage Point: Perspectives of the Presidency, 1963–1969* (New York, 1971), pp. 187–205.

22. *Ibid.*, pp. 151–53, 42–43. The Brogan essay is in *Harper's Magazine* (December 1952), pp. 21–28. LaFeber, *America, Russia, and the Cold War*, pp. 240–41.

23. Johnson, *The Vantage Point*, pp. 43–45, 64–65, 112–18. LaFeber, *America, Russia, and the Cold War*, pp. 242–44. Wittner, *Cold War America*, p. 246.

24. Goldman, *Tragedy of Lyndon Johnson*, pp. 474–79. Johnson, *The Vantage Point*, pp. 119–32.

25. Goldman, *Tragedy of Lyndon Johnson*, pp. 479–82. Johnson, *The Vantage Point*, pp. 132–34. Cooper, *The Lost Crusade*, pp. 328–30.

26. Kearns, *Johnson and the American Dream*, pp. 258–59, 268–69.

27. *Ibid.*, pp. 273–75, 280–84.

28. *Ibid.*, pp. 309–17. Goldman, *Tragedy of Lyndon Johnson*, pp. 590–93.

29. Kearns, *Johnson and the American Dream*, pp. 331–34.

30. *Ibid.*, chap. 12.

Chapter 9

1. Garry Wills, *Nixon Agonistes: The Crisis of the Self-Made Man* (New York, 1979 ed.), pp. 523–46, especially pp. 536–37.

2. Leuchtenburg, *A Troubled Feast*, p. 218 ff., especially pp. 218–27.

3. On Nixon's preference for foreign affairs, see Tad Szulc, *The Illusion of Peace: Foreign Policy in the Nixon Years* (New York, 1978), pp. 3–5, 15.

4. On Kissinger's background, see David Landau, *Kissinger: The Uses of Power* (New York, 1974), Prologue.

5. Richard M. Nixon, *United States Foreign Policy for the 1970's: Building for Peace* (New York, 1971), pp. ix–xiii, 1–11.

6. On Kissinger's role as a publicist, see Alan K. Henrikson, "Review

Essay: The Moralist as Geopolitician," *The Fletcher Forum: A Journal of Studies in International Affairs,* vol. 5 (Summer 1981), pp. 402–03. For the Kissinger quote, see Henry Kissinger, *Years of Upheaval* (Boston, 1982), p. 122.

7. Seyom Brown, *The Crises of Power: An Interpretation of United States Foreign Policy During the Kissinger Years* (New York, 1979), pp. 8–9.

8. Stanley Hoffmann, "The Case of Dr. Kissinger," *The New York Review of Books,* vol. XXVI (December 6, 1979), pp. 22–28.

9. Henry Kissinger, *White House Years* (Boston, 1979), pp. 226–30. Richard M. Nixon, *RN: The Memoirs of Richard Nixon* (New York, 1978), p. 349. On American distortions about Vietnam, see Frances Fitzgerald, *Fire in the Lake: The Vietnamese and the Americans in Vietnam* (Boston, 1972).

10. Nixon, *RN,* pp. 349, 380–82. Kissinger, *White House Years,* pp. 239–54. George C. Herring, *America's Longest War: The United States and Vietnam, 1950–1975* (New York, 1979), pp. 217–24.

11. *Ibid.,* pp. 224–26. Nixon, *RN,* pp. 404–11. Kissinger, *White House Years,* pp. 306–07.

12. Herring, *America's Longest War,* pp. 226–29.

13. *Ibid.,* pp. 229–31. Nixon, *RN,* pp. 445–52. Kissinger, *White House Years,* pp. 483–505, especially pp. 504–05.

14. Herring, *America's Longest War,* pp. 231–32. Kissinger, *White House Years,* pp. 509–17.

15. Herring, *America's Longest War,* pp. 233–39. Kissinger, *White House Years,* pp. 1016–46.

16. *Ibid.,* pp. 1097–99, 1305 ff. Herring, *America's Longest War,* pp. 240–44.

17. *Ibid.,* pp. 244–46. Kissinger, *White House Years,* pp. 1369, 1382, 1398–99.

18. Herring, *America's Longest War,* pp. 246–48. Nixon, *RN,* pp. 718, 734, 737.

19. Herring, *America's Longest War,* pp. 248–51.

20. *Ibid.,* pp. 252–72. Kissinger believes that "the consequences of totalitarian victory in Indochina, for the people concerned as well as for global stability, like all prospective dangers, were unprovable in 1973. There would be few who would doubt them at this writing (1981)." *Years of Upheaval,* p. 309. For his view of how Watergate affected the enforcement of the peace settlement, see pp. 318–21, 326–28; the quote is from p. 11.

21. Nixon, *RN,* pp. 544–80. Kissinger, *White House Years,* pp. 763–65, chap. XXIV, especially pp. 1058–60, 1066, 1069, 1074, 1085.

22. *Ibid.,* pp. 123–24, 1203–04.

23. Nixon, *RN,* pp. 611, 613–14. Kissinger, *White House Years,* pp. 1224–28.

24. Nixon, *RN,* pp. 609–10, 619–20. Kissinger, *White House Years,* p. 1208.

25. Hoffmann, "The Case of Dr. Kissinger," pp. 18, 20. The struggle with the bureaucracy is a central theme of Kissinger's memoirs; see especially chaps. XXIV and XXVIII for his feelings about the role of the bureaucrats at the summits. On the problems with SALT, see Szulc, *The Illusion of Peace,* pp. 578–79. Henrikson, "The Moralist as Geopolitician," p. 392.

26. LaFeber, *America, Russia, and the Cold War,* pp. 272–74. Szulc, *The Illusion of Peace,* p. 581. Kissinger, *White House Years,* pp. 1252–57; *Years of Upheaval,* pp. 122–27, 240–46, 982–85, 1028–31.

27. Kissinger, *White House Years,* chap. XXI, especially pp. 875–76, 885–86.

28. *Ibid.,* pp. 887, 894–902, 915–17. Nixon, *RN,* pp. 531–32. Szulc, *The Illusion of Peace,* p. 181.

29. Nixon, *RN,* pp. 489–90. Kissinger, *White House Years,* chap. XVII. Szulc, *The Illusion of Peace,* pp. 353–69, 480–86, 643–47, 720–25, especially pp. 361, 364, 366, 482–83, 643, 724. Although Kissinger describes "Nixon and his principal advisers" as "convinced that Allende represented a challenge to the United States and to the stability of the Western Hemisphere," he asserts that ". . . our government had nothing to do with planning his [Allende's] overthrow and no involvement with the plotters." Kissinger also acknowledges that the Nixon administration tried "to prevent Allende's accession to the Presidency," but he says that "there was no American involvement in coup plotting afterward." *Years of Upheaval, pp.* 374–77. Kissinger's version of what happened in Chile is in chap. IX.

30. Nixon, *RN,* pp. 476–85. Kissinger, *White House Years,* pp. 347, 353. Szulc, *The Illusion of Peace,* pp. 89–102, 328–31, 601–02, 704–07. Hoffmann, "The Case of Dr. Kissinger," p. 25. For Kissinger's analysis of why the administration was surprised by the Egyptian-Syrian attack, see *Years of Upheaval,* pp. 459–67; and for his estimate of the Soviet role, see pp. 469–70, where he concludes that Moscow "stopped short of encouraging the war but made no effort to halt it."

31. Kissinger, *White House Years,* pp. 348–59.

Index

Index

Index

Index

religion and religious thought, 92, 188; Scopes trial, 101; Social Darwinism and expansionism, 25, 26, 27, 28

Reston, James, 183, 248

Riesman, David, 188, 189–90, 215, 225–6

Rockefeller, John D., 38

Rogers, William, 273, 279, 281

Roosevelt, Franklin D., 107, 116–20; and China, 143, 150, 151; and Latin America, 105, 120–1; New Deal, xvii, 105, 110, 115, 118, 120, 124–5, 128, 136–7, 156–7; and Soviet Union, 117, 130, 141, 146, 150, 151, 160, 272; and trade policy and tariffs, 110–11; and World Court, 114–15, 117; and World War II, 128, 129–30, 134, 135, 141, 145–6, 147, 150, 152–3, 272

Roosevelt, Theodore, 28, 32–61; and Caribbean, 34–46, 60, 61, 65; and Far East, 47–56 *passim*, 60, 61, 73; international arbitration, role in, 56–60; and Japan, 52–6, 61; and Monroe Doctrine, xv, 43, 45–6, 105; and Panama Canal, 34, 36–41 *passim;* and Russo-Japanese War, 49–52 *passim*, 61; in Spanish-American War, 13, 16, 19–20, 21, 23, 33; "The Strenuous Life," 15; Woodrow Wilson, contrasted with, 62–3; World War I, views on, 76–7

Root, Elihu, 13, 39, 42, 44–5, 58, 59, 96

Root-Takahira Agreement, 55

Rosenberg, Ethel, 179

Rosenberg, Julius, 179

Rosenman, Samuel I., 152

Ross, Charles, 183

Rostow, Walt W., 233

Rubin, Barry, 200

Rumania, 160, 165

Rusk, Dean, 223, 235

Russia, 10, 101; and China and Far East, 10, 47, 48–9; Revolution, 86, 111; *see also* Soviet Union

Russo-Japanese War, 48–52 *passim*, 57, 61

Sacco, Nicola, 100–1

Sadat, Anwar, 280

Salisbury, Harrison E., 212–13

SALT talks, 273

Samoa, 8

Santo Domingo, *see* Dominican Republic

Saudi Arabia, 199

Schall, Thomas, 92

Schlesinger, Arthur, Jr., 221, 222, 226–7, 233, 235

Scopes trial, 101

SEATO (Southeast Asia Treaty Organization), 200, 208, 209

Sevareid, Eric, 222

Shafter, William R., 22

Shaw, Albert, 24

Sherman, John, 11

Sisco, Joseph, 281

Social Darwinism, 25, 26, 28

Sorensen, Theodore C., 221, 224

South Africa, 10, 29

Soviet Union: and Balkans, 152, 161, 163; and China, 162, 163; and China, Communist, 179, 182, 230, 231, 266, 275; and Cuba, 215, 223, 228, 230–1; and Czechoslovakia, 174–5, 175–6; and India, 275; and Middle East, 200–4 *passim*, 279–81; and nuclear energy, 152, 163, 166, 179, 192, 195, 216–17, 228–9, 229–30; and Poland, 160, 163; recognition of, 113, 117; and Vietnam, 229, 248; in World War II, 126, 130, 138–43 *passim*, 146, 150, 152, 153, 159, 272; *see also* Cold War and Communist threat; Russia

Spain, 8, 119; *see also* Spanish-American War

Spanier, John, 185

Spanish-American War, xi, xv, 4–5, 10–25 *passim*, 27, 28, 29, 30, 282

Spellman, Francis Cardinal, 168

Stalin, Joseph, 140, 141, 143, 152, 160–1, 163, 175, 192–3, 272

Stanton, Elizabeth Cady, 17

Stern, Fritz, xiv

Stevenson, Adlai, 204, 223

Stilwell, Gen. Joseph, 142

Stimson, Henry L., 104, 117, 147

Strong, Josiah, *Our Country*, 6–7

Study of History, The (Toynbee), 172

Suez Canal, 201–3

symbolic meaning (of foreign affairs), xiii, xiv, xv, xvi, 60, 105, 110, 220, 282; Spanish-American War, 4–5, 14, 15, 31, 282

Index

A NOTE ABOUT THE AUTHOR

Robert Dallek is a historian whose specialty is twentieth-century American diplomatic and political affairs. This is the sixth book he has written or edited, and articles by him have appeared in such publications as *The New Republic, The New York Review of Books,* the *American Historical Review,* and the *Journal of American History,* among others. Mr. Dallek received his B.A. from the University of Illinois, and his M.A. and Ph.D. degrees from Columbia University. He received the Bancroft Prize in 1980 for *Franklin Roosevelt and American Foreign Policy, 1932–1945,* and he has twice been nominated for American Book Awards in history. He is a Fellow of the Society of American Historians, teaches history at UCLA, and works as a Research Associate at the Southern California Psychoanalytic Institute. Mr. Dallek lives with his wife and two children in Los Angeles.

A NOTE ON THE TYPE

This book was set, via computer-driven cathode-ray tube, in a version of a type face called Baskerville. The face itself is a facsimile reproduction of types cast from molds made for John Baskerville (1706–1775) from his designs. Baskerville's original face was one of the forerunners of the type style known to printers as "modern face"—a "modern" of the period A.D. 1800.

Composed by American–Stratford Graphic Services, Inc., Brattleboro, Vermont
Printed and bound by R.R. Donnelley & Sons Co., Harrisonburg, Virginia

Designed by Virginia Tan